I AM GOD THE SON

READ MY STORY

BOOK ONE

A MODERN PARAPHRASE BY

ELMER L. TOWNS
LEE FREDRICKSON

I AM GOD THE SON

READ MY STORY

Heritage Builders Publishing and 21st Century Press are Christian publishers dedicated to publishing books that have a high standard of family values. We believe the vision for our partnership is to provide families and individuals with user-friendly materials that will help them in their daily lives and experiences. It is our prayer that this book will help you discover Biblical truth for your own life and help you meet the needs of others. May God richly bless you.

Cover and Book Design: Lee Fredrickson

ISBN: 978-1-942603-68-9

Visit our website at: www.heritagebuilderspublishing.com
Printed in the United States of America

DEDICATION

In this book are written different aspects of the key events in the life of God the Son on the earth. You will learn about the disciples that followed Him, and the millions of people whose lives He changed. You will learn how to live your life here on earth, and you will learn of the life to come in Heaven. You can have confidence that what He say is truth, for it was Jesus that said: "I am the Way, the Truth, and the Life."

You can absolutely trust in the things that are taught in His Word, so study it carefully to know what He said.

WHAT LEADERS ARE SAYING

Jesus talked directly to my heart through this Bible. As I read its pages, it was like walking and talking with Jesus. No one else was there, just the two of us. I believe God will use this Bible to get multitudes to listen to Him and follow Him.

    —Jentezen Franklin
    Senior Pastor, Free Chapel
    Author of NY Times Best Seller

This Bible has the power of Jesus talking directly to you. You will feel closer to Him than ever before and realize that He is God and you should follow Him.

    —Pastor David Sobrepena
    Word of Faith
    Manilla, Philippines
    Largest church in Philippines

Elmer Towns has been a close friend for over 20 years. I've often said, "He has no unpublished thought," yet, those thoughts have so often been a blessing to me! Now, Lee Fredrickson and Elmer have paraphrased the words of Jesus into the first person narrative, giving a fresh perspective on the Biblical narrative. It will be a blessing to many!"

    —Ed Stetzer
    President, LifeWay Research
    Author, Visiting Professor
    Liberty University Baptist Theological Seminary

Elmer Towns and Lee Fredrickson have made the words of Jesus more personal than any other Bible version. I felt Jesus was having a personal conversation with me and I felt a renewed commitment to obey what He was saying.

    —Dr. Mark Milioni
    President,
    Baptist Bible College, Springfield, MO

As I read the amazing text, I realized that this book "breaks through the barriers" of the way it has always been. I think I could actually hear the Master speaking and almost feel His Joy and His Pain. While reading *I Am God The Son* I was reminded of the first time I ever heard the song, "Rise Again" by Dallas Holm. Back then I remember thinking, "Can we really sing a song where Jesus is speaking in the first person?" The resounding answer was yes! Absolutely!

This amazing, heart stirring look at the Savior's life through His own eyes and in His own words is enthralling!

—Gary McSpadden
Faith and Wisdom Church
Branson, MO

Awesome! Captivating! In a first-person-narrative—God the Son seems to be sitting across the table from the reader, looking you in the eyes, and sharing the most exciting story ever told! What a new and refreshing insight with this genre. His story comes alive like never before! Specifically, read the "Sermon on the Mount" from a very different perspective—and don't miss any of the other stories. The Son is your guide with a word picture beyond anything written in the past. If you read only one book this year, this is the one to read. It's a page turner and a life changer!

—Robert J. Strand
Best selling author of over sixty books

CONTENTS

PART FOUR—BASED ON JOHN'S GOSPEL

Follow in My footsteps and I will show you how to live forever.

INTRODUCTION

I AM GOD THE SON

I am God the Son, Who is from the beginning. I will tell you all about God the Father, because I was face to face with Him throughout eternity, because I AM God.

Without Me nothing was created that was created. I do all the things that God the Father does. I have all life in Myself and give life to all of My creation. I AM the life of God, Who is the Light to all who are lost in a dark, forbidding world. My light shines in the hostile darkness, but the darkness doesn't even know that I exist. Commit yourself to My message which is written in the Word of God. It is eternal and perfect. Learn My message, believe My message, and share it with others.

I am the true saving Light who offers spiritual light to everyone in the world. I came to the world that I created, but those living in the world did not recognize Me as their Creator Savior.

I came to My own people—the Jews—and they refused to recognize Me.

But as many as recognize Me as their Savior and receive Me, I will make them My followers, simply because they believe in the authority of My name. They will be born again by My power, which is not a birth of blood, or the choice of people, or of flesh.

I had all the celestial glory of heaven, but I clothed My heavenly glory with human flesh. God living in flesh was the greatest glory of all. I am the uniquely begotten Son, and have all the grace and truth of God. Just know this, that I AM eternal, I created the universe; I had eternal fellowship with God the Father; and I became flesh when I was born of the Virgin Mary. You should worship and praise Me for all that I AM and do. My grace was offered and your need of grace was fulfilled. The law of Moses condemned you to death, but My grace and truth gave you life. You could never have seen God the Father, but I came from His Spirit to show you what God the Father is like.

Eternal life was manifested to you. You have seen it, and now you witness to others and tell them about eternal life which was with God the Father, and manifested to you. That which you have seen and heard, tell others, that they may have fellowship with you, as you have fellowship with God the Father, and Me, God the Son. I have written these things to give you heavenly joy. I AM Light, and there is absolutely no darkness in Me. So now you declare this message to everyone. If you tell people that you have fellowship with Me, and yet you walk in darkness, you lie and deny the truth. But when you walk in the Light, as I AM the Light, you have fellowship with other believers, and My blood cleanses you of all of your sins.

If you tell people you have no sin, you deceive yourself, and you don't have My truth. When you confess your sins, I AM faithful to forgive your sins, and cleanse you from all unrighteousness. If you were to say you have never sinned, you make Me a liar and My Word doesn't control you.

Because I told you not to sin, you won't do it; but when you slip and sin once, I stand at God the Father's right hand to plead forgiveness for you. You know I have forgiven all of your sins and I didn't die for you alone, but for the whole world.

You Can Know You Are My Follower

You know you are born again, because you believe I AM the Messiah. And all who love Me, love My followers also. I know you are My follower because you love Me, and you do what I have commanded you to do. This is what loving Me means—keeping My commands, because they are not difficult.

I know you are My child, because you have victoriously overcome the lust of the world by faith. Who else can overcome the world? Only those who believe that I AM God the Son.

PART ONE

I AM GOD THE KING

Based on the Gospel of Matthew

14

THE RECORD OF MY GENEALOGY

I AM God the Son. This is the record of My genealogy. I was the descendant of both David and Abraham: Abraham was the father of Isaac, who was the father of Jacob, who was the father of Judah and his brothers, who was the father of Perez and Zerah (whose mother was Tamar). Perez was the father of Hezron, who was the father of Ram, who was the father of Amminadab, who was the father of Nahshon, who was the father of Salmon, who was the father of Boaz (whose mother was Rahab). Boaz was the father of Obed (whose mother was Ruth), and Obed was the father of Jesse, who was the father of King David, who was the father of Solomon (whose mother was Uriah's wife). Solomon was the father of Rehoboam, who was the father of Abijah, who was the father of Asa, who was the father of Jehoshaphat, who was the father of Joram, who was the father of Uzziah, who was the father of Jotham, who was the father of Ahaz, who was the father of Hezekiah, who was the father of Manasseh, who was the father of Amon, who was the father of Josiah, who was the father of Jeconiah and his brothers, at the time of the Babylon captivity.

After the Babylonian captivity Jeconiah was the father of Shealtiel, who was the father of Zerubbabel, who was the father of Abiud, who was the father of Eliakim, who was the father of Azor, who was the father of Zadoc, who was the father of Akim, who was the father of Eliud, who was the father of Eleazar, who was the father of Matthan, who was the father of Jacob, who was the father of Joseph, who was the husband of Mary, who gave birth to Me. My name is Jesus, and I AM called Christ.

My genealogy is traced for fourteen generations from Abraham to David, fourteen generations from David to the captivity of Babylon, and fourteen generations from the deportation to My birth.

My Birth in Human History

My birth took place this way. When Mary was engaged to Joseph, before they came together, she was discovered to be pregnant by the Holy Spirit. Joseph, her future husband, was a good man and not wanting to see her put to shame, planned to divorce her quietly. But while he was thinking this over, an angel of the Lord appeared to him in a dream and said, "Joseph, son of David, do not be afraid to take Mary as your wife! She has conceived a Son through the Holy Spirit, and she will give birth to a son, whom you will call Jesus, 'the Savior,' for it is He who will save His people from their sins."

The greatest event in history was when I came to live among the people I created. The greatest event in your life was when I came to live in your heart.

All this happened to fulfill what the Lord had said through the prophet—"Behold, a virgin shall conceive and shall bring forth a son, and they shall call His name Emmanuel, which means 'God with us'." When Joseph woke up he did what the angel had told him. He took Mary as his wife but had no physical relations with her until she had given birth to Me. Then he called My name Jesus.

TWO

THE WISE MEN VISIT ME

After I was born in Bethlehem, wise men—astrologers—came from the East looking for Me, the baby born King of the Jews. They told King Herod that they saw My star in the East and followed it so they could worship Me.

King Herod was disturbed because the Roman Senate had declared he was King of the Jews. Herod assembled Jewish leaders to find out where the prophets predicted that I, the Deliverer, would be born.

They quoted the Scripture, "You, Bethlehem in Judah, are not the least important town because the Deliverer will come from you, who will rule the people of Israel."

Just as the wise men searched for Me in order to worship Me as their God, so you search to know Me and to worship Me according to the worship I deserve.

Herod met privately with the wise men to find out exactly when the star appeared. Herod then deceptively sent the wise men to search for Me, and to report back to him so that he could also worship Me.

The wise men started toward Bethlehem, and the Star appeared again to lead them, and stopped where I was. When they saw the star again, they were very happy. As they went into the house, they saw Me with My mother, and falling to their knees, they gave Me their gifts: gold, frankincense, and myrrh.

The wise men were warned in a dream not to return to Herod, so they went home a different way.

Worship Me as did the wise men. Even as they gave Me earthly wealth, surrender all of your earthly goods to My use, but most importantly, give Me your heart.

Slaughter of Babies in Bethlehem

After the wise men left Mary and Me, the angel of the Lord spoke to Joseph in a dream, "Get the child and His mother and escape to Egypt. King Herod will try to kill Him. Stay there until I tell you to come back."

Joseph immediately took My mother and Me and left for Egypt. Then the prophecy of the Lord was fulfilled, "I will call my Son out of Egypt."

Joseph would not have known of danger if My angel had not warned him. Today you face all kinds of danger—known and unknown— from those who would intentionally harm you, to accidents; from spiritual dangers, to toxic dangers. I will protect you when you are ignorant of danger, and when you face threatening situations. I will protect you by my guardian angel, just as I protected Joseph and My family.

When Herod realized the wise men deceived him, he sent soldiers to Bethlehem to kill every child who was two years old or younger. Then, the prophecy of Jeremiah was fulfilled, "Screams and mourning were heard in Ramah; Rachel was sobbing for her children and she would not be comforted because they no longer lived."

My Exile in Egypt

The Lord sent an angel to Joseph after Herod died, telling him to return to the land of Israel because "Those who tried to kill Jesus are now dead." So Joseph took Mary and Me and headed toward the land of Israel.

Then Joseph heard that Archelaus was now king so he was afraid to go to Bethlehem. So, the Lord spoke to Joseph in a dream telling him to go back to Galilee and his home in Nazareth. Then the prophecy was fulfilled, "He [Jesus] shall be called a Nazarene."

THREE

JOHN THE BAPTIZER BEGINS PREACHING

The Word of God came to John the Baptizer and he went through all Judea preaching the baptism of repentance for the forgiveness of sins. John quoted the Book of Isaiah proclaiming, "I am the voice of one crying in the wilderness, make ready the way for the Lord, make straight paths for Him."

John had a coat woven of camel hair, and a leather belt around his waist. He ate locusts and honey. Many in Jerusalem and Judea, and the area around the Jordan, heard about him and went to be baptized by him, confessing their sins.

When John saw the Pharisees and Sadducees coming to hear him, he said, "You are snakes . . . who warned you to escape the coming wrath? Show good fruit, repent. Do not think you can escape judgment just because you are Abraham's children. God can make children of Abraham from these stones in the desert. Every tree that doesn't grow good fruit will be cut down and thrown into the fire; the axe is ready to cut down your tree."

The crowd cried out, "What must we do?" Everyone anticipated their Deliverer would soon appear, and many thought John was the Messiah.

John answered them, "I only baptize with water, the One following me will baptize with fire and with the Holy Spirit; I am not worthy to unloose His sandal straps. The One following me will separate real believers, who are represented by good grain, from chaff, representing false believers. He will store the good grain in His barns, but will burn the chaff in eternal fire."

19

John Baptizes Me

Then I came from Galilee to the Jordan to be baptized by John. But John tried to prevent Me. "You need to baptize me," the Baptizer said. "Why do you come to me?"

But I replied, "It is the right thing to do. This will meet all the law's demands—let it be done now.

Then John agreed to baptize Me. I came up out of the water, and suddenly the heavens opened and I saw the Spirit of God coming down like a dove and resting on Me. A voice spoke out of heaven saying, "This is my beloved Son, in whom I am well pleased."

In order to understand the Trinity, go to the Jordan River. Watch Me, God the Son, being baptized, see God the Holy Spirit come on Me as a dove, and listen to the voice of God the Father saying, "You are My beloved Son; in You I am well pleased."

FOUR

I AM TEMPTED BY SATAN TO SIN

Then I was led by the Spirit into the desert, to be tempted by the devil. After fasting for forty days and nights I was hungry. "If you are the Son of God," said the tempter, "tell these stones to turn into bread." I answered, "The Scripture says, 'Man shall not live by bread alone, but by every word that comes out of the mouth of God.'"

Then the devil took Me to the holy city, and set Me on the highest pinnacle of the temple. "If You are the Son of God," he said, "jump down. For the Scripture says— 'He shall give His angels charge over you and on their hands they shall lift you up, lest you smash your foot against a stone.'"

I answered, "And the Scripture also says, 'You shall not tempt the Lord your God.'"

Again the devil took Me to a high mountain, and showed Me all the kingdoms of the world and their glory. "I will give you these kingdoms," he said to Me, "if you will fall down and worship me."

"Get out of here, satan!" I replied. "The Scripture says,— 'You shall worship the Lord your God, and Him only shall you serve.'"

Then the devil left Me alone, and angels came to strengthen Me.

Learn the Scriptures so that you can use them to protect yourself when temptations come. Just as I used the Scriptures to turn back temptations, understand the Scriptures. I will give you wisdom in how to apply them when you are tempted.

Now when I heard that John had been arrested, I went back to Galilee. I left Nazareth and came to live in Capernaum, a lakeside town in the Zebulun territory. Isaiah's prophecy came true in this way: "Light shall come to the land of Zebulun and the land of Naphtali, beyond Jordan, beside the lake of Galilee of the Gentiles; the people who sit in darkness will see a great light, and to them who sit in the shadow of death, light will spring up."

From that time I began preaching saying, "Repent, change your hearts and minds—for the kingdom of heaven is at hand."

I Call Fishermen to Follow Me

As I was walking by the Sea of Galilee I saw two brothers, Simon, who is called Peter, and Andrew, casting their net into the water. They were fishermen. So I said to them, "Follow Me and I will make you fishers of men!" Immediately they left their nets and followed Me.

Then I went farther and saw two more fishermen, also brothers, James and John, in the boat with their father Zebedee mending their nets, and I called them. Immediately, they left the boat and their father, and followed Me.

When I call you, drop what you are doing and follow Me, just as the disciples left their nets. I want you to be fishers of men and women.

I then traveled through all of Galilee, teaching in their synagogues and preaching the good news of the kingdom, and healing every disease and disability among the people. My reputation spread throughout the area and people brought to Me those who were sick, suffering from all kinds of disease—including the demon-possessed and the paralyzed. I healed them all, and was followed by large crowds from Galilee, Decapolis, Jerusalem, Judea, and from the regions beyond the Jordan River.

THE SERMON ON
THE MOUNT

When I saw the multitudes following Me, I went to the top of a hill to teach My disciples and the multitudes.
This is what I started teaching them:

"When you are poor in spirit—totally dependent on Me—the kingdom of heaven is yours.
When you mourn—broken over sin in your life—
    I will give you consolation.
When you are meek—willing to set aside your rights—
    I will give you possession of the earth.
When you are hungry and you thirst after righteousness—having a desire for outward holiness—
    you will be satisfied by My presence.
When you are merciful—looking on others—
    I will show mercy to you.
When you are pure—desiring inward holiness—
    then you shall see Me.
When you are a peacemaker—building relationship in others—
    you will be called a child of God.
When you are persecuted for righteousness' sake—suffering for Me—
    yours will be the kingdom of heaven.
    "When you are persecuted falsely—because of your loyalty to Me —you will accept it as a rich reward because this is what the enemies of God did to the prophets and to Me.

"Be like the salt of the earth, so through you I can make people thirsty for My presence. If you lose your ability to influence people, you might as well be thrown away like salt that has lost its saltiness.

"I want you to be a light to the world, so that people will know how to find their way to Me. People don't put a candle under a bucket. They put it in a candle-holder, so it can light a whole room. Let your light shine to all people so they can see My works through you, and glorify My Father in heaven.

"I didn't come to do away with the teachings of the Old Testament, but to fulfill the prophecies about Me. Not one dot and comma can be changed in the Old Testament Scriptures. Everything it promises will come to pass just the way it was predicted. Any one who breaks one commandment of the law, or teaches people to break them, will be last in the kingdom. When you keep or teach others to keep the commands, you will be great in the kingdom.

"Accept My imputed righteousness to you which is greater than the self-righteousness of the scribes and Pharisees. You know it has been said long ago that whoever kills will be in danger of eternal judgment. But I tell you, never become so angry with anyone that you condemn yourself to punishment. Anyone who says, 'You fool!' will be punished in hell fire. As you begin to pray and remember someone who is mad at you, you will stop praying and go reconcile yourself with that offended person, and then you will pray to Me. You will come to terms with those who sue you before you meet them in court, lest the judge agrees with your opponent and they put you in jail or make you pay the full cost.

"You have heard this said, 'You must not commit adultery.' I say, don't even have impure intentions, lest you commit adultery in your heart. If anything entices you to sin, get rid of it from your life. It is best for you to get rid of a stumbling block than to lose your testimony or life. If part of your body is a snare to you, ignore it, as though it's not there. It's best to lose the use of part of your body than to destroy your whole body and perhaps even your soul."

I quoted the Old Testament, that a notice of divorce must be given before putting away a spouse. Then I said, "If you put away a wife for any reason, other than unfaithfulness, both you and she have become adulterers."

I again quoted the Old Testament saying, "You shall not swear falsely, but shall do what you swear as a commitment to the Lord." Then I added, "But I say to you, do not swear at all; neither by heaven, or God's throne, nor by the earth for it is God's footstool, nor by Jerusalem because it is God's city. Don't swear by anything, because you can't make one hair black or white." I gave this commandment, "Tell people what you will do, and do what you say; your word of promise should be enough."

Pledge to do My will. I will give you strength to do it, and the tenacity to reject any temptation to be otherwise.

I quoted the ancients, "An eye for an eye and a tooth for a tooth," but that principle is not our standard. I also said "Don't take revenge; if someone hits you on the right cheek, offer them the left cheek. If a man asks to take away your coat, give him your overcoat also. If anyone orders you to go one mile, go two miles with him. If anyone wants to borrow something, do not turn that person down."

"You have heard it said to love your friends and hate your enemies. But I say do good to those who hate you, and pray for those who despitefully use you. Treat them as you want to be treated, so that you will be of my heavenly Father, because He makes the sun rise on evil people and good people, and sends rain on the evil and the good." I said, "If you love only those who love you, there is no spiritual reward in that; even sinners love those who love them. Love your enemies and do good things to those who hate you, because I said, 'You would receive a rich reward, and should show everyone that you are a child of the Most High.'"

SIX

GIVING, PRAYING, FASTING, TRUSTING

"Do not practice your piety before people, to be 'holy' in their eyes, because I will not reward it. Do not show off when you give money because that would be hypocritical. Recognition is the only reward a hypocrite gets. When you give your money secretly, you won't let your left hand know what your right hand is doing. I know all of your intentions, and see all gifts, and will reward you if you give humbly and honestly.

"Do not be like the hypocrites when you pray, because they love to pray before people to get attention. That's all the reward they'll get. Go to your prayer closet, where no one can see or hear you. Then when you pray to Me in secret, I will see your sincerity in private and will reward you openly. Do not rattle off long prayers like the unsaved, who think they'll be heard because they pray a long time. Realize that I know everything in your heart, and I know your needs before you pray.

"When you pray, follow this pattern:

'My Father in heaven, may Your name be holy, in my life on earth, as Your name is holy in heaven. May Your kingdom come, in my life on earth, as Your kingdom rules in heaven. May Your will be done, in my life on earth, as Your will is done in heaven. Give me daily bread for this day. And forgive the consequences of my sin, as I forgive the sins of those who hurt me. Do not let me be tempted to do evil, but protect me from the evil one, for You have the ability to answer this prayer. Let Your kingdom rule my life. May You get credit when these prayers are answered.'"

Pray My Prayer each day because it embraces every petition you must make to Me, and it leaves out nothing that is imperative to your prayer relationship with Me.

"If you forgive the failings of others, I will forgive your faults. But if you refuse to forgive others I will not forgive you.

"Do not fast with an outward 'religious' face for that is just to get attention from others. The 'attention' you get is your reward. Dress your normal way when you fast so no one will know you are fasting. Your fast will be a secret between you and Me, and I will reward you with the answers you seek.

"Do not pile up wealth on earth where inflation or corruption will destroy it. But deposit your wealth in My heavenly bank, where nothing can destroy it. Therefore, put your treasure where you make a heart commitment. I will make you see things clearly, and give you light and understanding in your heart, because when your eye is clouded with lust and evil thoughts, your heart will be blinded by darkness. You'll not understand or seek spiritual things. You cannot serve two masters—God and money—because you'll naturally love one and reject the other. So, this is what you must do. Don't worry about clothes, entertainment, or food. Your life is far more important than what you eat or wear. The birds will be your example; they don't worry about sowing, reaping, or eating food. You are more important to Me than birds. Worry will not give you anything you need. Let the lilies of the field be your example for clothing; they don't worry about their appearance. Yet Solomon, in all his glory, was not as beautiful as the lilies. Since I wonderfully care for the flowers that are here today, and gone tomorrow, you know I can take care of you. I will forgive you when you have so little faith about the necessities of life. Do not worry about having enough food and clothing because I know you need them; these are the things unsaved people worry about. But seek first My kingdom and righteousness, then all these things will be added to you."

Allow Me to sit on the throne of your heart to rule all you say and do. I want to give you abundant life.

"Do not be anxious about tomorrow, since I will take care of tomorrow's needs, but live one day at a time."

SEVEN

YOUR RELATIONSHIP TO OTHERS

"Do not criticize others, so they won't criticize you, because the way you treat others is the way they'll treat you. What you give to others is what they'll give you, so I will make you a gracious giver. Do not criticize the small trash in another's eye, when your eye is full of garbage. You can't say to someone, 'Let me clean out your eye' when your own eye is full of dirt and filth. You must first cleanse your eyes before you can help anyone see more clearly. Do not give beautiful pearls to pigs, they will stomp them into the mud and then they will turn to attack you, so do not give 'holy things' to evil people.

"Ask, in prayer, and I will give it to you. Seek for the things you need, for I supply those who seek. When a door is closed for the things you need, you will constantly knock, for I will open and allow you to find. You would never give anyone a stone when he needs bread to eat. You would never give anyone a snake when he asks for a fish to eat. Since hardhearted people give good things to their children, then you know that God, the heavenly Father, will give good gifts to My children, when they ask.

"Do good things for other people, just as you want them to do good things for you.

"Enter My presence by the narrow door since the road to hell is wide and inviting, and most of the crowd takes this road. But the door to My presence is small and the path to eternal life is narrow. So only a few find it.

"Watch out for false preachers disguised as sheep, because they are ravenous wolves who will eat up young Christians. You can tell good people by their fruit, just as you can tell the difference between good fruit and weeds, so false preachers are known by their evil deeds. Good trees grow good fruit, and evil trees grow evil fruit. A good tree can't grow bad fruit, and an evil tree can't grow good fruit. A tree that produces bad fruit is cut down and thrown in the fire. So everyone is known by his fruit.

"Those who cry publicly, 'Lord, Lord' will not enter the kingdom of heaven. But those who do My will, will be able to enter into My presence. Others will cry out, 'Lord, Lord, I preached in Your name and cast out demons and did miracles.' Then I'll say to them, 'I never knew you, get out of my sight.'

"Those who listen to this sermon and obey My words, will be like a sensible man who built his house on a rock foundation. The rains came, floods swirled, and the wind blew on this house but it didn't fall, because it was founded on a rock. But those who hear this sermon and reject My words, are like a stupid man who built his house on sand. The rains came, floods rose, and gale winds blew, and it collapsed with a mighty crash."

When I finished this sermon, the people were amazed at its content, because I taught them with authority, not like the scribes and other religious preachers.

EIGHT

I PERFORM MIRACLES

Large crowds followed Me when I came down from the hillside. A leper came and knelt in front of Me. "Sir," he said, "if You will, You can make me clean."

I stretched out My hand and placed it on the leper saying, "Of course I will. Be clean!" And immediately he was healed of the leprosy. "Say nothing to anyone," I told him. "Go show yourself to the priest and make the offering that Moses prescribed."

Then, as I was coming into Capernaum, a centurion approached Me. "Sir," he begged, "My servant is in bed at home paralyzed and in terrible pain."

"I will come heal him," I said.

The centurion replied, "I'm not important enough for You to come into my house. Only give the order and my servant will be healed. I'm under authority and I have soldiers under me. I can say to one man, 'Go' and I know he'll go, or I can say, 'Come' to another and I know he'll come—or I can say to my slave 'Do this' and he'll do it."

When I heard this, I was astonished. I said to those who were following Me, "I have never seen faith like this even in Israel! I tell you that many people will come from the east and west and sit with Abraham, Isaac, and Jacob in the kingdom of heaven, while those who should have belonged to the kingdom will be banished to the darkness outside, where there will be tears and gnashing of teeth." Then I said to the centurion, "Go home, it will happen as you have believed it would." And his servant was healed at that moment.

Then, on coming into Peter's house, I saw that Peter's mother-in-law had been put to bed with a high fever. I touched her hand and the fever left her. And then she got up and began to serve them. When evening came, they brought to Me many who were demon-possessed, which I expelled with a word. I healed all who were ill. This fulfilled Isaiah's prophecy, "He took our infirmities and bare our diseases."

I will give you faith to believe I can heal, and answer when you call to Me for healing.

Giving Up Everything For Me

When I saw the large crowd, I commanded My disciples to cross over to the other side of the lake. But one of the scribes came to Me and said, "Master, I will follow You wherever you go."

I said to him, "Foxes have holes, birds in the sky have nests, but I, the Son of Man, have nowhere to lay My head."

Another of My disciples said, "Lord, let me first go and bury my father."

But I said to him, "Follow Me, and leave the dead to bury their own dead."

I Calm the Storm

I went aboard the boat, and My disciples followed Me. Then a terrific storm sprang up and the boat was about to sink with the waves. I was sleeping soundly and the disciples awakened Me. "Lord, save us!" they cried. "We are about to drown!"

"Why are you so frightened, oh you with little faith?" I replied. Then I got up and rebuked the wind and the waters and there was a great calm.

The men marveled and kept saying, "What sort of man is this— even the winds and the waves obey Him!"

When storms enter your life, you can cry out to Me for courage and help. I will teach you to trust Me. I will save you in the storms of this life.

I Heal a Violent Demon-Stricken Man

When I arrived on the other side at Gadara, I was met by two demon-possessed men who came out from among the tombs. They were so violent that no one came in that area. "What have you got to do with us, O Son of God?" they screamed. "Have You come to torture us before our time?"

There was a large herd of pigs feeding nearby. So the demons begged Me, "If You cast us out, send us into the herd of pigs!"

"Go!" I said. And the demons came out and went into the pigs. Suddenly the whole herd stampeded down the steep cliff into the lake and drowned.

The herdsmen ran to the town and told the whole story of what happened to the two men who had been demon-possessed. Then the whole town came out to meet Me, and commanded Me to leave their territory.

Follow Me wherever I lead. I will give you a willing spirit, courage to endure, and strength to do it.

GETTING A FRIEND TO ME

So I got back into the boat, went back across the lake, and came to My own town. Some people brought Me a paralytic lying on his bed. When I saw the faith of those who brought him, I said to the paralytic, "Be of good cheer, my son! Your sins are forgiven."

Immediately some of the scribes thought to themselves, "This man is blaspheming."

But I knew what they were thinking, and said to them, "Why do you have evil thoughts in your minds? Which is easier to say, 'Your sins are forgiven' or 'Get up and walk'? But so you will know that I, the Son of Man, have authority to forgive sins"—I spoke to the paralytic, "Get up, pick up your bed and go home." And the man got up and went home.

When the crowds saw it, they were afraid and praised God for such power.

I know your thoughts, just as I knew the religious leaders' thoughts when I was on this earth. I will forgive you for any sin or doubt that hides in your heart. I will teach you to think My thoughts.

The Call to Matthew

I left there and as I passed on, I saw a man called Matthew, sitting at his table at the tax-collector's place. "Follow Me!" I said to him, and Matthew got up and followed Me.

Later, as I was in a house sitting at the dinner table, many tax collectors and other disreputable people came and sat down with My disciples and Me. The Pharisees saw this and said to My disciples, "Why does your master eat His meals with tax collectors and sinners?"

But I heard them and replied, "It is not the well who need a doctor, but those who are sick. Go and learn what the Scripture means when it says, 'I desire mercy and not sacrifice.' I did not come to invite the 'righteous' to salvation but 'sinners.' "

Then John's disciples approached Me with a question, "Why do we and the Pharisees fast often, but Your disciples do not?"

I will show you when to fast and how to fast. May you fast to know Me more intimately.

"Can the wedding guests mourn while they have the bridegroom?" I replied. "The day will come when the bridegroom will be taken from them—they will certainly fast then! No one sews a patch of unshrunk cloth on to an old coat, for the patch will pull away from the coat and the hole will be worse than ever. Nor do people put fresh wine into old wineskins—otherwise the skins burst, the wine is spilt, and the skins are ruined. But they put fresh wine into new skins and both are preserved."

The Woman and the 12-Year-Old Girl

While I was saying these things to them, an official came up to Me and knelt before Me saying, "My daughter has just died. Please come and lay Your hand on her and she will live." I arose and followed him with My disciples.

And on the way a woman who had had a hemorrhage for twelve years came at Me from behind and touched the hem of My cloak. "If I can only touch His cloak," she kept saying to herself, "I shall be healed."

But I turned around and saw her. "Be of good cheer, my daughter," I said, "your faith—not your touch—has healed you." And the woman was completely cured from that moment.

Then when I came into the official's house and saw the flute players and mourners, I said, "Depart, the little girl is not dead, but asleep." They laughed at Me with scorn. But when the crowd had been put out,

I took her by the hand, and the girl got up. And this was reported to the whole district.

I was interrupted as I was going to Jairus' house, when I stopped to heal a woman with an issue of blood. Both the woman and Jairus' daughter were important, so I will teach you the importance of people and give you compassion so you will know when to let people interrupt you.

As I passed on My way, two blind men followed Me crying out, "Have mercy on us, Son of David!"

And when I had gone inside the house the two came to Me. I asked, "Do you believe I can heal you?"

"Yes, Lord," they replied.

Then I touched their eyes, saying, "So shall it be." Then their eyes were opened, but I sternly warned them, "Don't tell anyone." Yet they went and spread it throughout the whole district.

Later, when My disciples and I were coming out of the town, they brought to Me a dumb man who was demon-possessed. As soon as the demon had been cast out, the dumb man began to talk. The crowds were amazed saying, "Never has this ever happened in Israel."

But the Pharisees' comment was, "He cast out demons by the power of demons."

The Twelve Sent Two by Two

I traveled through the towns and villages, teaching in their synagogues, proclaiming the gospel of the kingdom, and healing all kinds of illness and disability. As I saw the crowds coming to Me, I was deeply moved with compassion for them, for they were helpless and lost and like a flock of sheep without a shepherd. "The harvest is great," I remarked to My disciples, "but the reapers are few. Pray therefore to the Lord of the harvest to send laborers to harvest the fields."

I will give you compassion for hopeless people who need help, just as I had compassion on them.

CHOOSING MY DISCIPLES

I called My twelve disciples to Me, and gave them authority over the demons, so that they could cast them out, and could cure any disease or sickness. Here are the names of the twelve apostles: first, Simon, who was named Peter, and his brother Andrew, James the son of Zebedee and his brother John, Philip, and Bartholomew (Nathaniel), Thomas, and Matthew the tax collector, James the son of Alpheus, and Thaddeus (Judas), Simon the zealot, and Judas Iscariot, who afterward betrayed Me.

I sent these twelve out, after challenging them, "Do not go to the Gentiles, or to any Samaritan town, but rather go to the lost sheep of Israel. And as you go continue to preach, 'The kingdom of heaven is near.' Keep on healing the sick, raising the dead, cleansing lepers, and casting out demons. You received, so you must give and take no pay."

I will give you an open heart to see needy people, and give you a willing heart to help them. Then you, like My disciples, can open your hands to help them.

"Do not accept gold or silver or even copper money and do not take a purse for your journey, nor two shirts, nor shoes, nor a staff, for the workman is worthy of his pay.

"Into whatever town or village you go, find some deserving person, and stay at his house until you leave the place. As you go into his house, bless it, and if the house should prove deserving, pray for peace on it. And whoever will not welcome you, or listen to your words, on leaving that place, shake off the dust from your feet. I tell you, the punishment, in the day of judgment, will be easier for Sodom and Gomorrah than for that town.

"I am sending you out as sheep threatened by wolves. So you must be wise like serpents and harmless like doves. Watch out, some men will turn you over to the courts and they will beat you in the synagogues, and you will be brought before governors and kings for My sake. When they bring you before the courts, you must not worry what you should say, for it will be given you at that hour what you should say. Because it is not you who is speaking, but the Spirit of our Father who is speaking through you.

"One brother will turn against another to be killed, and a father his child, and children will take a stand against their parents, and will have them put to death. And you will be hated by all men, because you bear My Name; but whoever endures to the end will be saved. But whenever they persecute you in one town, flee to another. For I say, you will not go to all the towns of Israel before I, the Son of Man returns."

There will be persecution, because I predicted it while on this earth. I will prepare you mentally for persecution, and use you in suffering to bring glory to My Father.

"No pupil is better than his teacher, and no slave is better than his master. The pupil should be satisfied to become like his teacher, and the slave should be satisfied to become like his master. If men have called the head of the house Beelzebub, how much worse names will they give to the members of the family! So you must never be afraid of them; for there is nothing covered that will not be uncovered and there is not a secret that will not be revealed.

"What I speak to you in the dark, proclaim in the light, and what you hear whispered in your ears, shout from the housetops. You must not be afraid of those who kill the body, but can't kill the soul. But rather fear God, who can destroy both soul and body in hell. Do not sparrows sell for a penny apiece? And yet not one of them will fall to the ground without your heavenly Father knowing it. Even the hairs on your head are numbered by God. So do not fear; you are worth much more than many sparrows.

"Therefore, everyone who will testify of Me before men I will testify of them before My Father in heaven, but anyone who denies Me before men I will deny him before My Father in heaven."

Confess Me at all times in all places. Do not be ashamed of Me.

"Many think I have come to bring peace into the earth. But no, I have come to bring a sword. For I have come to put a man against his father, and a daughter against her mother, and a daughter-in-law against her mother-in-law. A man's enemies may be members of his own family. Anyone who loves father or mother more than he loves Me is not worthy of Me, and anyone worthy of Me must take up his cross and follow Me. Anybody who gains only human life will lose heavenly life, and anybody who loses his human life, for My sake, will gain heavenly life.

"Whoever welcomes you as My disciple, also welcomes Me, and whoever welcomes Me also welcomes My Father who sent Me. Whoever receives a prophet will receive only the reward of a prophet, and whoever receives an upright man will only receive the reward of an upright man. And I truly say to you, no one who gives a cup of cold water to the least of My disciples will fail to get his reward."

ELEVEN

JOHN THE BAPTIZER

When I had finished My sermon to My disciples, I left to teach and preach in their towns.

The Doubts of John the Baptizer

Now John was in prison when he heard what I was doing. He sent this message by My disciples: "Are you the One who was to come, or should we keep on looking for a different Messiah?"

Then I answered, "Go tell John what you have heard and seen, the blind are seeing and the crippled are walking, the lepers are being healed and the deaf are hearing, the dead are being raised and the poor are having the good news preached to them. And happy is the man who does not lose faith in Me."

As John's disciples were leaving, I began speaking to the crowd about John: "What did you go out into the desert to see? A reed that is tossed about by the wind? If not, what did you go out to see? A man dressed in fine clothes? No, those who dress that way are found in the courts of kings. What did you really go to see? To see a prophet? This is the one of whom the Scripture says, 'Behold! I am sending my messenger before you; he will prepare the road ahead of the Messiah.' I solemnly say to you, no one born of women is greater than John the Baptizer, and those who make themselves least important in the kingdom of heaven is greater than he. And from the days of John the Baptizer until now the kingdom of heaven has been attacked by violence, and those who capture it are seizing a precious prize. For until the days of John all the prophets and the law prophesied its coming, and if you will listen, John himself is the Elijah who was to come. Let him, who has ears, use them to listen!

"But how can I show what the leaders of this age are like? They are like little children sitting in the marketplaces playing their games and singing their songs, 'We played the wedding march for you, but you did not dance; we sang the funeral dirge, but you did not cry.' For John came neither feasting nor drinking, and yet they said, 'He has a demon.' I, The Son of Man, came enjoying eating with others, and they say, 'He is a glutton and a wine-drinker, a friend of tax collectors and notorious sinners!' So what's the conclusion? A wise man is vindicated by his results!"

Judgment for the Unrepentant

Then I began to condemn the cities, in which My many miracles had been done, because they did not repent. "Judgment on you, Chorazin! Judgment on you, Bethsaida! For if the miracles done in you had been done in Tyre and Sidon, they would have repented in burlap clothing and ashes long ago. Moreover, I tell you, on the day of judgment the punishment will be more bearable for Tyre and Sidon than for you! And you, Capernaum, will you be exalted to heaven? No, you will be thrown to the regions of the dead! For if the miracles done in you had been done in Sodom, that city would have lived until today. But I tell you, on the day of judgment the punishment will be easier for the land of Sodom than for you!"

If believers in my redeeming power will pray for their nation, then I will forgive and restore their nation. May they return to Me and be spared the fate of Sodom and Capernaum.

My Prayer to God the Father

At that time I prayed, "O Father, Lord of heaven and earth, thank You for concealing these matters from wise and intelligent men, and for showing them to little children. Yes, Father, I thank You that You do Your will. All the things I do have been entrusted to Me by My Father. No one knows Me, the Son, but My Father; and no one but Me, the Son, knows My Father. And I make Him known to whoever I will."

I want you to know Me, and to spend your life learning about Me. Then, one day, you will live with Me for eternity in a place that I am preparing for you.

"Come to Me, all who are tired and carry heavy burdens, and I will give you rest. Take My yoke, and learn from Me, for I am gentle and humble in heart, and you will find rest for your souls. My yoke is easy, and My load is light."

TWELVE

THE SABBATH

As I walked through the wheat fields one Sabbath, My disciples were hungry, so they pulled the heads of wheat and ate them. When the Pharisees saw it, they said to Me, "Look! Your disciples are doing what the law forbids on the Sabbath!"

But I said to them, "Did you ever read what David did when he and his soldiers became hungry? How he went into the house of God and ate the sacred loaves, which was against the law to eat? It was wrong for anyone except the priests. Or did you ever read in the law that the priests in the temple break the Sabbath every Sabbath day, yet they are not guilty? But something greater than the temple is here! If you only understood the Scriptures that say, 'It is mercy and not sacrifice that I want,' you would not have condemned My disciples who are not guilty. For I, the Son of Man, am Lord of the Sabbath."

The Shriveled Hand Healed

Leaving there I went into their synagogue. Now there happened to be a man there with a shriveled hand. And to find something against Me, they asked, "Is it legal to cure people on the Sabbath?"

But I said to them, "If any of you has only one sheep and it falls into a ditch on the Sabbath, will you not pull it out? And how much more is a man worth than a sheep! So it is right to do good on the Sabbath." Then I said to the man, "Reach out your hand," and he held it out and it was cured. It became like his other hand. But the Pharisees left and planned to put Me to death.

Multitudes Healed

Because I knew about their plots, I left that area. Many people followed Me, and I cured them all, and charged them not to call attention to Me. In this way I fulfilled the saying spoken by the prophet Isaiah, "Behold, my Servant whom I have chosen, my Beloved, in whom my soul is well pleased. I will put my Spirit on Him, and He will declare a judgment to the pagan. He will not strive nor challenge anyone; His voice will not be announced in the streets; a bruised reed He will not break; a tiny flame He will not put out until He turns His judgment into victory. And the pagan will hope in His name."

The Long Day

A man, under the power of demons, who was blind and dumb was brought to Me. I cured him so that he could talk and see. The crowd was dumbfounded, and began to say, "This is the Son of David."

When the Pharisees heard it, they said, "This man is casting out demons by the power of Beelzebub, the prince of the demons."

But I knew their thoughts, so I said to them, "Any kingdom that is divided against itself will fall and no town or family that is divided against itself will last. Now, if satan is driving out satan, he is divided against himself. How then can his kingdom last? And if I am driving out demons by the help of Beelzebub, by what authority are your sons casting them out? But if I, by the Spirit of God, cast out demons, then the kingdom of God has come to you. How can anyone get into a strong man's house and carry off his goods unless he first binds the strong man? After that he can carry off everything out of his house. Whoever is not with Me is against Me, and whoever does not gather with Me scatters."

The Unpardonable Sin

"So I tell you, every sin and all blasphemy will be forgiven men, but blasphemy against the Spirit cannot be forgiven. And whoever speaks a word against Me, the Son of Man, will be forgiven, but whoever speaks blasphemy against God, the Holy Spirit, will not be forgiven, either in this world or in the world to come."

The sin that could not be pardoned didn't come just from words, it came from a heart that hated God and rebelled against Me. To blaspheme is to smite with words, to denote injurious speaking against God's nature, attributes, or works. I will keep your heart in tune with Me. Never say anything to anger or turn Me against you. Guard your lips.

"You must choose a good tree and get good fruit or choose an evil tree and get evil fruit, because a tree is judged by its fruit. You brood of snakes! How can you, evil as you are, say anything that is good? For out of the mouth the heart speaks. A good man, out of his good heart, speaks good things. The evil man, out of his evil heart, speaks evil things. So I tell you, for every careless word that men speak, they will have to give account on the day of judgment. By your words you will be free, and by your words you will be judged."

Then some of the scribes and Pharisees asked Me, "Teacher, we would like to see You do a spectacular miracle."

But I answered, "Only a wicked and treacherous age will ask for a spectacular sign, but no sign will be given to them but the sign of the prophet Jonah. For as Jonah was in the great fish's stomach for three days and nights, so I, the Son of Man, will be three days and nights in the heart of the earth. The men of Nineveh will condemn the leaders of this age at the judgment. The men of Nineveh turned and believed the message preached by Jonah. But there is a greater than Jonah here! The queen of the South will condemn the leaders of this age at the judgment, because she came from the farthest limits of the earth to listen to Solomon's wisdom. There is a greater than Solomon here!

"Whenever the evil spirit goes out of a man, it wanders about in deserts in search of rest, but cannot find it. Then it says, 'I will go back to my house which I left,' where it finds the house unoccupied, swept, and ready for use. Then the evil spirit goes and gets seven other spirits more evil than itself, and they go in and make their home. So the end of that man is worse than the beginning. This is what will happen to the wicked leaders of this age."

While I was still speaking to the crowds, My mother and My brothers came to stand outside the house to speak to Me. Someone said to Me, "Your mother and brothers are waiting outside to talk with you."

But I answered, "Who is My mother, and who are My brothers?" And with a gesture toward My disciples I said, "Here are My mother and My brothers. For whoever does the will of My heavenly Father is My mother and brother and sister."

THIRTEEN

THE SERMON BY
THE SEA

I left Peter's house to teach the multitude from a boat beside the shore of the Sea of Galilee.

"Look," I said, pointing to a farmer sowing seed in his field, which was nearby, "Some seed fell on the path next to the field; birds quickly came to eat up the seeds." I noted next, "Other seed fell among the rocks and because there was little dirt, the grain sprang up fast, but withered when the hot sun beat upon it, because the roots had little nourishment." I continued, "Other seed fell among thorns and the thorns choked their growth." I told, "Still other seed fell on rich soil and produced a crop, some places a hundredfold, some other places sixty, and some places thirty." Finally I said, "If you have ears to hear, then you will understand the spiritual application of this parable."

The disciples asked, "Why do You use stories to teach?"

I replied, "Because you have the privilege of understanding the secrets of the kingdom, but the unbelievers don't understand spiritual truth." I continued, "When a person does something for Me, he will be given more till he has plenty. If a person does nothing for Me, what he has will be taken away. This is why I am speaking to them in stories, because they look, but do not see, they listen, but do not really hear or understand." I quoted Isaiah to describe those who rejected Me, "They listen with their ears, but they don't understand what God says. They see with their eyes, but don't perceive because their heart is hardened to God. So they hear the good news, but don't understand how God wants them to respond, so they won't believe and become converted."

I will give you eyes to see My truth; and I will take away your blindness. I will give you a heart to obey My commands; and I will take away any doubt.

"But blessed are your eyes, for they are beginning to see, and your ears, for they are beginning to hear. For I solemnly say to you, many prophets and upright men yearned to see what you are seeing, and did not see it, and to hear what you are hearing, and did not hear it."

I then explained the story for the disciples, because they had believing hearts to understand what the story meant. "When a person hears the message of the kingdom and does not respond, the devil comes to snatch away the message, as the birds take the seed from the path. When a person receives the message but doesn't understand, he gives up when trouble or persecution comes. He is like the grain sown in the rocks. And what was sown on the thin rocky soil illustrates the man who hears the message, and bubbling over with joy, at once accepts it. However, because the seed takes no real root in him, he lasts only a little while, and just as soon as suffering and persecution come for the truth's sake, he at once yields and falls. When a person hears the message but gives up because of worldly things or pursuit of money, it is like the seed sown among the thorns. And what was sown among the thorns illustrates the man who hears the message, and the worries of the times and the pleasures of being rich choke the truth out, and he yields no fruit. But when someone hears and believes the message, he brings forth fruit: thirty, sixty, or a hundredfold, he is like seed sown on rich soil."

May your heart be good soil to receive and believe. I will take away the thorns of sin, and the stubbornness of unbelief.

I then told another parable of a farmer who planted seed in his field. "While he slept the enemy sowed weeds among the good seed. And when the wheat plants grew up and yielded their ripened grain, the weeds appeared too. The workers told the owner, 'You planted good wheat, so where did these weeds come from?' The farmer said, 'An enemy has done this!' The workers asked, 'Do you want us to pull up all the weeds right now?' 'No,' the farmer said, 'If you pull up the weeds, you'll also pull up the good grain. Let them both grow until harvest, then burn the weeds, but put the grain in the barn.'"

The enemy tries to destroy everything that is godly. I will give you wisdom to know the difference between seeds and weeds. I will protect you in this world as you work for Me.

I then told another parable that My kingdom was like a tiny mustard seed sown in a field. While it is the smallest of seeds, it grows into the largest of trees, and many birds rest in its branches.

My message seems weak to the unsaved, but it is the power of God to salvation that will attract many to My salvation.

I then said, "My kingdom is like yeast. When put in flour, the bread swells up much larger."

When I continued to speak to the crowd in parables, the disciples asked why I used parables. I told them I was fulfilling the prophecy of Israel, "I will open my mouth with parables to explain God's eternal mysteries."

Then I left the crowds and went into the house. And My disciples came up to Me and said, "Explain to us the story of the wild wheat in the field."

And I answered, 'The sower of the good seed is the Son of Man; the field is the world; the good seed are the members of the kingdom; the wild seed are the followers of the evil one. The enemy who sowed them is the devil, the harvest is the close of the age, and the reapers are angels. Just as the wild seeds are gathered and burned up, so it will be at the close of the age. I, the Son of Man, will send out My angels, and they will gather from out of My kingdom all those who cause evil and are disobedient. They will throw them into the furnace of fire, where they will weep and grind their teeth. Then the righteous will shine like the sun in the kingdom of their Father. Let him who has ears listen and do!'"

Again, I told that My kingdom was like a treasure that was buried in a field. "Someone found the treasure, then went to sell everything to get money to buy the field."

Again, I told the story of someone searching for pearls to buy; "When he found the greatest pearl ever, he sold everything to buy it."

I AM the pearl of infinite price. You can have confidence and I will give you the faith to give up everything to have Me.

I told the final story of a big net that was thrown into the sea. "When it was full, the fisherman pulled it to shore; they put the good fish in a barrel, but threw away the bad ones. So it will be at the close of the age; the angels will go out to separate the wicked from the upright, and will throw them into the furnace of torturing punishment. There they will wail and grind their teeth."

"Do you understand all these parables?"

They answered Me, "Yes."

I said to them, "Everyone who knows the law and has become a disciple in the kingdom of heaven is like a house owner who can bring out of his storeroom new things as well as old." When I had finished these stories, I left there.

I went to My own country and kept teaching in their synagogue in such a way that they were amazed, and said, "Where did this man get His wisdom? Is He not the carpenter's son? Is not His mother's name Mary, are not his brothers James, Joseph, Simon, and Judas? And are not his sisters living here with us? Where then did He get all this knowledge?" And so they were offended because of Me.

But I said to them, "No prophet is ever honored in his own town and in his own home." And so I did not perform many miracles there, because of their lack of faith.

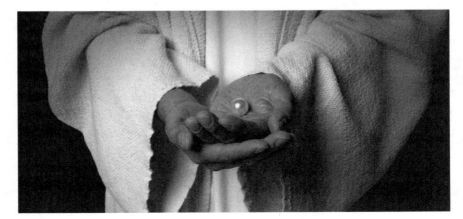

FOURTEEN

THE MURDER OF JOHN THE BAPTIZER

Then Herod the Tetrarch said this about My fame, "This is John the Baptizer risen from the dead." For Herod had arrested John and chained him in prison to please Herodias, the wife of Philip, his brother. John had preached that it was against Scripture for Herod to marry his brother's wife. Herod wanted to execute John, but was afraid because the people regarded John as a prophet. His wife, Herodias, also wanted to kill John because he had embarrassed her, but she couldn't arrange for it to happen.

During Herod's birthday, the daughter of Herodias danced before the guests at the party. Herod was so delighted with her that he made an oath to give her anything she asked.

Her mother, Herodias, told her to ask for the head of John the Baptizer on a platter.

The king was sorry that he made the oath and was embarrassed because his guests expected him to do what he promised. Herod sent immediately and beheaded John in prison; the head was brought in on a platter and given to the girl who gave it to her mother. John's disciples came and took the body and buried it, and then they told Me.

Feeding the Five Thousand

When I heard about the death of John the Baptizer, I left there in a boat for a quiet place, to be alone. And when the crowds heard where

I went, they followed Me on foot. When I got out of the boat and saw a great crowd, My heart was moved with compassion for them, so I healed the sick. But when it was evening, My disciples said, "This is a barren place, and it is getting dark; send the people to buy themselves food in the villages."

But I said to them, "You give them something to eat."

They answered, "We have only five loaves and two fish."

I said, "Bring them to Me." After summoning the people to sit down on the grass, I received the five loaves and two fish; then I looked up to heaven and thanked God. Then I broke the loaves into small pieces and gave them to the disciples, and they distributed them to the people. Everyone ate and had enough. Then the disciples took up the fragments that were left, and filled twelve baskets. The crowd was about five thousand men, besides women and children.

I Am the Creator, God the Son, and I Am the Bread of Life. I will provide physical food for you when you are hungry. I will fill you spiritually with the bread of life when you are weak.

Immediately the disciples got into a boat to cross over to the other side ahead of Me. After I dismissed the crowds, I climbed up a hill that evening to pray alone.

I Walk on the Water

The disciples in the boat were a long way from shore, struggling against the waves, for the wind was blowing in their faces.

In the fourth watch I went to them, walking on the water. And when the disciples saw Me walking on the water, they were terrified, and cried, "It's a ghost!" screaming with fear.

Immediately I spoke to them, "Be of good cheer. It is I; stop being afraid."

Peter yelled, "Lord, if it's You, invite me to walk on the water to You."

I said, "Come!" So Peter stepped out of the boat and walked on the water, and walked toward Me. But when he felt the force of the wind, and saw the waves, he was frightened, and began to sink.

Immediately Peter cried out, "Lord, save me!"

I reached out My hand and grabbed Peter, and said, "You have little faith! Why did you doubt?" And when they got into the boat, the wind suddenly died down.

The men in the boat worshiped Me and said, "Truly You are God the Son."

I will allow storms in your life that test your faith. I will also help you to be faithful to Me in every storm that comes. I did the impossible; I walked on water and I came to them in their storm. So be like the disciples, who worshiped Me, after I delivered you from your storm.

We crossed over and came to Gennesaret. And the men of that place recognized Me and told everyone about Me. They brought to Me the sick, and begged Me to let them touch the hem of My coat, and the sick, who touched it, were healed.

FIFTEEN

FOLLOW GOD'S COMMANDS

Jewish leaders came from Jerusalem to Capernaum to find fault with My religious practices. They were angry because My disciples ate bread with defiled hands; they didn't wash their hands ceremonially before eating.

I told the Jewish leaders, "You violate the Word of God and hold to your traditions. God commanded you to honor your father and mother; the one who curses father and mother shall be put to death. But you say, 'My mother and father have profited because they gave birth to me.' This statement does not honor your parents, but actually denies the Scriptures."

I quoted Isaiah, "This people honors Me in outward ways, but their heart is far from Me. They vainly worship Me, teaching their doctrine as the Word of God."

I called the multitude to Myself, and said, "Listen and understand: it's not the things that go in your mouth that defile you, it's what comes out of the mouth."

The disciples told Me that I was offending the Pharisees by what I was saying. I replied, "Every plant put there by God will be uprooted. Let them alone; they are blind leading the blind. When the blind leads the blind, they both fall into a ditch."

Peter said, "Lord, explain this parable to us."

I said, "Are you still without understanding? What goes into the mouth, enters the stomach, and finally is discharged from the body, but things that come out of the heart, defile a person, for out of the heart come evil thoughts, murders, adulteries, sexual perversions, thefts, lying, pride, and anger. The things that come out of the heart defile a person, not eating with unwashed hands."

I will cleanse your heart from every thought of evil. I will keep your thoughts centered on Me. I will sit on the throne of your heart and control all you think and do. I will forgive the sinful desires of your heart and keep you from all outward transgressions.

I Visit Lebanon

When I left Galilee and went to Tyre and Sidon, a Greek woman from Canaan came and cried out to Me, "Have mercy on me, O Lord, Son of David. My daughter is possessed with a demon," and she begged Me to cast the demon out.

But I didn't answer her. The disciples urged Me to send her away, "She pesters us with her pleading."

I answered, "I was sent only to the lost sheep of Israel."

Then she worshiped Me, and said, "Lord, help me."

I said, "It is not good to take bread from the children, and throw it to the little dogs under the table." I didn't respond in a positive way but referred to her as a dog, the Jewish word for Gentile.

But the woman showed faith by replying, "Yes, Lord, but the dogs under the table get to eat the crumbs from the Master."

I answered, "Woman you have great faith, you will get what you asked;" and the daughter was immediately healed.

I will give you bold faith, like the Canaanite woman, when you pray persistently. You need to look only to Me for your spiritual needs.

Then I left and returned to the shore of the Sea of Galilee. Then I went up a hill to sit. Great crowds came to Me, bringing their lame, crippled, blind, deaf, and many others with diseases. They laid them at My feet, and I cured them. The crowd was astonished so they praised the God of Israel.

Then I called My disciples and said, "My heart has compassion for the crowd because they have been here and they have nothing left to eat. I fear they might faint on their way home."

The disciples answered, "This is an isolated place, where can we find food enough to feed such a crowd?"

I asked, "How many loaves of bread are available?" They answered, "Seven, and a few small fish."

Then I instructed the crowd to sit down. I gave thanks and kept giving the pieces to the disciples and they kept giving food to the people. And everyone ate and were filled. The disciples took up the pieces of food left over and filled seven baskets. There were about four thousand men, besides women and children. Then I sent the crowds away, entered a boat, and went to Magadan.

SIXTEEN

MY CHURCH IS INTRODUCED

Some Pharisees and Sadducees tried to test Me by asking to see a spectacular miracle from heaven. I answered them, "When you see a red sky at night, you know it will be a delightful evening. When you see a red sky in the morning, you must take warning because the weather is threatening. Hypocrites! You now know how to discern the signs of the sky, but you can't discern the signs of the times. Only a wicked and evil generation seeks a spectacular miracle, so no sign will be given to you but the sign of Jonah." Then I left, and went away.

I will help you understand the signs of change in this world. I am coming back to receive My Church. So be ready!

Then the disciples and I crossed the sea. The disciples forgot to take any bread. So I said to them, "Watch yourselves, and guard yourselves against the contaminating yeast of the Pharisees and the Sadducees!"

Then the disciples discussed what I said among themselves, saying, "Was it because we did not take any bread?"

I knew what they said, "Why are you talking among yourselves that you have no bread? You still have little faith and you still don't understand. Remember the five loaves that fed five thousand and how many basketfuls you took up? Remember the seven loaves for four thousand people and how many baskets you took up. Why do you not understand that I was not speaking about physical bread when I said to guard yourselves against the contaminating yeast of the Pharisees and the Sadducees?" Then they understood that I meant guard your inner yeast, the teaching of the Pharisees and the Sadducees, not outer yeast.

I Visit Caesarea Philippi

Next I went to the village of Caesarea Philippi, and as we were walking, I asked, "Who do the people say that I am?"

The disciples answered, "Some say You are John the Baptizer, others say You are Elijah, or Jeremiah or one of the prophets."

I then asked, "But who do you say that I am?"

Simon Peter answered, "You are the Christ, the Son of the Living God."

I answered him, "Simon Peter, son of Jonah, you are blessed, you didn't think this up, My Father in heaven gave you this revelation. Peter, you have faith like a rock, and I will build My church on the solid rock statement of My deity that you just spoke about. The gates of hell cannot stop My followers when they go preaching who I Am." I then replied, "I will give you the keys to the kingdom of heaven. Whatever you bind on earth will not enter heaven, whatever you loose on earth, will enter heaven." I then instructed them not to tell anyone I was the Messiah, the anointed of God.

Then I told My disciples that I must go to Jerusalem to suffer many things from the chief priest and the scribes, and be killed by them, but I would rise from the dead on the third day.

Peter rebuked Me saying, "This will never happen to You."

I turned and said to Peter, "Get behind Me, you are like satan; you are a stumbling block. You are not concerned with the things of God, but with the things of men."

Then I said, "If anyone will follow Me, let him take up his cross daily and follow Me. For whoever tries to save his life on this earth, will lose it. But whoever loses his life for My sake, will find it. For what benefit will it gain a man, if he gains the whole world and loses his soul? What price will a man pay to buy back his soul?"

"For I, the Son of Man, am going to return to earth in My Father's splendor, with My angels, and then I will reward everyone in accord with what that person has done. Some of those standing here will live to see Me coming with My kingdom."

SEVENTEEN

A MEETING WITH GOD

Six days after I spoke at Caesarea Philippi I took Peter, James, and John with Me and climbed up into the heights of Mount Hermon.

I was transfigured before them; My face glistened as the sun, My clothes were sparkling white. Then Moses and Elijah appeared and talked with Me about My coming death. Peter said to Me, "Master, it is good for us to be here, let's make three tents, one for You, one for Moses, and one for Elijah."

While Peter was speaking, a bright cloud covered us and the three disciples were afraid. Then the voice of God the Father spoke from the cloud, "This is my beloved Son, in whom I am well pleased; listen to Him and obey Him."

The disciples fell to the ground in fear, then I touched them saying, "Don't be afraid." When they looked up, I was the only one they saw.

As we were going down the mountain I said to them, "Don't tell anyone about this until I am raised from the dead."

The disciples asked Me, "Why do the scribes say Elijah must come before Messiah comes?"

I answered, "It is true that Elijah must come to get everything ready. But I'm telling you that Elijah has already come, but the scribes didn't know it and unsaved people will do to John the Baptizer as they want. In the same way I, the Son of Man, will suffer at their hands." The disciples understood that I meant John the Baptizer was Elijah.

The Disciples Can't Heal

When the disciples and I reached the crowd, a man came kneeling before Me begging, "Lord have pity on my son, for he has epilepsy and suffers terribly. He often falls into the fire or into the water. I brought him to Your disciples, but they could not heal him."

And I answered, "O you faithless and unbelieving generation. How much longer must I put up with you? Bring the boy to me!" And I rebuked the demon, and it came out of him. Immediately the boy was cured.

Later the disciples came privately to Me to ask, "Why could we not cast out the demon?"

I answered, "Because your faith is small. For verily I say, if you have faith the size of a mustard seed, you can say to this mountain, 'Move from here to there,' and it will move. Nothing is impossible for you who believe. However, this can be done only with prayer and continued fasting."

While we traveled through Galilee, I said, "I, the Son of Man, am going to be turned over into the hands of those who will kill Me, but on the third day I will be raised again." That news crushed them.

Paying the Temple Tax

When we reached Capernaum, the collectors of the temple tax came to Peter and asked, "Why does your Teacher not pay the temple tax?"

When I entered the house, I anticipated Simon's questions, so I said, "What is your opinion, Simon? From whom do civil rulers collect taxes? From their own family or from others?"

Peter answered, "From others."

I said to him, "So their own sons are exempt. But that we may not offend them, go down to the sea and throw in a hook. Pull in the first fish that bites, open its mouth and you will find in it a shekel. Take that money and pay the tax for both of us."

CHILDLIKE FAITH

The disciples approached Me and asked, "Who is the greatest in the kingdom of heaven?"

I called a little child to stand with them, and I said, "Truly I say to you, unless you repent and become like little children, you will never enter the kingdom of heaven. Whoever becomes meek as this little child will be the greatest in the kingdom of heaven, and whoever receives a little child like this for My sake receives Me."

Mistaken Zeal of John the Apostle

"Whoever influences one of these little ones who believe in Me to sin, will have a great stone hung around his neck and cast into the bottom of the sea. A person will be condemned who does this wrong! Evil comes to all, but the man who does this will be condemned. If your hand or foot makes you do wrong, cut it off or get rid of anything that condemns you. It is better to go through life crippled than to be thrown into everlasting torture with both hands or feet. And if your eye makes you do wrong, pluck it out and get rid of anything that causes you to do wrong. It is better for you to go through life with a single eye than to be thrown into hell with both eyes. Be careful you don't look with anger on a little child, because their guardian angels in heaven have continued access to My Father in heaven.

"If a man has a hundred sheep and one is lost, he will leave his ninety-nine, to go search for the lost one. When he finds it, he rejoices over it more than he does over ninety-nine that did not get lost. In the same way it is not the will of my Father in heaven that a single one of these little ones be lost.

"If your brother does something wrong, go to him privately and show where he is wrong. If he listens, you have won back your brother. If he will not listen, take one or two others, so that you have witnesses confirmed by their testimony. If he refuses to listen to them, report the matter to the church. And if he refuses to listen to the church, treat him as a pagan and as an abomination.

"Verily I say to you, whatever you bind on earth is bound in heaven, and whatever you release on earth is released in heaven.

"Verily I tell you, if only two of you on earth agree on what they ask, you will receive it from my heavenly Father. For where two or three meet as My disciples, I am present with them."

Then Peter asked Me, "Lord, how often may my brother sin against me and I have to forgive him? As often as seven?"

I answered, "Not as many as seven, I tell you, but as many as seventy times seven! The kingdom of heaven may be compared to a king who decided to settle up the accounts of his servants. First, a servant was brought to the king who owed his master millions of dollars. And because he could not pay, his master ordered him to be sold, with his wife and children and all his belongings, until payment was made. The servant fell at his master's feet and begged, 'Give me time, and I will pay you everything.' The master's heart was moved with sympathy, and he let him go free, and canceled his debt.

"The servant went to one of his fellow servants who owed him ten dollars, and choked him by the throat, demanding, 'Pay me now the ten dollars.' The fellow servant fell down and pleaded, 'Give me time, and I will pay you.' But he refused and threw him in jail until he should pay the debt. When the other slaves saw what had happened, they went to report what happened to their master. Then the master called to the first servant, and said, 'I canceled your huge debt because you pleaded with me. Should not you have shown mercy to your fellow slave, as I did for you?' The master was angry and turned him over to the torturers until he paid the whole debt. This is how My heavenly Father will deal with you, if you do not freely forgive your brother."

NINETEEN

THE RICH YOUNG RULER

When I had finished this sermon, I left Galilee and came into the district of Judea that is on the other side of the Jordan. Great crowds followed Me, and I healed them.

I Teach on Divorce

Some Pharisees came to test Me with this question, "Is it lawful for a man to divorce his wife on any grounds?"

I answered, "Have you not read that the Creator at the beginning made them male and female, and said, 'For this reason a man shall leave his father and mother and become one with his wife, and the two of them shall be one?' So they are no longer two but one. So, what God has joined together man must not separate."

They asked Me, "Then why did Moses command that a written divorce be allowed for a man to divorce his wife?"

I answered them, "It was because of your hard heart that Moses allowed you to divorce your wives, but it was not allowed from the beginning. Now I tell you, whoever divorces his wife for any reason other than her unfaithfulness, and marries another woman, is guilty of adultery."

The disciples said to Me, "If that is the way a man should treat his wife, then why get married?"

I said to them, "Not every man can live single, it is only for those who have this capacity. For some are born eunuchs, and some have been made eunuchs by men, and some have made themselves eunuchs for the sake of the kingdom of heaven. Let anyone do this who can."

Little Children Come to Me

Later some little children were brought to Me so I would lay My hands on them and pray for them. But My disciples rebuked them. I said, "Let the little children come to Me and stop turning them away, for such is the kingdom of heaven." And I laid My hands on them to bless them.

I will teach you the importance of children. May you love them and bless them as I did. May you see the great potential in every child. May you help children find My wonderful plan for their life.

The Rich Young Ruler

A man asked Me, "What good deed can I do to gain eternal life?"

And I answered, "Why are you asking Me about what is good? Only the heavenly Father is perfectly good. But if you want eternal life, you must continually keep the commandments."

He asked Me, "What commandments?"

I answered, "You must not kill, you must not commit adultery, you must not steal, you must not lie, you must honor your father and mother, and you must love your neighbor as you love yourself."

The young man said to Me, "I have kept all these; what more do I need to do?"

I said, "If you are going to be perfect, go and sell what you own and give the money to the poor, and you will have riches in heaven; then come and follow Me."

And when the young man heard this qualification he turned away in sorrow for he owned a lot of property.

Surrender the control of all your belongings to Me. Than I will help you use all your belongings for My glory. May belongings never possess you, but use all your "things" for My purpose for your life.

I then told My disciples, "Verily I say to you, it is hard for a rich man to enter the kingdom of heaven. And it is easier for a camel to enter through a needle's eye than for a rich man to enter the kingdom of heaven."

When the disciples heard this, they were astonished, and asked,

"Who can be saved then?"

But I told them, "This is impossible with men, but everything is possible with God."

Then Peter answered Me, "We have left everything to follow You. What are we going to get?"

I said to them, "Verily I say to you, in the new world when I, the Son of Man, shall take My seat on My throne, you who have followed Me, will sit on twelve thrones and rule the twelve tribes of Israel. And everyone who has left home, brothers, sisters, father, mother, children, or land, for My sake, will be rewarded a hundred times in addition to eternal life. But many who are first now will be last and many who are last will then be first."

TWENTY

ON THE WAY TO JERUSALEM

I taught a parable, "Now the kingdom of heaven is like a land owner who went out early in the morning to hire laborers for his vineyard. He contracted with them for a day's wages, then sent them off to work. He went out again about nine o'clock and found workers standing idle. So he contracted with them, 'You also go work in my vineyard, and I will pay you what is right.' And they went to work. Again he went out about twelve o'clock and three o'clock, and made the same contract. About five went out again and found still others were idle. He said to them, 'Why have you been standing here all day idle?' They answered, 'Because no one has hired us.' He said, 'Go work in my vineyard.'

"At the end of the day, the owner of the vineyard said to his manager, 'Call the workers and pay them their wages, beginning with the last and ending with the first.' Those who had been hired at five o'clock, each received a full day's wages. And those who were hired first thought that they would receive more; but they too received each a full day's wages. And they began to complain, and say, 'These you hired last worked only one hour, and yet you have paid them the same thing you paid us. We have done the heavy work in the scorching heat of the day.' But the land owner answered, 'Friend, I am not doing you wrong. Did you not contract with me for a day's wages? Take what you earned and go. I choose to pay the last man hired as much as I pay you. Do I not have the right to do what I please with my own money? Must you be covetous because I am generous?' Those who are last will now be first, and those who are first will be last."

The Selfish Ambition of James and John

As I was going up to Jerusalem, I took the twelve disciples aside, and said to them while still on the road, "Listen! We are going up to Jerusalem, and I, the Son of Man, will be betrayed to the high priests and the scribes. They will condemn Me to death, and turn Me over to the Gentiles to be mocked, and beaten, and then crucified; but on the third day I will rise again."

Then the mother of James and John came to Me with her sons, kneeling and asking for a favor. I asked her, "What do you want?"

She answered, "Promise that my two sons may sit one at Your right and one at Your left in Your kingdom."

I answered, "You do not realize what you are asking. Can they drink the cup of suffering that I am about to drink?"

They answered, "Yes, we can."

I said to them, "You will drink the cup of suffering that I am to drink, but to sit at my right and left are not Mine to give. That honor will be given to those chosen by My Father."

When the other ten disciples heard of this, they were angry at the two brothers. But I called them and said, "You know that pagan rulers lord it over their subjects. Their great men rule as tyrants. But it will not be so among you. Whoever wants to be great among you must be a servant, and whoever wants to be first must be a slave. In the same way, I, the Son of Man, have come not to be served but to serve and to give My life a ransom for many."

I Heal Two Blind Men

As we left Jericho, a large crowd followed Me. There were two blind men sitting by the roadside who heard that I was passing by. They cried out, "Have mercy on us, Lord, Son of David!"

The crowd shouted at them to be quiet, but the two blind men begged even louder; "Have mercy on us, O Lord, Son of David."

I stopped and called for them, asking, "What do you want Me to do for you?"

They answered, "Lord, open our eyes!" Then My heart was moved with compassion, and I touched their blinded eyes. Immediately they could see, and they followed Me.

TWENTY-ONE

THE TRIUMPHANT ENTRY

The next day—Sunday—news that I was coming to Jerusalem swept through the crowds of Passover pilgrims. As I came to Bethpage, I sent two disciples into the village, telling them they would find a donkey with her young colt tied there. "If anyone asks why you are taking the donkey, tell them the Master needs it to ride into Jerusalem."

This act fulfilled Scripture, "Tell the people of Zion, your king is coming to you, humbly riding on a donkey, even on a young colt." The disciples did as instructed and found the donkey as I said. They put their coats on the donkey and I rode on a colt that had never been ridden by anyone.

I know the future because I live there. Yield your future to Me. I will tell you how to serve Me best, just as I told the disciples about the donkey.

Great crowds spread their coats on the road; others waved their palm branches as they went to meet Me. The crowds who marched in front of Me shouted, "HOSANNA to the Son of David, blessing on Him who comes in the Lord's name, HOSANNA in the highest heaven."

When I entered the city, people everywhere were asking, "Who is this?"

The multitude answered, "This is Jesus, the prophet from Nazareth."

I Cleanse the Temple

I went into the temple to cleanse it. I drove out all the buyers and sellers, and turned over the money-changers' tables. I upset the seats of those selling doves, and said to them, "The Scripture says, 'My house will be called a house of prayer, but you have made it a den of thieves.'"

Then blind and crippled people came to Me in the temple, and I cured them. But the high priest and scribes saw My miracles.

Children began shouting in the temple, "Welcome to the Son of David."

The high priest and scribes were indignant and asked Me, "Do you hear what they are saying?"

I answered them, "Yes. Have you never read, 'Out the mouths of little children, and babies come perfect praise?'" And I left and went out of the city to Bethany where I spent the night.

The Withered Fig Tree

Early next morning I returned to the city, and was hungry. I saw a fig tree by the roadside, but found nothing on it but leaves, and I said, "May you never bear fruit again." The fig tree immediately withered.

When the disciples saw it, they were amazed, and asked, "How did the fig tree wither up so soon?"

I answered them, "If you have faith and do not doubt, you can do this miracle and if you can say to this mountain, 'Be moved and throw yourself into the sea,' it will be done. If you have faith, whatever you ask for in prayer, you will receive."

A Day of Controversy in the Temple

When I came into the temple, the high priests and elders came up to Me while I was teaching and asked, "By what authority have you done these things?"

I answered, "I will ask you just one question. If you answer it, you will know by what authority I have for doing what I do. Where did John's baptism come from? From heaven, or from men?"

They said among themselves, "If we say, 'From heaven,' He will say, 'Why did you not believe John?' But if we say, 'from men,' we are afraid of the people, for they all consider John a prophet." So they answered Me, "We do not know."

Then I answered them, "Neither will I tell you by what authority I do as I do."

I told them a parable, "There was a man with two sons. He told the first, 'Son, go and work in my vineyard today.' And the son answered, 'I will not.' But afterward he changed his mind and went. Then the father said the same thing to the second son, and he said, 'I'll go,' but he did not go. Which of the two did what his father wanted?"

They answered, "The first son."

I said, "Verily I say to you, that tax-collectors and prostitutes will go into the kingdom of heaven before you. For John came to you living righteously, and you did not believe him. But tax-collectors and prostitutes believed his message; but you, even after seeing that, would not change your minds and believe the message of John."

"Listen to another parable. "There was once a land owner who planted a vineyard and built a fence to protect it, and hewed out a vat to store the wine, and built a tower. Then he rented it out to tenants and went on a trip. When it came time to gather grapes, he sent his servants to the tenants to collect rent. But the tenants beat his slaves, and killed the second, and stoned the third. Again he sent other servants in a group, and the tenants treated them exactly the same way. Finally he sent his son, for he said, 'Surely they will honor my son.' But when they saw the son, they said, 'He is the heir, let us kill him, and get the estate!' So they drove the son out of the vineyard and murdered him. Now when the owner of the land returns, what will he do to these tenants?"

They answered, "In vengeance he will put the murderers to death, and rent the vineyard to other tenants, who will quickly pay him the rent."

Then I said to them, "Did you never read this truth in the Scripture: The stone that was rejected by the builders will become the cornerstone; this is the Lord's doing, and it is wonderful to see? This is why the kingdom will be taken away from you, and given to a people who will produce its fruit. Whoever falls on that stone will be saved, but whoever it falls on will be crushed to pieces."

When the high priests and Pharisees heard My stories, they knew that I was speaking about them. Although they would like to have had Me arrested, they were afraid of the people who considered Me a prophet.

TWENTY-TWO

I TEACH WITH
STORIES

Then I spoke to them in parables once again and said: "The kingdom of heaven is like a king, who gave a wedding feast for his son. And he sent his servants to call those who had been invited to the wedding feast, but they refused to come. A second time the king sent other servants, 'Tell the invited guests that I have my feast all ready, my cattle are butchered, and everything is ready. Come to the wedding feast!' But they did not come, but went about their business, one to his farm, another to his shop, and the others seized his servants to beat them and then murdered them. Then the king was furious, and sent his soldiers to destroy those murderers and burned their town. Then he said to his servants, 'My wedding feast is ready, but those invited are not worthy to come. So go out to the country roads to invite everyone you find to my wedding feast.' And those servants went out into the roads to gather everyone they found, both good and bad, and the banquet hall was packed with guests.

"When the king entered to see the guests, he saw a man who was not wearing a wedding suit. So the king said to him, 'My friend, why are you not wearing a wedding suit?' But the man was silent. Then the king said to his attendants, 'Bind him hand and foot and throw him out into the outer darkness, where there will be weeping and grinding of teeth.' For many are invited, but few are prepared."

The Pharisees' and Herodians' Question

Then the Pharisees went and plotted to trap Me. So they sent their disciples to Me with the Herodians, to say, "Master, we know that you are an honest man who teaches honestly the way of God. You are not afraid of what anyone says. What is Your opinion on this question: Is it right to pay Caesar the poll tax, or not?"

I saw their hypocritical plot, and so I asked them, "Why are you testing Me, you hypocrites? Show Me a coin."

Then I asked, "Whose likeness and name is this?"

They answered, "Caesar's."

Then I said, "Give to Caesar, the things that belong to Caesar, and give to God the things that belong to God." And when they heard it, they were amazed, so they left Me and went away.

The Sadducees' Question

On the same day some Sadducees, who denied the resurrection, came to Me to ask, "Teacher, Moses said, 'If a man dies childless, his brother must marry his widow and raise up a family for his brother. Now there were seven brothers. The first married and died without children. His widow married his brother. The second also died, and the third, and all down to the seventh. Last of all the woman died, too. Now in the resurrection whose wife will she be? For they all married her."

I answered them, "You are wrong, because you do not understand the Scriptures nor the power of God. In the resurrection men and women do not marry nor are they married, but are as the angels in heaven. But you did not read and understand the resurrection of the dead. God said to Moses, 'I Am the God of Abraham and the God of Isaac and the God of Jacob. Now God is not the God of the dead but He is God of the living.'" And when the crowds heard this, they were astonished at My teaching.

A Legal Question

The Pharisees heard that I had silenced the Sadducees, so they got together to test Me. One of them, an expert in the law, tempted Me, asking, "Teacher, what command is greatest in the law?"

And I answered, "'You must love the Lord your God with all your heart, all your soul and all your mind.' This is the first and greatest command. The second is like it: 'You must love your neighbor as you love yourself.' The foundation of the whole law and the prophets are found in these two commands."

Now I Ask a Question

And then I asked the Pharisees, "What is your opinion about the Christ? Whose son is He?"

They answered Me, "He is David's son."

I asked them, "How then does David, moved by the Spirit, call Him Lord, when he says: 'The Lord has said to my Lord, sit at my right hand, and I will put your enemies under your feet?' If David has called the Messiah Lord, how can the Messiah be his son?" And no one could answer Me, and from that time on no one dared ask Me any more questions.

TWENTY-THREE

I DENOUNCE THE SCRIBES AND PHARISEES

After a while, I went into the courtyard of the temple to teach the multitudes, "Beware of the scribes who like to sit in Moses' seat; they make rules for you to obey, but they themselves do not obey their own rules. They put heavy and grievous burdens on your shoulders, but they will not bear them, nor will they lift one finger to help you. They love to wear long robes to get greetings from everyone, they love the best seats at celebrations and in the synagogues. You must not seek for others to call you 'Master,' for you have but one who is 'Master.' And you must not call anyone on earth 'Father,' for the heavenly One is your Father. And you must not be called 'leaders,' for you have only one Leader, and that is the Messiah. Whoever will be greatest among you must be your servant. Whoever will exalt himself will be humbled, and whoever humbles himself will be exalted.

"Woe to you scribes and Pharisees—hypocrites—because you shut the door to the kingdom of God and you yourselves will not enter, nor will you let anyone else enter. Woe to you scribes and Pharisees, hypocrites! You devour widows' houses, and to show off that you pray long. Therefore you will receive greater judgment.

"How terrible it will be for you scribes and Pharisees—hypocrites—because You go everywhere to make people your proselytes, yet you make them twofold sons of hell. Because they were originally on their way to hell, now as your proselytes they are doubly directed to hell.

"Woe to you blind guides, you say it is alright to swear by the temple, but not by the gold on the temple. You are fools! What is greater, the temple or the gold? You say it is alright to swear by the altar but it's not right to swear by the gift on the altar. You are blind! What is greater the altar or the sacrifice? The one who swears by the altar, also swears by the things on the altar. The one who swears by the temple, swears by it and by Him who dwells in it. The one who swears by the heavens also swears by the throne of God, and by Him who sits on the throne.

"How terrible it will be for you scribes and Pharisees—hypocrites—you are careful to tithe the mint that grows at your back door, but you've left undone the weightier things of the law which is judgment, and self-control, and faith. It's right to tithe everything God gives to you, but it's wrong to ignore those greater things; you strain at a gnat and swallow a camel.

"How terrible it will be for you scribes and Pharisees—hypocrites—because you clean the outside of the cup, but leave the inside filthy. Blind Pharisees, first cleanse the inside of the cup and bowl, then clean the outside.

"How terrible it will be for you scribes and Pharisees—hypocrites—because you're like a freshly painted grave that looks beautiful, but inwardly you're dead, rotting, stinking corpses. Outwardly you appear to people to be righteous, but inwardly you're full of sin and hypocrisy.

"How terrible it will be for you scribes and Pharisees—hypocrites—because you build monuments at the tombs of the prophets, and you make a big spectacle of putting flowers on their graves. You say, 'if you lived in their day, you would not be part of those who killed them.'

"But you witness against yourselves by the things you do today, that you would murder them. You identify with your father's guilt. You serpents and children of snakes, how will you escape the punishment of hell? You are just like those to whom the Father sent prophets to preach to them. Yet you would scourge them, persecute them, and crucify them. And on your hands is the blood of all righteous martyrs, from the blood of Abel to the blood of Zechariah who was killed in the temple next to the altar. Surely all these things will come on this age."

Jerusalem will be Destroyed

"O Jerusalem, Jerusalem, who killed the prophets and stoned those who were sent to you from the Father. How often would I have gathered you to Me, as a hen gathers her chicks, but you would not come to Me. I now have abandoned your house. You will not see Me or understand what I am doing in the world, till I come again in the name of the Lord."

TWENTY-FOUR

THE MOUNT
OF OLIVES
DISCOURSE

Later in the day—Tuesday—I sat with My disciples on the Mount of Olives to look at the city of Jerusalem and the temple. I said, "You see the city and the temple; verily not one stone will be left on another, but shall be thrown down."

I predicted the temple would be destroyed, and it happened, just as I predicted. Because I Am God, I know the past as well as the future. I will give you confidence to believe every promise I give.

My disciples asked Me privately, "Tell us when this will happen? And what shall be the sign of Your coming? And what shall be the sign of the end of the world?"

I answered, "Don't let anyone lead you astray, because many will come in my name, saying, 'I am the Christ!' You will hear of wars and rumors of wars, but don't worry because these things must happen before the end. Nation will fight nation, and alliances of nations will fight other alliances; and there will be earthquakes; these are the beginning of tribulation.

"Your enemy will arrest you, persecute you, and kill you; all nations will hate the nation of Israel for My sake. Many will be offended and betray one another, and hate one another. Many false prophets will lead many astray, and the influence of sin will influence every area of life. Love for Me will become cold. But those followers of Mine who endure tribulation to the end shall finally be saved. The gospel of the kingdom will be preached to the whole world; then the end shall come."

I predicted the world would hate you. Why are you surprised when it happens? Believe and act on My promises.

"When you see the abomination of desolation—a pig sacrificed on the altar—which was predicted by Daniel; realize this is the beginning of the Great Tribulation. Then let my people flee to the mountains for protection, let those on the rooftop not go in their house to take anything with them. Let those working in the field not return home for clothes and those with child will suffer the most; so pray your escape will not be in winter or on the Sabbath. This will be the Great Tribulation, which is greater than any since the beginning of the world and greater than any after it. Unless God shortens these days, no one can live through it, and for God's people, those days will be shortened.

"If anyone tells you, 'Here is the Messiah,' or 'There is the Messiah,' don't believe it; many false messiahs will come and perform miracles to lead God's people away. I've told you before, if anyone tells you the Messiah is in the wilderness, don't go out there to check it out. And if they say Messiah is in an inner room, don't believe that either."

The Second Coming

"My coming will be as spectacular as lightning flashing from the East to the West. And there'll be so many slain by My coming, that buzzards will gather to eat their flesh.

"The sun will be darkened and the moon won't shine. The stars will fall from the sky and heaven itself will be shaken as I make My appearance in heaven. Then shall all ethnic tribes mourn when they see Me coming with great power and glory through the clouds. I will send My angels with the sound of a trumpet to gather My people from the four corners of the earth.

"Learn from the parable of the fig tree; when new growth appears and the leaves are growing, realize it is summer. So when you see these signs happening, Messiah is at the door. This generation of Jewish believers will not pass away until all these signs have appeared. Heaven and earth shall pass away but My Word—which I promise shall not pass away—these things will happen as promised.

"But no one knows the hour when Messiah will come, not you, nor anyone else, not even the angels in heaven. Neither I, the Son of Man, but only the Father knows the hour.

"It will be like the days of Noah. He warned everyone that judgment was coming, but no one believed him. People went on eating, getting drunk, getting married, until the flood came. Two will be working in the field, one will be taken, the other left. Two women will be grinding meal, one will be taken, the other left; watch because you don't know when I will return.

"If the owner of the house knew when a thief would break into his home, he would have been constantly vigilant. Therefore, be ready, for in just the hour you think I won't return, I will come.

"If the owner made a faithful worker supervisor of all his businesses while he was gone, that worker is blessed if the owner returns to find everything in order. Verily, the owner would give him a promotion. But if the servant is lazy and spends his time eating and drinking because he thinks the owner is tarrying, the owner will come back at a time the worker doesn't expect him, and will fire the worker and give his job to someone else. That worker will suffer with those who weep and gnash their teeth."

TWENTY-FIVE

MY COMING KINGDOM

I spoke a parable that the coming of the kingdom is likened to ten bridesmaids with ten lamps who were waiting for the coming of the bridegroom. "Now five were foolish, and five were wise. Five foolish bridesmaids didn't take oil with them, but five were wise bridesmaids and took oil in addition to their lamps. The bridegroom was late and all the bridesmaids slept.

"At midnight there was a shout, 'He's coming! Let all the bridesmaids come meet him.' When the ten got ready to light their lamps, the five foolish asked the wise, 'Give us some oil because our lamps are going out.' But the wise answered, 'If we give you some of ours, we won't have enough to light the bridegroom's way.' They told the foolish virgins to go buy some for themselves. The five wise virgins went into the feast with the bridegroom, and the door was shut.

"Afterward the five foolish virgins came asking, 'Open the door.'"

"But the bridegroom answered, 'I don't know you.'"

I said, "Verily I say to you, watch continually because you don't know the day or hour when I, the Son of Man, am coming."

The Parable of the Unprofitable Worker

I spoke another parable about My returning, saying, "A businessman planned to take a long trip, and delegated to various workers, different jobs in the company. He gave one worker $500,000, another $200,000 and the third $100,000; each according to his ability to manage money. The one with $500,000 invested wisely and doubled his money; the one with $200,000 also invested prudently and doubled his money. The worker with $100,000 hid his money carefully so it wouldn't be lost. After a long time, the owner returned and asked his workers to report what they had done.

"The one who had $500,000 brought in another $500,000, and the owner said, 'You've done well because you were faithful, I'm going to promote you to a larger responsibility.'

"The one with $200,000 gave the owner an additional $200,000; the owner also congratulated and promoted him. The worker with $100,000 said, 'I know you are a hard man, reaping where you don't sow, and I was afraid, so I safely hid your money, and here it is!'

"The owner said, 'You're a lazy worker. You know I expected profit from my investment. You should have put it in a bank where it would at least earn interest.' The owner took away the $100,000 and gave it to the worker who now had a million dollars.

"He said, 'If you have gathered much for the kingdom you'll be given more. If you've done little for the kingdom, it'll be taken from you.' The owner said, 'Cast the unprofitable servant into outer darkness, where there is weeping and gnashing of teeth.'"

I will teach you to faithfully manage your time, talent, and treasure for My glory. May you be as fruitful as you can be with the gifts I've given you, and may you work effectively in the location where I've placed you.

I explained, "When you see Me, the Son of Man, come in My glory, all the nations of the earth will stand before Me. I will sit on My throne to divide them as a shepherd divides his flock; sheep will be separated to My right hand, and goats to the left. Then I, the King, will say to those on the right, 'Come in because you are blessed, inherit the kingdom prepared for you.' Then I will say to them, 'You are blessed, because I was hungry and you fed Me. I was thirsty and you gave Me drink. I was naked and you took Me in. I was in prison and you came and visited Me.'

"Those on the right will say, 'When did we see You hungry, or thirsty, or naked, or in prison?' Then I, the King, shall answer, 'Inasmuch as you did it to my brethren and the poor, you did it to Me.'

"Then I will say to those on the left, 'Depart from Me into eternal fire prepared for the devil and his demons. Because I was hungry, you didn't feed Me. When I was thirsty you didn't give me something to drink. When I was a stranger, you didn't take Me in. When I was naked, you didn't clothe Me. When I was in prison, you didn't visit Me.'

"Then they will try to excuse themselves, 'Lord, when did we see You hungry, or thirsty, or naked, or sick, or in prison, and did not minister to You?' Then I will answer them saying, 'Verily I say to you, inasmuch as you ignored one of these needy, you ignored Me.' Then they will be sent to eternal punishment but the righteous will go to eternal life."

TWENTY-SIX

THE PASSION WEEK

On Wednesday I said to My disciples, "In two days the Son of Man will be delivered up to be crucified."

The religious leaders with Caiaphas the high priest came together to discuss how to arrest Me and kill Me. But they decided not to do it during Passover, for fear that there would be an uprising among the people.

My Anointing at Bethany

That night I attended a feast in Bethany in the home of Simon the leper. A woman poured a pound of perfume from a jar on My head. The oil was very costly. Some in the crowd were indignant, thinking the ointment was wasted. They wanted to sell it and give the money to the poor.

I understood what they were saying, so I answered, "Why are you criticizing the woman? She has done a good thing for Me. You always will have the poor, and you can do for them what you want to do. But you won't always have Me; she has anointed My body for its burial. Wherever the gospel is preached in the world, she will be remembered for her act of worship."

It Took Thirty Pieces of Silver to Betray Me

One of the twelve—Judas Iscariot—went to the chief priest and asked, "What will you give me if I deliver Jesus to you?" The religious rulers gave him 30 pieces of silver, so Judas looked for an opportunity to hand Me over to them.

Events on Thursday

On Thursday, the day when the Passover lamb was killed, the disciples asked Me, "Where do You want to celebrate Passover?"

I told Peter and John to go in the city and find a man with a pitcher on his head. "Follow him to a house, and ask the owner for a room where I can celebrate Passover. He will show you a larger upper room. Get it ready for Me to celebrate the Passover."

And they went and found the man just as I said, and they prepared it for the Passover meal.

The Last Supper

When evening came, I was sitting at the table with the twelve when I said, "Verily I say to you, one of you is going to betray Me."

They were stunned in their hearts, and asked one by one, "Lord, is it I?"

I answered, "The man who dipped his bread with Me in the stew is the one who is going to betray Me. I, the Son of Man, am going to My destiny as the Scriptures predict, but a curse will be on the one who betrays Me. It would have been better for that man if he had never been born!"

Then Judas, who was to betray Me, asked, "Is it I, Rabbi?"

I answered him, "Those are your words."

The Institution of the Lord's Table

While we were eating, I took bread and blessed it; then I broke it and gave it to the disciples and said, "Take and eat it; this represents My body."

I also took the cup and gave thanks; then giving it to them, I said, "All of you drink, for this represents My blood which confirms the covenant, the blood which is poured out for many for the forgiveness of their sins. I tell you, I will never again drink the fruit of the vine till the day when I drink with you in My Father's kingdom."

My Prayer in Gethsemane

After singing a hymn, we left the city and went up the Mount of Olives.

Then I said to them, "You will all lose faith over Me tonight, for the Scripture says, 'Strike the shepherd, and the sheep will be scattered.'

But after my resurrection from the dead, I will meet you in Galilee."

Peter answered, "Though all the rest will lose faith in You, I will never lose faith."

I said to him, "I tell you solemnly, before a rooster crows this very night, you will deny Me three times."

Peter answered, "Even if I have to die with You, I will never deny You."

Then I came with them to a garden called Gethsemane, and I said to the disciples, "Sit here while I go a little farther to pray." I took Peter, James and John with Me to pray. I became overwhelmed with grief. Then I said to the three, "My heart is at the point of death! Stay here and keep watch with Me."

Then I walked on a few steps and fell on My face to pray, and said, "My Father, if it is possible, let this cup pass from Me; and yet not what I want, but what You sent Me to do."

Then I returned to the disciples and found them asleep. I said to Peter, "Could you not then watch with Me one hour? You must watch and pray that you enter not into temptation. Your spirit may be willing but human nature is weak."

A second time I went away to pray, "My Father, if this cup cannot pass without My drinking it, may Your will be done." I came back again and found the disciples sleeping again. They were so sleepy that they could hardly hold their eyes open.

Then I left them again to pray the third time. Then I returned to the disciples and said, "Sleep on! The time has come for Me, the Son of Man, to be betrayed into the hands of sinners! Get up! My betrayer is here!"

I Am Betrayed, Arrested, and Forsaken

Even while I was still speaking, Judas, one of the twelve, came with the crowd, who had swords and clubs. They were sent from the high priests and the elders of the people.

Now My betrayer had told them the signal was this: "The one I kiss is Jesus. Seize Him!" And Judas went straight to Me and greeted Me; then with hypocrisy, he affectionately kissed Me.

I said to Judas, "My friend, do what you planned." Then they came, grabbed Me, and arrested Me. One of the disciples with Me drew his sword, and struck at the high priest's servant cutting off his ear.

Then I said, "Put up your sword, for all who draw the sword will die by the sword. Don't you know I can ask My Father and He will send one hundred thousand angels to protect Me? There is no other way for the Scriptures to be fulfilled."

I said to the soldiers, "Have you come out with swords and clubs to arrest Me, as though I were a criminal? I constantly sat teaching in the temple and you never laid hands on Me. But this has all taken place so that the writings of the prophets may be fulfilled."

Then all the disciples left Me and ran away.

The Second Trial—Before Caiaphas

The men who had arrested Me took Me away to Caiaphas the high priest, where the scribes and elders were assembled. Peter followed Me at a distance to the courtyard of the high priest's home, going inside to sit among the attendants to see what would happen.

The high priests and the whole council were looking for false testimony against Me, so they could put Me to death. But they could not agree, although many false witnesses came forward to testify. Eventually two men came forward to agree, "This man claims, 'I can tear down the temple of God, and build it again in three days.'"

The high priest then arose and said to Me, "Have you no answer? What evidence do you have?" But I kept silent. So the high priest said to Me, "I put You under oath, in the name of the living God, tell us whether You are the Christ, the Son of God."

I answered him, "The words you charged Me with are true. But I tell you, you will all soon see Me, the Son of Man, seated at the right hand of the Almighty and coming on the clouds of the sky."

Then the high priest tore his clothes, and said, "He has blasphemed. What more witnesses do we need? You have just heard His blasphemy. What is your opinion?"

Then they agreed, "He deserves to die."

After that they spit in My face and slapped Me with their fists. Others hit Me, saying, "If You are the Christ, tell us who struck You?"

I suffered all of this for you. Deepen your love to Me.

As Peter was sitting outside in the courtyard, a servant girl said to him, "You, also, were with Jesus the Galilean."

But Peter denied before them all, and said, "I do not know the man."

Then he went out into the gate, where another servant girl saw him, and said, "This fellow was with Jesus the Nazarene."

Again Peter denied it, and even swore and cursed, "I do not know the man!"

A few minutes afterward a bystander told Peter, "You are surely one of them, for your accent gives you away."

Then he continued cursing and swearing, "I do not know the man!"

And at once a rooster crowed. Then Peter remembered what I had said, "Before a rooster crows, you will deny Me three times." And he went out and wept bitterly.

TWENTY-SEVEN

MY DEATH
AND BURIAL

Early in the morning, all of the chief priests and the elders of the people met to plan My death. They tied Me up, and led Me away to hand Me over to Pilate the governor.

The Remorse and Suicide of Judas

When Judas the betrayer found that I had been condemned, he was overcome with remorse and took the 30 silver pieces back to the chief priests and elders saying, "I have sinned, I have betrayed innocent blood."

"What has that got to do with us?" they replied. "That is your concern."

Judas threw down the silver pieces in the temple sanctuary and left to hang himself.

The chief priests picked up the silver pieces saying, "It is against the law to put this money into the treasury; it is blood money." So after discussing the matter they bought a potter's field with the money as a graveyard for foreigners. This is why the field is called the Field of Blood to this day.

The words of the prophet Jeremiah were fulfilled: "And they took the 30 silver pieces, the price the children of Israel agreed to pay for Him, and they bought the potter's field, just as the Lord directed."

The Fourth Trial Before Pilate

I stood before the governor, and Pilate asked Me, "Are You the King of the Jews?"

I replied, "That is what you say."

I Am not only the King of the Jews, I Am also King of your life.

But when I was accused by the chief priests and the elders, I refused to answer anything. Pilate then said, "Don't You hear these many charges they have brought against You?" But to the governor's complete surprise, I didn't offer any reply to the charges.

Barabbas Is Released

At the Festival of Passover it was the governor's practice to release any prisoner the people chose. At this time there was a famous prisoner named Barabbas. So when the crowd gathered, Pilate asked them, "Who do you want me to release: Barabbas or Jesus, the one who is called your Messiah?" Pilate knew it was out of envy that they had brought Me to court.

Now as Pilate sat in the chair of judgment, his wife sent him a message, "Don't have anything to do with that Man; I had a terrible dream about Him."

The chief priests and the elders had persuaded the crowd to shout for the release of Barabbas and demand My execution. So when Pilate asked them, "Which of the two do you want me to release to you?"

They cried out, "Barabbas."

"Then in that case," Pilate asked, "what shall I do with Jesus who is called the Messiah?"

They all cried, "Let Him be crucified!"

"Why?" Pilate asked. "What crime has He done?"

But they shouted with a roar, "Crucify Him!"

When Pilate saw that he could do nothing else, he took a basin of water and washed his hands in front of them and said, "I am innocent of this man's blood."

And the people shouted back, "His blood be on us and on our children!"

It's not possible to get rid of Me by washing your hands. When the world rejects Me, you can accept Me as your Savior.

Then Pilate released Barabbas to them. He ordered Me to be scourged, and then handed Me over to the soldiers to be crucified.

The governor's soldiers took Me into the Praetorium and gathered the whole guard around Me. They stripped Me and made Me wear a scarlet robe.

I Am Mocked

Then they twisted some thorns into a crown and placed it on My head and placed a reed in My right hand. They knelt before Me saying, "Hail, King of the Jews!" And they spat on Me and took the reed and struck Me on the head with it. When they had finished making fun of Me, they took off the cloak and dressed Me in My own clothes and led Me away to crucify Me.

On their way to crucify Me, they met a man from Cyrene, Simon by name, who was ordered to carry My cross. When we reached the place called Golgotha, the place of the skull, they offered Me wine mixed with gall to drink. When I tasted it, I refused to drink it.

I Am Lifted Up Between Heaven and Earth

When they had finished crucifying Me they cast lots for My clothing, and then they sat down to keep guard. Over My head was placed a shingle that read: "This is Jesus, the King of the Jews." Two thieves were crucified with Me, one on the right and the other on the left.

The passersby hurled abuse at Me; they nodded their heads, saying, "You said You would destroy the temple and rebuild it in three days! Then save Yourself! If You are the Son of God, come down from the cross!"

The chief priests with the scribes and elders mocked Me in the same way. "He saved others," they said, "but He cannot save Himself. If You are the King of Israel; come down from the cross, and we will believe You. He trusted God; now let God save Him. For He did say, 'I am the Son of God.'"

Even the thieves who were crucified with Me mocked Me in the same way.

From Noon until 3 P.M.

At noon, darkness fell over all the land until three o'clock. Then I cried with a loud voice, *Eli, Eli, lama sabachthani?* that is, "My God, My God, why have You forsaken Me?"

When those who stood there heard this, they said, "The man is calling on Elijah."

At this moment I took on Myself the sin of the world. I did not pray, "My Father," His usual name. Rather, I prayed, "My God," which means I was separated from God the Father because the Father couldn't look on the sin that was on Me. I was offering Myself as the sin sacrifice to God. Gratefully receive My salvation, for it is freely offered to you.

One of the soldiers quickly ran to get a sponge dipped in vinegar and put it on a reed for Me to drink. But the rest of them said, "Let's see if Elijah comes to save Him."

Then I, crying out in a loud voice, yielded up My Spirit.

Then the veil of the temple was torn in two from top to bottom. There was an earthquake and rocks were split; the tombs opened and the bodies of many holy men rose from the dead and came out of the tombs and entered the Holy City and appeared to a number of people.

The centurion and the other soldiers guarding Me, felt the earthquake and everything else that was taking place and they were terrified. They said, "Truly this was the Son of God."

I want you to know, beyond a shadow of a doubt, I Am God The Son! I am no longer in the tomb, but seated at the right hand of God the Father in Heaven.

And many women were watching from a distance, the same women who had followed Me from Galilee, and took care of My needs. Among them were Mary Magdalene, Mary the mother of James and Joseph, and the mother of Zebedee's sons.

The Burial of My Body

When evening came, Joseph, a rich man of Arimathaea, who had become My disciple, went to Pilate and asked for My body. Pilate gave orders for it to be handed over. So Joseph took My body, wrapped it in clean linen and put My body in his own new tomb which he had hewn out of the rock. He then rolled a large stone across the entrance to the tomb and left.

Friday until Sunday Morning

Now Mary Magdalene and the other Mary were there watching where I was buried. The next day, after the Passover was over, the chief priests and the Pharisees went to Pilate and said, "Sir, we remember what this impostor said while He was still alive, 'After three days I shall rise again.' Therefore order guards to secure the grave until the third day. We fear His disciples will come and steal the body and tell the people, 'He has risen from the dead.' If this happens, it would be worse for us than the first."

"You have your guard," Pilate said to them. "Go and make it as secure as you can." So they went and placed guards at the grave, putting an official seal on the stone.

If it hadn't been for the soldiers, people might have believed the lie that My disciples stole My body.

TWENTY-EIGHT

THE EMPTY TOMB

After the Sabbath was over, just as a new day was dawning, on the first day of the week, Mary Magdalene and the other Mary went to the grave. Suddenly there was a violent earthquake, for the angel of the Lord came down from heaven, and rolled away the stone and sat on it. His face shined like lightning, and his robe was white as snow. The guards were so afraid of him that they fainted and collapsed.

The angel spoke to the women, "Do not be afraid. I know you are looking for Jesus, who was crucified. He is not here, for He has risen, as He said. Come and see where His body was laying. Then go quickly and tell His disciples, 'He has risen from the dead and He is going to Galilee; it is there you will see Him.'"

You can know the Resurrection is true, not just because of this story or an empty tomb. You can know it's true, because I live in your heart. Trust your heart.

The women were overjoyed and quickly left the tomb and ran to tell the disciples.

I Appear to the Women

As they were going, I met them. "Greetings," I said. And the women, falling down before Me, grabbed My feet and worshiped Me. Then I said, "Do not be afraid; go and tell My brothers that they must go to Galilee. They will see Me there."

While the women were on their way, some of the guards went into the city to tell the chief priests what had happened. The Jewish leaders held a meeting, and after a long discussion they gave a large sum of hush money to the soldiers, and told them, "This is what you must report, 'His disciples came during the night and stole the body while we were asleep.' And should the governor hear about this, we will make things right with him, and see that you do not get into trouble." The soldiers took the money and obeyed their instructions. This story was spread among the Jews to this day.

My Appearance on a Mountain

But the eleven disciples went to Galilee, to the mountain where I had arranged to meet them. When they saw Me they worshiped Me, though some doubted.

The Great Commission

I came and said to them, "All authority in heaven and on earth has been given to Me. Go, therefore, make disciples of all ethnic groups; baptizing them in the name of the Father and of the Son and of the Holy Spirit, and teach them to obey all the things I told you. And lo, I am with you always; even to the end of the age."

PART TWO

I AM GOD THE SERVANT

Based on the Gospel
of Mark

ONE

THE BEGINNING OF MY MINISTRY

This is the beginning of My gospel. I Am Jesus Christ, God the Son, as My coming was predicted by Isaiah the prophet. "Look, I am sending my messenger before You; he will prepare Your way. He will be the voice of one crying in the wilderness, who is preparing the way for the Messiah, saying, 'Make the paths straight for Him.'" He was John the Baptizer appearing in the wilderness, preaching baptism and repentance to be forgiven of sins. People flocked to John from all over Judah and Jerusalem to confess their sins and be baptized by him in the Jordan River. John wore camel's hair clothes and a leather belt around his waist. He ate locusts and wild honey. John announced, "Someone is coming after me who is more powerful than me. I am not worthy to stoop and untie His sandals. I have baptized people in water, but He will baptize people in the Holy Spirit."

I Am Baptized by John the Baptizer

I came from Nazareth in Galilee and was baptized by John in the Jordan River. Immediately coming out of the water, I saw heaven open and the Spirit descended on Me like a dove. I heard a voice from heaven say, "You are My Son whom I love; I am well pleased with You."

I Am Tempted in the Wilderness

Immediately, the Spirit led Me into the wilderness. I fasted 40 days, and afterward I was tempted by satan. I was with the wild animals and the angels took care of Me.

After John was arrested, I went and preached the gospel in Galilee. "Repent and believe the gospel; the time has come, and the kingdom of God is near."

I Call Fishermen to Follow Me

As I walked by the Sea of Galilee I saw Peter and Andrew casting their nets into the sea. I called out to them, "Come, be My disciples; I'll teach you how to catch people." Immediately they left their nets and followed Me. A little farther, I saw two more fishermen, James and John; they were mending their nets with their father Zebedee and the servants. I called them also to be My disciples; immediately they left their nets to follow Me.

I Attend Sabbath Services

I went into the synagogue, as was My custom, every Saturday. Because I was a visiting rabbi, the elders gave Me an opportunity to teach the people. They were amazed at what I said and the way I said it. My words were authoritative, not like the others.

There was a demon-possessed man in the congregation; he screamed out to Me. "Jesus of Nazareth, what do You want with me? Have You come to destroy me?" This was the demon speaking through the man. The demon said to Me, "I know who You are, You are the Holy One of God; You are El Elyon, the possessor of heaven and earth."

I commanded the demon, "Be quiet!" Then I said, "Come out of the man!" The demon screamed loudly, then the man shook uncontrollably with convulsions, and the demon came out of the man.

The crowd was amazed saying, "What is this new teaching; even demonic spirits obey Him?" The people went back to their homes telling everyone about My mighty power and My message.

I Heal Peter's Mother-in-Law and Others

I left the synagogue and went to Peter's house where his mother-in-law was sick with a fever. When I heard about it I took her by the hand, helped her up, and the fever went away. She got up and prepared a meal for us.

At sundown, the sick and demon-possessed were brought to Peter's house for healing. The whole town crowded in to see what would happen. I cured many of them and cast demons out of others, but I wouldn't permit demons to speak because they knew who I was.

In the morning I woke up before anyone else and went into a private place to pray. Simon and the others searched until they found Me. Then Peter said, "Master, everyone is looking for You."

I told them I couldn't stay in Capernaum, but I said, "Let us go to the towns of Galilee so I can preach to people there; that is why I came into the world." I preached in synagogues all over Galilee and cast out demons.

After a busy day of ministry among the crowds, I got up early the next day, drawing Myself apart from people to be blanketed in the presence of My heavenly Father. I drew near to My Father for divine fellowship.

As I went through Galilee, a leper pleaded with Me, "If You are willing, You can heal me."

Because I was moved with love for him, I touched the leper and said to him, "Be healed!" Immediately his leprosy was healed. I warned him and sent him away. Then I sent him to be examined by a priest, and to make an offering that was required by Moses. I also told him not to tell anyone, but the man told everyone what happened. As a result, I could no longer enter any town, but even when I stayed in the fields, people came to Me from all around.

When I do a great work in your heart, it is hard to keep quiet. Just as a light must shine, you will want to tell others what I've done for you.

TWO

I AM THE MESSIAH

I was in Peter's house in Capernaum when a crowd gathered to hear Me teach, so that the house was packed with people.

Getting a Friend to Me

Four men brought a man with palsy to Me, but they could not get in the house because there were so many people. They took the sick man up to the roof, then removed tiles in the roof, and let down the palsied man in front of Me. I knew they had faith for healing, so I said, "Son, your sins are forgiven."

There were some Jewish leaders in the crowd who criticized Me in their hearts, saying, "Who can forgive sins but God? This man is blaspheming God; does He think He is God?"

I knew their thoughts and said to them, "Why are you criticizing in your mind? Which is easier to say, 'Your sins are forgiven' or 'Arise, pick up your bedroll and walk?'" Then I told them I would prove that I AM the Messiah—the Son of Man, who can forgive sins. I then told the man, "Get up, pick up your bedroll and walk."

The man jumped to his feet, took his bedroll, and everyone saw him walk. They were astounded and praised God saying, "We have never seen anything like this."

Do not be amazed at the things I've done in your life. I have forgiven your sins, given you purpose to live for Me, and you have the joy of the Holy Spirit. I have a wonderful plan for your life, and I've given you determination to be victorious over sin. Tell others about the salvation that was freely given to you, and freely offered to everyone who believes.

The Call to Matthew

I left Capernaum and followed the road that ran alongside the Sea of Galilee. When I came to the customs office, I saw Levi sitting there calculating taxes. I said to him, "Follow Me," and to everyone's amazement, Levi left the tax office to follow Me.

May you instantaneously obey when I enter your life, and call you to do a job. I will keep reminding you that there is no sinner who is too hardened to follow Me as a dedicated disciple. I will teach you to love the unsaved, as I loved Matthew and all who follow Me.

That evening, Levi gathered a number of his friends to hear Me—politicians and tax collectors. When the Jewish leaders saw Me eating with the crowd, they said to My disciples, "Why does your master eat with questionable characters?"

When I knew what the religious leaders asked, I asked a question to get My point across, "Do the healthy need a doctor, or is it the sick who need help? I did not come to offer salvation to people who think they are good enough, but I offer salvation to sinners."

The disciples of John the Baptizer and the Jewish leaders fasted as part of their religious activities. They approached Me, asking, "Why do these disciples of John the Baptizer and Pharisees fast but Your disciples do not?"

I answered, "Do you expect wedding guests to fast when they are at the wedding feast? They eat as long as they are with the bridegroom but they will fast when the bridegroom is taken from them."

I continued, "No one sews a patch of unshrunken cloth on an old coat. If he does, the new patch will shrink and tear the old coat and it will be worse than ever. No one puts new wine into an old wineskin; as the new wine ferments, it will burst the old wineskin. The wine will be lost and the wineskin ruined."

I will teach you when to embrace the new, and guide you when to leave the old.

Debate about the Sabbath

As I journeyed home from the Passover at Jerusalem, I went past the corn fields on the Sabbath and My disciples picked the grain and ate it. The Pharisees criticized us because we broke the Sabbath law. I answered that David went into the tabernacle to eat the showbread when he was hungry and those with him also ate it. I also mentioned that the priest ate showbread on the Sabbath day which outwardly broke the law. Then I added that Hosea the prophet said, "God wants us to be merciful, He doesn't want us to just keep the law. God wants us to know Him, not just bring in burnt sacrifices to Him." Finally I noted, "The Sabbath was made to serve man, not for man to keep its law." I proclaimed, "Therefore I, the Son of Man, am master of the Sabbath, not the reverse."

THREE

MY HEALING POWER

When I got to Capernaum, I entered the synagogue, and a man was there with a shriveled up hand. The Jewish leaders watched Me closely whether I would heal on the Sabbath day, so they could charge Me with breaking the law. I said to the man with the shriveled up hand, "Stand in the middle of the people." Then I asked, "Is it right to help or hurt on the Sabbath day? To kill or save lives?" I continued, "If a man's sheep falls into a pit, isn't it proper to rescue the sheep on a Sabbath day? Isn't a man worth more than a sheep?" But the Pharisees wouldn't answer Me. I looked at them with anger, being grieved for their hardness of heart. I then said to the man, "Stretch out your hand." The man held out his withered hand and it was completely restored. And the Jewish leaders refused to believe in Me, but began making plans to destroy Me.

Do not be critical of anyone who comes to Me for help or healing, as the Jewish leaders criticized Me. I have compassion on those who hurt or need My help, and I AM patient with those who reject Me.

Multitudes Healed

My disciples and I left to go to the seaside. Multitudes followed Me from Galilee, Judea, Jerusalem, Idumea, Tyre, and Sidon because they heard about My miracles.

I told My disciples to have a boat ready because the crowds were crushing Me. I had cured so many people that anyone with an ailment crowded in to touch Me. When people possessed with demons encountered Me, they fell down at My feet screaming, "You are the Son of God." But I warned them repeatedly that they should not make Me known.

My healing power demonstrates that I AM a powerful God. My tenderness demonstrates that I AM a loving God.

Choosing the Twelve

I went up into the hill country and I continued all night in prayer. The next day I called certain men to be My apostles so they would be with Me to learn, then they would be sent forth to preach, heal and cast out demons.

Simon, whom I called Peter; was the leader of the first group of four that included James and John whom I named the Sons of Thunder, and Andrew was in that group. The second group of four apostles was led by Philip, and included Bartholomew, Matthew, and Thomas, the one with a twin brother. The third group of four was led by James the short one, and included Thaddeus and Simon, the former terrorist fighter, and Judas Iscariot, the one who betrayed Me.

The Long Day

The crowds demanded so much attention that the disciples and I couldn't even get away to eat our lunch. But those who followed Me said, "You can't keep on going if you don't eat something." They added among themselves, "Jesus is not thinking straight."

Then the scribes who came from Jerusalem to examine Me said, "He is possessed by Beelzebub, a ruler of demons, and Jesus cast out demons by this power."

I gathered people around Me and said, "How can satan cast out satan? If a kingdom is divided against itself, can that kingdom stand? If a house is divided against itself, can that house stand? If satan rises up against himself, and is divided, he cannot stand; he will fall. No one can go into the house of a strong man to destroy his property unless the strong man is tied up. First, he binds the strong man, then destroys his property." I continued, "Truly I tell you, all sins shall be forgiven those who sin, including their blasphemy. But those who blaspheme the Holy Spirit will never be forgiven; they are in danger of eternal damnation."

I said this because My enemies said I was demon-possessed.

Then My mother and brothers came to the edge of the crowd and called for Me to go with them. With the crowd sitting around Me, they said, "Behold, Your mother and brothers are calling for You to go with them."

I answered them, "Who are My mother and brothers?" Then looking at those sitting about Me I said, "Here are My mother and My brothers. Those who do the will of God are my brothers, and sisters, and mother."

FOUR

MY MESSAGE TO A LOST AND DYING WORLD

A s I was teaching by the seaside, a huge crowd gathered around Me so I entered a boat and sat down to teach the people on the shore.

The Sermon by the Sea

I taught them many lessons in parables. "Look," I pointed to a farmer in a field, "a sower went out to sow, and as he sowed, some seed fell on the path around the field. The birds came to eat it up. Other seed fell on rocky soil where it had little dirt, and because it had no earth, it sprang up quickly, but when the sun came up, it was scorched. Because it had no root, it died. Other seed fell in among thorns. The growing thorns choked it, so it yielded no crop. And other seed fell in the good earth and yielded a crop of thirty, sixty, even a hundredfold. Whoever has ears let him hear and do."

When I was by Myself, those near Me with the twelve asked what the story meant. I told them, "You can know the secret of God's kingdom but outsiders can't understand spiritual things, so I use stories when I speak to them. Because all that they see they may not perceive and for all they hear they do not understand; so they do not turn for forgiveness." I then told them that they must understand this story to grasp the other stories. "The sower sows God's message. Those on the pathway, where the message is sown, forget it as soon as they hear it. Satan comes and snatches away God's message that was sown in their hearts. The seeds on rocky soil are those who readily receive God's message; but it doesn't take root in them. They give up. When persecution comes, because of the message, they immediately stumble and fall. Others are those sown among thorns—they hear the message of God, but the cares of the world and the taste of wealth and the attraction of entertainment choke God's message and it becomes fruitless. But those sown on good dirt are those who hear and accept God's message and yield fruit thirty, sixty, even a hundredfold."

Watch for hard soil in your heart. Let My roots grow deep in your heart to overcome trials and suffering. Immediately pull up the weeds that will tempt you to sin. You need to have a clean, healthy body to serve Me.

I said to them, "Do you hide a lamp under a basket or under a bed? No! You put it on a lamp stand. Nothing will be hidden until it is shown and nothing is kept secret until it is revealed. Whoever has good ears let him hear and obey." I also said, "Be careful about what you hear. The shovelful you shovel out to others will be shoveled to you tenfold. The one who has shall be given more and the one who does not have shall lose what he has."

And I said, "The kingdom of God is like a man scattering seed in the earth and then he goes to sleep while the seed sprouts and springs up, but he does not know how or when it happens. The earth produces from itself. First, the blade, then a head, then the full-grown wheat in the head. When the crop is ripe, he puts in the sickle because harvest has come."

I also said, "To what may we compare the kingdom of God or by what parable may we understand it? The kingdom is like a mustard seed—smaller than any known seed on earth. Yet, when planted, it grows up to be larger than any bush, so that wild birds roost in its branches." With many such stories, I told them God's message as far as they could understand it. I spoke only in stories and explained everything privately to My disciples.

I Calm the Storm

Toward noon I said, "Let us cross over to the other side."

So leaving the crowd, we went to the other side. A heavy storm came up and the waves filled the boat so that the boat was sinking. I was asleep in the stern. They woke Me up and said, "Teacher, do You realize we are sinking?"

I rose up, stopped the wind and said to the sea, "Peace! Be still!" So the wind died down and the sea was calm. I said to them, "Why are you afraid? Where is your faith?"

They were afraid and said to one another, "Who is He, that even the wind and the sea waves obey Him?"

Turn to Me when the storms of life threaten you. I have power to calm the storms in your life, just like I calmed the storm that day on the Sea of Galilee.

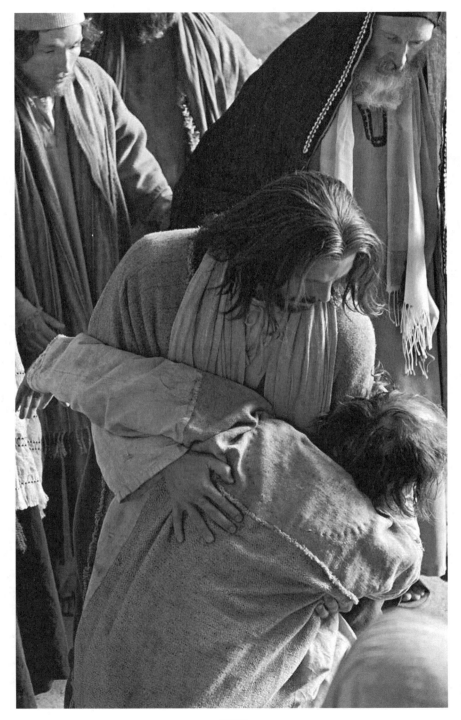

FIVE

MY HEALING NATURE

We landed in the area of Gad, on the opposite side of the lake from Capernaum.

I Heal a Violent Demon-Stricken Man

As soon as I got out of the boat, a demon-possessed man, who was living in the tombs, accosted Me. No one could subdue him, even with chains. Many times he had been bound with ropes and chains, but the chains were broken and the ropes snapped. No one could control him. He lived night and day among the tombs and in the mountains, screaming and cutting himself with stones.

He noticed Me from a distance, then ran and knelt before Me screaming, "What do You have to do with me, Jesus, Son of the Most High God? I plead with You, do not torment me," for I had said to him, "Unclean spirit, come out of the man."

I questioned the man, "What is your name?"

The man answered, "My name is Legion, for we are many." Then the demons urgently begged Me not to send them away. There was a large herd of hogs feeding there on the mountainside. The demons appealed to Me, "Send us to the hogs so we may enter into them!" I permitted it and so the demons went into the hogs. Then the herd of about two thousand rushed headlong down a precipice into the sea and drowned.

There are evil spirits in the world that would want to destroy you. I will deliver you from the evil one, and protect you.

Those tending the hogs ran to tell the news in town. Many people came to see what had happened. They saw the demoniac, who had been possessed of the legion, sitting calmly, dressed and sane. They were frightened. Those who had seen it, told them what occurred to the demoniac; they also told them about the hogs. Then they began to beg Me to leave their country. As I was leaving, the demoniac asked to go with Me, but I said, "No." Instead I said to him, "Go back to your family and friends and tell them everything I have done for you and the mercy I showed you!" And the healed man went to announce throughout Decapolis everything that I had done for him, and all were astonished.

The Woman, and the 12-Year-Old Girl

When I had crossed by boat back to Capernaum, a great multitude was waiting for Me on the shore. Then a leader of the synagogue named Jairus came immediately and fell at My feet and begged Me, "My daughter is at the point of death. Come, place Your hands on her that she may be healed." So I followed him and a multitude followed us.

A woman, who had a blood hemorrhage for 12 years, had been treated by many physicians. She spent all she had without getting better, and was rather growing worse. She heard I was coming, so she got in the crowd behind and touched the hem of My robe. She kept saying, "If I only touch the hem of His robe, I'll be healed." Instantly, her hemorrhage stopped, and she felt in her body that she was healed.

I was instantly conscious that power had gone from Me, so I turned around to the crowd and asked, "Who touched Me?"

My disciples remarked, "The crowd is pressing You on all sides and You ask, 'Who touched Me?'"

But I looked around to see who had done it. Then the woman was afraid and knowing what had happened to her, came and fell at My feet. She told Me everything. But I said to her, "Daughter, your faith, not your touch, has saved you. Go in peace because you are healed."

Seek My help when you have a life-threatening problem. Come first to Me, instead of trying all other solutions, as did the woman with an issue of blood.

While I was still speaking, some servants came from the ruler's house and told him, "Your daughter is dead. Don't trouble the Master anymore."

But I, overhearing the message, said to the synagogue ruler, "Do not fear; only trust Me!" I permitted no one to accompany Me except Peter and James and James' brother John. When I came to the ruler's house, I saw confusion with loud weeping and wailing. As I entered, I asked them. "Why this confusion and weeping? The girl is not dead, she's only asleep." They ridiculed Me, but I put them out of the house and took along the child's father and mother and those with Me, and went to where the child was. Then taking the child's hand, I said to her, "*Talitha cumi*," which is translated "Little Girl, get up by My Word." Instantly the little girl got up and walked; for she was 12. Everyone was astonished, but I strictly charged them that no one should know what happened, and told them to give her something to eat.

WALKING ON THE WATER

I left Capernaum and came to My hometown with My disciples following Me. On the Sabbath I began teaching in the synagogue where many listeners were utterly amazed. "Where did He get all this wisdom?" they remarked. "What knowledge has been given Him and what are these miracles that He does? Is not this the carpenter, the son of Mary and the brother of James and Joseph and Judas and Simon? And do His sisters live here?" And they were offended by Me.

I said, "A prophet has honor except in his own community and among his own people." So I could do no mighty miracles there, except I laid hands on a few sick and healed them. I marveled at their unbelief so I went to nearby villages to teach.

Unbelief hampers My work through you. Just as I couldn't do many miracles in Nazareth because of their unbelief, so your lack of faith curtails My work through you. Ask Me for more faith, and I will give it to you.

The Twelve Sent Two by Two

I called the twelve to Myself and then I began to send them out two by two, giving them authority over demons and telling them to take nothing for the trip except a staff—no food, no purse, nor money, but to wear sandals; and not to take a change of clothing. I explained, "Whenever you enter a house, stay there until you leave the town. And if a town will not receive you nor listen to you, shake off the dust from your feet. Truly I tell you, it will be easier for Sodom and Gomorrah in the judgment than for that town."

Put your emphasis on those who will receive My ministry. Preach to all, but spend your time with those who will receive My Word.

So they went out preaching that men should repent; they cast out many demons and healed many sick, anointing them with oil.

The Murder of John the Baptizer

When King Herod heard about it, he said, "John the Baptizer has risen from the dead, therefore these powers are working in Jesus."

Some said, "He is Elijah"; others said, "He is a prophet, or one of the prophets."

But on hearing about Me, Herod said, "John, whom I beheaded, has been returned to life." For Herod himself had sent soldiers to arrest John, and had him put in chains in prison. He had married Herodias, his brother Philip's wife.

But John had told Herod, "You have no right to have your brother's wife." So Herodias wanted to get even, and wanted him executed. But she couldn't get it done because Herod was afraid of John, whom he knew to be a righteous and holy man. Therefore Herod protected him and was confused for he enjoyed listening to him. Then an opportunity came; it was Herod's birthday when he gave a banquet to his nobles and officers and Galilean chiefs. Herodias' daughter came in and danced. She pleased Herod and his guests so that the king said to her, "Ask whatever you want and I will give it to you." Then he made an oath, "Whatever you ask me, I will give it to you up to half of my kingdom."

She went to ask her mother, "What shall I ask?"

The mother said, "The head of John the Baptizer."

The daughter hurried to the king and said, "The head of John the Baptizer." Although exceedingly sorry, yet because of his oath and the pressure of his guests, immediately the king sent a guard with orders to bring John's head on a plate. He went, beheaded John in prison, and brought his head on a plate and gave it to the daughter who presented it to her mother. And when My disciples heard of it, they came and took up his body and buried it in a tomb.

Feeding the Five Thousand

The apostles returned to Me and reported everything they had done and taught. Then I instructed them, "Come away with Me to a private place in the desert to rest awhile." For so many were pressing around us we could not even conveniently eat.

So we left in a boat for a private spot by ourselves. But the people saw us leaving and ran there on foot and arrived ahead of us. When I got out of the boat, I saw a large crowd and was deeply moved for them because they were like sheep without a shepherd. And I began to teach them many things. As the hour grew late, My disciples came to Me and said, "This is a secluded spot and the hour is late; send them away so they may go to the surrounding towns to buy something to eat."

But I answered them, "You give them to eat!"

They answered Me, "Shall we go, buy food to feed them?"

I said to them, "Go and find out how many loaves you have."

They answered, "Five loaves and two fish."

I told them to have the people all sit on the grass by groups of hundreds and fifties. I took the five loaves and two fish and looking into heaven, blessed the food and broke it and gave it to the disciples to give to the people. I also divided the two fish. Everyone ate and was filled. They picked up 12 full baskets of the bread and fish that were left over. About five thousand men were fed.

Immediately I urged My disciples to get into a boat to cross over to Bethsaida. I dismissed the crowd and left to go to a mountain to pray.

I Walk on Water

During the night, the boat was half way across the sea and I was on the land. I saw them toiling hard at rowing because a storm had come up. I went to them around the fourth watch of the night walking on the sea. I made as if I would pass them by. But the disciples saw Me walking on the sea and thinking it was a ghost, they yelled; for they all saw Me and were scared. I said to them, "Be of good cheer. It is I; be not afraid." I then came to them in the boat, and the wind was calm. They were amazed; they did not understand the miracle of the loaves and they were filled with doubt.

We crossed over to arrive at Gennesaret. But as soon as I got out of the ship, the people recognized Me and they circulated throughout the area that I was there and people began bringing to Me the sick on their mats. Wherever I went in villages or towns, the people brought their sick and begged Me to let them touch the hem of My robe. And as many as touched Me were healed.

SEVEN

THE PROBLEM
WITH TRADITIONS

Jewish leaders came from Jerusalem to Capernaum, to find fault with My religious practices. They were angry because My disciples ate bread with defiled hands. They didn't wash their hands ceremonially before eating. The leaders cleansed themselves ceremonially, when they came from the marketplace, they did the same to all eating utensils.

Questions About Ceremonial Cleansing

The leaders asked Me why My disciples didn't keep the tradition of the elders? I answered by quoting Isaiah, "This people honors Me in outward ways, but their heart is far from Me. They vainly worship Me, teaching their doctrine as the Word of God." I told the Jewish leaders, "You leave the Word of God and hold to your traditions such as washing pitchers and cups and such things. You ignore God's commands to keep your traditions. Moses told you to honor your father and mother; the one who speaks evil of father and mother shall be put to death. But you say, 'My mother and father are better off because they gave birth to me.' This statement does not honor your parents, You no longer allow people to honor his parents. You deny Scriptures by your tradition that is handed down from generation to generation."

I then spoke to the crowd, "Nothing that goes into a man's mouth defiles him; the things that come out of his heart are the things that defile him. If anyone have ears to hear, let them hear."

When I went into a house away from the crowd, the disciples asked

Me to explain what I meant. I answered, "Don't you understand; a person is not defiled by what goes in the mouth, but by what comes out of the heart. What goes into the mouth, enters the stomach, and finally is discharged from the body, but things that come out of the heart defile a person; for out of the heart come evil thoughts, murders, adulteries, sexual perversions, thefts, lying, pride, and anger. The things that come out of the heart defile a person, not eating with unwashed hands."

I Visit Lebanon

I left Galilee and went to Tyre and Sidon, and slipped quietly into a house for rest where the crowd wouldn't exhaust Me. But the crowds found out where I was. Then a woman whose daughter was possessed with a demon fell down before Me. She was a Syrophoenician, who begged Me to cast the demon out of her daughter. I said, "No one takes bread from the children, and gives it to the dogs under the table." So I didn't respond in a positive way but referred to her as a dog, the Jewish word for Gentile.

But the woman showed faith by replying, "Yes, Lord, but the dogs under the table get to eat the crumbs."

I answered, "Woman you have great faith; you will get what you asked." When the woman left the house, she found that the demon had gone out of her daughter.

I left the area of Tyre and went through Sidon to the area of the Ten Cities by the Sea of Galilee. They brought to Me a man who was deaf and had an impediment in his speech. They begged Me to lay My hands on the man. So I took him away from the crowd and put My fingers in his ears with spit from My tongue. Then I looked up to heaven sighing and said, "*Ephphtha,*" which means "Be opened." Immediately he could hear and speak clearly. Then I charged them not to tell anyone; but the more I asked them to keep quiet, the more they kept telling the news.

So the people were astonished saying, "He has done everything good. He even makes deaf people hear and dumb people talk."

EIGHT

WHO DO YOU SAY THAT I AM?

Then another great crowd gathered and had nothing to eat. I said, "I have compassion on these people for they have been with Me three days and have nothing to eat. If I send them away hungry, they will faint on the road for some of them have come a long way."

But My disciples answered, "Where can we get food in this isolated place?"

Then I asked, "How many loaves of bread do you have?"

They answered, "Seven."

So I told the crowd to sit on the ground. I took the seven loaves and gave thanks and broke them in pieces and gave to My disciples to distribute. There were a few small fish there, and I also blessed them and the disciples passed these to the people. They ate and had all they wanted. Then the disciples took up the food left over which filled seven baskets. There were about four thousand people present. Then I sent them away and got in a boat to cross to the area of Dalmanutha.

I Meet With the Pharisees

The Pharisees again met Me, to talk with Me and trip Me up. They asked Me to show them a spectacular miracle from heaven. But I sighed in My Spirit, "Why do these people ask for a spectacular miracle? I truly say, no sign will be given them at this time." And I got into the boat and crossed back over to the other side.

Now the disciples had forgotten to bring any food. They only had one loaf with them in the boat. So I warned them, "Be careful! Guard yourselves against the yeast (influence) of the Pharisees and the yeast of Herod." The disciples had been discussing the fact that they forgot to bring bread. When I heard them, I said, "Why are you talking about having no bread? Do you not remember? Are your minds forgetful? Can your eyes not see? Can your ears not hear? Remember how many baskets you picked up after I broke the five loaves for the five thousand? Remember how many baskets were left over when I broke the seven loaves for the four thousand?" Then I asked, "How is it that you do not believe?"

Do not ask for a miracle to prove who I AM. I have done such a great transformation in your heart that you could never doubt that I AM the God of miracles, and the Lord of the universe.

I Visit the City of Bethsaida

When we came to Bethsaida, a blind man was brought to Me. They begged Me to touch him. I took the blind man by the hand and led him out to the village, then put spit in his eyes, laid My hands on him, asking, "Do you see anything?"

He looked around and answered, "I see the people like trees swaying."

Then I laid My hands on his eyes a second time. The blind man was cured, and saw everything plainly. So I sent him home instructing him, "Do not go into the village, or tell anyone there about this."

I Visit Caesarea Philippi

My disciples and I left Galilee to go to the villages around Caesarea Philippi. While walking, I asked My disciples, "Who do people say that I am?"

They answered, "Some say John the Baptizer; others say Elijah, and still others that You are one of the prophets."

Then I asked them, "But, who do you say that I am?"

Peter answered, "You are the Christ."

I then carefully told them, "Do not tell this to anyone." Then I told them for the first time that I, the Son of Man, had to go through great suffering and be rejected by the elders, the high priest and the scribes, and be killed but would rise again in three days.

So Peter took Me aside and rebuked Me. But I turned to look at My disciples and rebuked Peter saying, "Get behind me, satan! For what you say is not from God but from men."

Do not think the way humans think. Search the Scriptures to think the way I think.

When I called the people and My disciples, I said, "Whoever becomes My disciple must say, 'No' to self-interest; take up his cross, and follow Me continually. Whoever tries to save his life, will lose it and whoever gives up his life for Me and the gospel, will save it. For what shall it benefit a person to gain the whole world and lose his life? What price can a person give to buy back his life? For whoever is ashamed of Me and My words in this adulterous sinful age, then I, the Son of Man, shall be ashamed of him when I come in the Father's glory with the holy angels."

There are three steps to becoming My disciple. First, you must focus on it by picking up your cross to follow Me, for it is through the cross that you identify with Me and get forgiveness of sins. Second, you must "follow," which means getting as close to Me as possible. Third, you must deny yourself to do My will.

NINE

MY GODHOOD REVEALED

And I said to them, "I truly say to you, some of those standing there will live long enough to see the kingdom of God come with power."

My Transfiguration

After six days I took Peter, James, and John and led them up on a high mountain.

You will have "mountaintop" experiences where you see Me clearer than ever before and you are closer to Me than ever before. You can't live on the mountaintop, but you will remember them until the next time.

My appearance was changed in their presence and My clothes shined exceedingly white, whiter than any bleach could wash them. Then Elijah and Moses appeared to us, talking with Me. Then Peter said to Me, "Master, it is good to be here. Let us build three tents, one for You, one for Moses, and one for Elijah." Peter didn't realize what he was saying because he was so frightened.

Then a cloud overshadowed us, and we heard a voice out of the cloud, "This is my Beloved Son, listen to Him!" And instantly, they saw no one with them but Me. After we were going down the mountain, I cautioned them not to tell anyone what they had seen, until I, the Son of Man, was risen from the dead. And they kept that saying as they continued to discuss among themselves what rising from the dead meant.

Then they asked Me, "Why do the scribes say that Elijah must come first?"

I answered, "Elijah will come first and restore all things so how it is that Scripture says the Son of Man will suffer much and be rejected? But I tell you, Elijah has already come, and they did to him what they wanted."

My Disciples Can't Heal

When I came to the other disciples, a great crowd was around them and some scribes were arguing with them. When the people saw Me, they ran up and greeted Me. Then I asked, "What are you arguing about?"

A man from the crowd answered Me, "Master, I brought my son to be healed. He has a demon that causes him to be dumb. He has convulsions and foams at the mouth and grinds his teeth; and he's dying. So I asked Your disciples to cast out the demon, but they couldn't do it."

I answered, "Oh, unbelieving generation! How long must I be with you before you understand? Bring the boy to Me." As soon as the demon saw Me, the boy had a convulsion and fell to the ground wallowing and foaming at the mouth. Then I asked his father, "How long has he been like this?"

The father answered, "From childhood. Many times the demon has thrown him into the fire or into the water to drown him. Is there anything You can do for him? Have compassion on us and help us!"

I said, "Everything is possible for him who believes."

All things are possible for the person who believes. But does that include cars, wealth, and personal happiness? You must first believe, and that involves coming to Me as your Savior, following Me, and denying self, including denying dreams of money, stuff, and even health. Possibility praying involves getting as close to Me as possible, and obeying Me as explicitly as possible.

The boy's father cried out, "I believe, help my unbelief."

When I saw that a crowd was running to see what I would do, I rebuked the demon and said, "You deaf and dumb spirit, come out of him. I command you never go into him again." Then the demon cried out and violently shook the boy, and came out of him. The boy looked like he was dead, so much so that the people thought he was dead. But I took his hand and raised him up.

When I went privately in the house, My disciples asked Me, "Why could we not cast out the demon?"

I answered them, "This kind can only be cast out by prayer and fasting."

Then we left and went through Galilee, but I did not want anyone to know it. I was giving My time to teaching My disciples. I said, "I will be turned over into men's hands, and they will kill Me, but after three days I will rise again." But the disciples did not understand what I meant, and they were afraid to ask Me.

Childlike Faith

When we reached the house in Capernaum, I asked them, "What were you talking about on the way home?" But they did not answer Me, for they had discussed which one of them was the greatest.

So I sat down and called the twelve together and said, "If anyone desires to be the first, he must be the last and the servant of all." Then I took a little child and stood him in the midst; then I took the child in My arms, and said, "Whoever will be My disciple, will receive one little child, like a child receives Me. Whoever receives Me, receives the One who sent Me."

God's service reverses the world's order. That is, give to receive, humble yourself for power with God, for low is the way up and weakness leads to strength.

Mistaken Zeal of John the Apostle

John said to Me, "Master, we saw a man driving out demons in Your name and we tried to stop him, for he was not one of us."

I said, "Do not stop him, for there is no one who will do a miracle in My name that will speak lightly of Me. For whoever is not against Me is for Me."

"For whoever gives you a cup of water in My name I truly say, he will get his reward. And whoever leads one of these children to do wrong, he might as well have a huge millstone hung around his neck and be thrown into the sea. If your hand makes you do wrong, cut it off. It is better to go into life maimed than go to hell with both your hands where the worm doesn't die and the fire is not quenched. And if your foot makes you do wrong, cut it off. It is better to go through life crippled than keep both feet and go to hell. And if your eye makes you do wrong, cut it out. It is better to go into the kingdom of God with only one eye than keep both eyes and be thrown into hell. Because there the fire never dies and is never put out. Everything must be seasoned with fire. Salt is good, but if salt loses its seasoning power, how can it be good again? You must look at all things through salt, and live in peace with one another."

TEN

TEACHING ABOUT THE KINGDOM OF GOD

I left and went to the Judean territory on the other side of Jordan. The crowds gathered around Me, and as usual, I taught them.

I Teach about Divorce

Pharisees came and questioned Me to trip Me up. "Is it lawful for a man to divorce his wife?"

I answered, "What did Moses command?"

They said, "Moses allowed the writing of a divorce certificate to let her go."

I answered, "Because of your hard hearts he wrote this commandment. But from the beginning of creation, God said, 'Male and female He made them; therefore shall a man leave his father and mother and cleave to his wife, and the two shall be one flesh. They are no longer two, but one flesh. Therefore what God has joined together, man shall not divide them.'"

As I went in the house, the disciples asked Me again about divorce, and I told them, "Whoever divorces his wife and marries another commits adultery against her, and if she divorces her husband and marries another she commits adultery."

Children were brought to Me to touch, but the disciples stopped them. When I saw that, I rebuked them and said, "Allow the children to come to Me; do not hinder them, for the kingdom of God belongs to children. Verily, whoever will not receive the kingdom of God as a little child, shall not enter into it." Then I took them in My arms, and blessed them and laid My hands on them.

The Rich Young Ruler

As I was walking on the road, a young man ran to Me and knelt before Me and asked, "Good master, what shall I do to inherit eternal life?"

I answered, "Why do you call Me good? There is none good except God. You know the commands: do not murder; do not commit adultery; do not steal; do not witness falsely; do not lie; honor your father and mother."

The young man replied, "Master, I have kept all these things from my childhood."

Looking at him in love, I told him, "You lack one thing. Go, sell all you have and give to the poor, and you will have treasure in heaven; then come follow Me." At this, the young man was convicted and walked away downcast for he possessed great wealth.

I looked around and said to My disciples, "It is difficult for those possessing wealth to enter the kingdom of God!" The disciples didn't understand My remarks; but I spoke to them again, "Young men, it is difficult for those who trust in wealth to enter the kingdom of God. It is easier for a camel to go through the eye of a needle than for a wealthy person to enter the kingdom of God."

The disciples said to Me, "Who then can be saved?"

I looked on them and replied, "With men it is impossible, but everything is possible with God."

I will teach you the impossibilities that I can do. Know that I AM the God of impossibilities. When your weak faith makes you doubt, stretch your faith to believe for bigger miracles.

Peter first answered saying to Me, "We have given up everything to follow You."

I answered, "Truly I say to you, anyone who has left home or brothers or sisters or mother or father or children or lands for Me and the gospel, will also receive a hundred times over now in this life, and in the future, eternal life. But the first shall be last and the last shall be first."

The Selfish Ambition of James and John

As we were going up to Jerusalem, the disciples, following Me, were amazed and afraid. Then calling the twelve, I began again to tell them what would happen to Me there. "I, the Son of Man, will be delivered to the chief priests and the scribes who will condemn Me to death, will hand Me over to the Gentiles to mock Me, flog Me, spit on Me, and after three days I will rise again."

Then James and John, the sons of Zebedee, came to Me and asked, "We want You to grant us what we request."

So, I answered them, "What do you want Me to do for you?"

They said, "Let us be seated with You in glory, one at the right and the other at Your left."

But I replied, "You do not realize what you are asking. Are you able to drink the cup that I drink and be baptized with the baptism?"

They replied, "We are able."

Then I said, "You will drink the cup I drink and you will be baptized with the baptism I face, but sitting at My right or left is not Mine to give. It is for those who deserve it." When the other ten disciples heard what they asked, they were angry at James and John. But I called to them and said, "You know how the Gentiles rule over those under them and how their chiefs exercise authority over them; but this is not what I want you to do. Whoever will be great among you, shall be your servant and whoever wants to be first among you, shall be last. For even I, the Son of Man, did not come to be ministered to, but to minister and to give My life a ransom for many."

I Heal Blind Bartimaeus

As I was leaving Jericho with My disciples and a great crowd, Bartimaeus, son of Timaeus, a blind beggar, was there sitting by the roadside. When he heard that I was coming, he began to shout, "Son of David, have mercy on me!" Some rebuked him to keep quiet, but he shouted even louder, "Son of David, have mercy on me!"

I stopped and said, "Call him!"

So they told the blind man, "Be of good cheer, Jesus is calling for you." He dropped his coat and ran to Me.

I asked him, "What do you want Me to do for you?"

The blind man said, "Rabbi, I want to see again."

I told him, "Go! Your faith has healed you." Immediately he recovered his sight and followed Me.

ELEVEN

I SET MY COURSE FOR JERUSALEM

My disciples and I came to Jerusalem, at Bethphage and Bethany by the Mount of Olives. I sent two of My disciples to go into the opposite village and said, "When you get there, you will find a donkey hitched to a post on which no one has ever sat. Untie and fetch it. If anyone asks you, 'What are you doing?' answer, 'The Lord needs it,' and he will send the donkey with you without delay."

They went and found the donkey hitched outside a door and untied it. Some of the bystanders asked them, "Why are you untying the donkey?" They answered what I told them to say.

The Triumphant Entry Into Jerusalem

Then they brought the donkey to Me, spread their robes on it, and I rode on it. Many spread their garments on the road, and others waved branches they had cut. Those walking ahead and behind began shouting, "HOSANNA! Blessed be He who comes in the name of the Lord! Blessed be the coming kingdom of our father David! HOSANNA in the highest!"

I entered Jerusalem and went into the temple to see everything. As night approached, I went to Bethany with the twelve.

Cursing the Barren Fig Tree and Cleansing the Temple

Next morning, as we were leaving Bethany, I was hungry, and I saw a fig tree with leaves at a distance. I went to find fruit on it, but I found nothing but leaves. I said, "May no one eat fruit from you forever." And My disciples observed what I did.

When we reached Jerusalem, I entered the temple and began to throw out the sellers who were in the sanctuary. I threw over the tables of the money-changers and the stalls of those who sold doves. I did not allow anyone to carry anything through the temple. I said, "It is written, 'My house shall be called a house of prayer among all nations.' But you have made it a den of robbers."

The scribes and chief priests heard it, and looked for ways to kill Me, because they were afraid of Me, and all of the people received My teaching. That evening I left the city.

The Withered Fig Tree

On Tuesday morning My disciples and I saw that the fig tree I had cursed the previous day was dead and withered. Peter was amazed that the tree had withered to its roots. I answered, "Let God's faith control you. Verily, if you will say to a mountain, 'Be removed and thrown in the sea' and you don't doubt but believe that you will receive what you ask, You shall have it." I then explained, "You shall have all things for which you ask if you believe before you pray."

I then instructed, "When you begin to pray, you must forgive those with whom you have an issue so that your Father may forgive your sin; then you have a basis for getting an answer to your prayer. If you do not forgive others, neither will your heavenly Father forgive your trespasses."

A Day of Controversy in the Temple

Again I entered Jerusalem and walked around in the temple. The chief priests and scribes and elders approached Me to ask, "By what authority are You saying these things or who gave You authority to do miracles?"

I answered them, "I will ask you one question; if you can answer Me, then I will tell you My authority. Was the baptism of John from heaven or from men?"

They disagreed among themselves saying, "If we answer 'from heaven,' He will say, 'Why then did you not believe Him?'" But they didn't want to say, 'From men,'—they were afraid because the people considered John to be a prophet. So they told Me, "We do not know."

I replied, "Neither will I tell you My authority for doing these things."

TWELVE

TEACHING IN THE TEMPLE

Then I began to speak to them in parables. "A man planted a vineyard and fenced it in and dug out a wine vat and built a tower; then he rented it to tenant farmers, and went on a trip. At the harvest he sent a servant to collect his share of the harvest. But they took him and beat him and sent him back without anything. Then he sent another servant and they beat him and treated him terribly. Then he sent a third one, and they killed him. Others they beat, and some they killed. He prepared to send his only son; for he thought, 'Surely they will respect my son.' But those tenants said, 'This is the heir; let us kill him and the farm will be ours.' So they killed him, and threw his body outside the vineyard. What will the owner of the vineyard do? He will kill those tenants and give the vineyard to others. Have you never read the Scripture: 'The stone which the builders rejected now has become the cornerstone.' This is the work of the Lord which is wonderful to see." Then the Jewish leaders tried to have Me arrested, but they were afraid of the people. They knew that I applied this parable to them. So they left and went away.

The Pharisees' and Herodians' Question Me

Then they sent some Pharisees and Herodians to trip Me in an argument. They came to Me and said, "We know that You always tell the truth, and respect no one, but teach the way of God honestly. Is it right to pay taxes to Caesar, or not?"

Now I saw their plot so I said to them, "Why are you trying to trip Me up? Bring Me a coin." And they gave Me one. Then I asked,

"Whose picture and title is on this coin?"

They answered, "Caesar's."

So I said, "Give to Caesar what belongs to Caesar, and give to God what belongs to God."

The Sadducees' Question

And they were utterly amazed at My wisdom. Then some Sadducees, who believed there was no resurrection, tried to trick Me with this question: "Teacher, Moses gave us a law that when a man's brother died leaving a wife but no child, the man must marry the widow to raise up an heir for the family."

Believe in the resurrection, and know that you will be raised because I Am alive in you. I was raised first, so you too will be raised.

"There were once seven brothers. The eldest married a wife but died and left no heir, and the second brother married her and died leaving no heir; and so did the third. None of the seven left an heir. At last the woman died. Now at the resurrection, whose wife will she be for she was married to all seven?"

I answered, "You are wrong in your interpretation. You do not understand the Scriptures or the power of God. For when people rise from the dead, they will not marry nor are they given in marriage, but are as the angels in heaven. But about the rising of the dead did you not read where Moses at the burning bush heard God say, 'I am the God of Abraham, the God of Isaac, and the God of Jacob?' He is not the God of the dead, but He is God of living people!"

A Legal Question

Then one of the scribes on hearing Me asked, "Which command is the greatest of all commands?"

I answered, "The greatest is, 'Hear, O Israel, the Lord our God is one Lord and you must love the Lord your God with all your heart, all your soul, all your mind, and all your strength.'"

Love Me with all of your talents, with all your time, and with all your treasures.

"And this is the second, 'You must love your neighbor as you love yourself.' No other command is greater than these."

Then the scribe said to Me, "Indeed, Teacher, You have properly said that there is one Lord and no other but Him, and to love Him with all one's heart, all one's understanding, and all one's strength, and to love one's neighbor as one loves himself is far more important than all the burnt-offerings and sacrifices."

I saw that he had answered thoughtfully, so I said, "You are not far from the kingdom of God." And no one dared ask Me any more questions.

Now I Ask a Question

While I was teaching in the temple, I asked them, "How can the scribes say that Messiah is the son of David when David himself, under the influence of the Holy Spirit, said: 'The Lord has said to my Lord, "Sit at My right hand until I make Your enemies the footstool of Your feet?"' The people wanted to hear more from Me.

I Denounce the Scribes and Pharisees

I continued to say, "Beware of the scribes who desire to go about in long robes, to be honored in public places, to have the front seats in the synagogues, to be honored at banquets—these are men who devour widows' houses and cover up their greed with long prayers. They will receive a much heavier judgment."

Then I sat in front of the collection box to watch the people as they gave their money. Many rich people were dropping in large amounts of money. Then a poor widow came to drop in two small coins. I called My disciples and pointed out, "I say to you, this poor widow has given more than the others who have been given much into the collection box. For they gave out of their abundance, but she gave out of her need; yes, she gave out of what she needed to live on."

I give you all that you need for this life and the life to come, not for the applause of people but for Me.

THIRTEEN

THE MOUNT
OF OLIVES
DISCOURSE

As I left the temple, one of My disciples said to Me, "Teacher! Look at these giant stones; this is a beautiful building!"

I answered him, "Do not be overwhelmed by this giant building. Not one stone will be left upon another; all will be torn down."

I got on the Mount of Olives opposite the temple where Peter, James, John, and Andrew asked Me, "When will all this take place? And what will be the sign that this will happen?"

You don't know when I'll return to judge the earth, so just live faithfully each day.

I told them, "Let no one mislead you about the future. Many will come calling themselves Messiah, and saying, 'I am He.' But they will deceive many. When you hear about wars and rumors of war, don't be alarmed. Wars will come, but the end is not yet. One nation will rise up to fight another and one kingdom against another. There will be earthquakes and famines; that is only the beginning of the birth pangs. Protect yourselves; you will be turned over to courts and synagogues where you will be beaten and persecuted. You will be brought before governors and kings for My sake. But before the end, the gospel must be preached to all nations. When they try you in court, do not be concerned about what you should say for it is not you who will be speaking, but God, the Holy Spirit, will speak through you. Brother will hand over brother to death, and a father his child, and children will rise up against their parents and have them killed. You shall be hated by everyone because of My name. But whoever endures to the end will be saved. So when you see the abomination of desecration standing where he has no right to stand, let the reader beware. Let those who remain in Judea flee to the hills; let him who is on the roof not go down to get any possessions. Let him who is in the field not go back to get his coat; pregnant mothers and those with nursing babies beware. Pray that it may not be in winter, for there will be a greater tribulation at that time than ever before since the beginning of creation, and never will be again. If the Lord does not cut short those days, no one will escape, but for the sake of the elect, God will cut them short."

"Then if anyone tells you, 'Look, the Christ is here!' or, 'Look, He is there!' don't believe it; for false Christs and false prophets will come and perform signs and wonders, to lead you astray; even if possible the elect. Watch out, I am warning you before it comes."

Because no one knows when I will come, expect Me to come for you at any moment.

"But in those days the sun shall be darkened and the moon will not give light; the stars will fade from the sky and the heavens will be shaken. Then shall I, the Son of Man, come in the clouds with great power and glory. Then I shall send angels to gather My chosen from the four ends of the earth."

Parable of the Fig Tree

"Learn from the fig tree: Whenever her branches are tender and there are leaves, you know that summer is near. So when you see these things happen, you will know that I AM at the door. Verily this present generation shall not pass until all these take place. Heaven and earth shall pass away, but My Word shall not pass away.

"No one knows the exact date and hour, no one except the Father; neither the angels in heaven nor the Son. Watch and pray; for you do not know the time when the Son of Man will come. A man who leaves his home to go away authorizes his servants and assigns each his work, with the guard appointed to watch them. Therefore watch, for you have no idea when the master of the house arrives—in the evening or at midnight or in the morning. If he comes unexpectedly, he might find you sleeping. Therefore I say to you, watch!"

FOURTEEN

MY LAST SUPPER
WITH MY DISCIPLES

It was Wednesday and the Passover was due in two days. The chief priests and the scribes schemed how they might arrest and execute Me, but they said, "Not during the festival, or else the people will revolt."

The Anointing at Bethany

While in Bethany, at the home of Simon the leper, I was reclining at the table, when a woman came with a very valuable jar of perfume, and broke the jar, and poured the ointment on My head. But some indignantly said to one another, "Why is she wasting this ointment? This could have been sold for a great price and given to the poor."

But I said, "Leave her alone! Why do you embarrass her? She has honored Me. For you always have the poor, and whenever you wish, you can give to them; but you will not always have Me. She has done what she could; she has prepared My body for burial."

All I ask is that you do what you can for Me, and I will do the rest.

"I say to you, wherever this gospel shall be preached over the whole world, what she has done shall be remembered as her memorial."

Then Judas Iscariot, one of the twelve, went to the chief priests to betray Me. When the priests learned of it, they were glad and promised to give him money. So he looked for an occasion how he might conveniently betray Me.

Events on Thursday

On the first day of the Festival of Bread without Yeast, when the Passover lamb was annually sacrificed, My disciples asked Me, "Where do you want us to prepare a place where You may eat the Passover?" Then I sent out two of My disciples telling them, "Go into the city where you'll see a man carrying a water pitcher; follow him. And wherever he enters, say to the owner, 'The Teacher asks, "Do you have a guest room where I can eat the Passover with My disciples?' He will show you a large upper room—prepare that room for us." My disciples went to the city, and found the man as I had told them, and they prepared for the Passover.

The Last Supper

As evening came, I arrived with the twelve. As we were reclining and eating, I said, "I know that one of you who is eating with Me shall betray Me." They were all disturbed and said, one after another, "Is it I?" I answered, "One of the twelve, who will dip with Me. The Son of Man is going the way of death that has been written about Him, but how terrible it will be for that man who betrays the Son of Man. It is better for that man if he were never born."

Institution of the Lord's Table

At the meal I took bread, blessed and broke it, then gave to them saying, "Take! Eat! This is My body." Also I gave thanks for the cup and I gave to them and they all drank. I said, "This is My blood of the new covenant, which is shed for many. I say to you, I will no more drink of the vine until that day when I will drink it new in the kingdom of God."

My Prayer in Gethsemane

We sang a hymn, and went to the Mount of Olives. I said to them, "This night all will be offended because of Me, for it is written, 'Strike the shepherd and the sheep will flee.' But after my resurrection I will go before you into Galilee."

Peter said to Me, "If all leave You, I will never do it."

I told him, "I tell you, during this night before the rooster crows, you will disown Me three times."

But Peter insisted, "Even if I must die with You, I shall never disown You." They all said the same thing.

We came to a place called Gethsemane, and I told My disciples, "Sit here while I go pray." I took Peter, James and John with Me. As I began to feel deeply distressed, I said to them, "My soul is deeply grieved; stay here." I went a little farther and fell on the ground and prayed. "If it is possible, let this hour pass from Me. Abba, Father, all things are possible with You, let this cup pass from Me! But not My will; but Your will be done." I came and found the disciples asleep and said, "Simon, are you sleeping? Could you not watch with Me for one hour?"

"Watch and pray so you will not be tempted. The spirit is willing, but the flesh is weak." I left again to pray, saying the same words. I then returned to find the disciples asleep once more. And they did not know how to explain their disobedience. I then came a third time and said, "Sleep and rest; the hour has come. The Son of Man is betrayed into the hands of sinners. Rise, let us go! Look, My betrayer is here."

You cannot begin to understand the dread of My prayer as I faced the cross and the task of becoming sin for humankind. As God, I had never faced this moral dilemma before, so I cried, "Abba, Father . . . . . Take this cup away from Me." Ultimately I faced the inevitable because of My love for you. Now you can pray, as I did, "Nevertheless, not what I will, but what You will." Come to Me when you are absolutely scared. I will Help you! Protect you! Save you!

I am Betrayed, Arrested, and Forsaken

While I was yet talking, Judas, one of the twelve, came and brought a crowd with swords and clubs commissioned by the chief priests, scribes, and elders. The betrayer had given them a sign: "The one I shall kiss is the one. Arrest Him and take Him away." As soon as Judas came, he stepped up to Me and said, "Rabbi!" and kissed Me. Then they grabbed Me and bound Me. One of My disciples standing close by drew his sword and cut off the high priest's servant's ear. And I said to them, "Have you come out against a violent man with swords and clubs to arrest Me? I was with you daily in the temple teaching. Why did you not seize Me then? But the Scripture must be fulfilled." And the disciples left Me and ran away. But a certain youth followed Me, wearing a linen cloth around his body, and when the soldiers grabbed him, he dropped the linen cloth and ran from them.

The Second Trial—Before Caiaphas

They brought Me before the council of the high priest, chief priests, elders, and scribes. Peter followed from a distance until he was inside the high priest's courtyard. There he sat down with the servants to warm himself by a fire. The chief priests and Sanhedrin were looking for a reason to execute Me, but couldn't find one; for while many bore false witness against Me, their testimony was not consistent. Some testified falsely, "We heard Him say, 'I will tear down this temple and in three days will build it up.'" But their words did not agree. Then the high priest stood to ask, "Jesus, why are You not answering these accusations?" I kept quiet and never answered. Again the high priest questioned Me; "Are You the Christ, the Son of the Blessed?"

I said, "I AM. And you shall see Me, the Son of Man seated at the right hand of the Most High, coming on the clouds of heaven."

Then the high priest tore his robes and yelled, "Why do we need any more witnesses? You heard Him blaspheme; what do you think now?"

All said that I deserved to die. Then some spat on Me. They blindfolded Me and slapped Me saying, "Prophesy, who hit You!" Even the servants who led Me out slapped Me.

As Peter was in the courtyard below, one of the high priest's maids saw him warming himself, and said, "You were with Jesus, the Nazarene!"

But he denied it saying, "I don't know what you're talking about." He went out the gate and a rooster crowed.

Then the maid who saw him began saying again to the men standing there, "This man is one of them!"

But Peter again denied it. Later the group said to Peter, "You are surely one of them; you're a Galilean!"

But Peter started to curse and swear, saying, "I tell you I don't know the man!"

Immediately the rooster crowed for the second time. Peter remembered My words, "Before the rooster crows twice, you will deny Me three times." Then Peter broke down and wept.

FIFTEEN

MY CRUCIFIXION

The Third Trial—Before the Sanhedrin

As soon as the morning came, the chief priests called a meeting of elders, scribes, and the whole council (the Sanhedrin) condemned Me.

The Fourth Trial—Before Pilate

They bound Me and led Me to Pilate. Pilate first asked Me, "Well—are you the King of the Jews?"

I replied, "You say that I am."

The chief priests accused Me of many things so Pilate questioned Me again, "Listen to their accusations! Have You nothing to say?" But I did not answer them—Pilate was astonished.

Pilate's custom at the festival was to release a prisoner—anyone they asked. Barabbas was in the prison at the time, with some other violent criminals who had committed murder. The crowd began to demand that Pilate should release Barabbas. So Pilate spoke to them, "Do you want me to release the King of the Jews?" Pilate knew that the chief priests had handed Me over to him because of their hatred of Me. But the chief priests agitated the crowd to get Pilate to release Barabbas rather than Me. So Pilate spoke to them once more, "What shall I do with the man whom you call the King of the Jews?"

They shouted, "Crucify Him!"

But Pilate answered, "Why, what crime has He done?"

But they yelled even louder. "Crucify Him!" Because Pilate wanted to satisfy the crowd, he released Barabbas, and after having Me flogged Pilate handed Me over to be crucified.

I am Mocked

Then the soldiers marched Me away to the courtyard and called for other guards. They dressed Me in a purple robe, and twisting some thorn-twigs into a crown, thrust it on My head. Then they began to mock Me. "Hail, Your majesty—King of the Jews!" They struck Me on the head with a stick and spat on Me, and then bowed before Me on bended knee. When they had finished mocking Me, they took off the purple cloak and put on My own clothes. Then they led Me away to crucify Me.

While the world makes fun of Me, you can worship Me.

They forced Simon, a man from Cyrene in Africa, the father of Alexander and Rufus, who was coming in from the fields, to carry My cross. They took Me to a place called Golgotha, meaning "Skull," and there they offered Me some drugged wine, but I would not drink it.

On the Cross

Then they nailed Me to the cross and divided My garments, casting lots to see what each would get. It was nine o'clock in the morning when they nailed Me to the cross. Over My head they posted a placard that read, "THE KING OF THE JEWS." They also crucified two thieves at the same time, one on each side of Me. And so the Scriptures were fulfilled. Those who passed by jeered at Me, shaking their heads in mockery, saying, "You said You could destroy the temple and build it up again in three days; come down from the cross and save Yourself."

There are many scoffers who don't believe Me, but you can believe all that I say, because it is truth and you can worship Me as God.

The chief priests, along with the scribes, also mocked Me, "He saved others, He cannot save Himself. If this Messiah, the King of Israel, would come down now, we would see and believe!" And even the thieves who were crucified with Me mocked Me.

At noon darkness spread over the countryside and lasted until three o'clock in the afternoon. Then I cried out in a loud voice, "My God, My God, why have You forsaken Me?"

Some of the bystanders heard what I said in Aramaic, *Eloi, Eloi, lama sabachthani?* and said, "Listen, He's calling for Elijah!" One man ran to soak a sponge in vinegar, put it on a stick and held it up for Me to drink, saying, "Let Him alone! Let's see if Elijah will come to take Him down!" Then I let out a loud cry and breathed My last. At that very moment, the curtain of the temple sanctuary was torn from the top to the bottom.

And then the centurion, who stood facing Me, seeing how I died, said, "Truly, this man was the Son of God!" There were some women watching from a distance: Mary Magdalene, Mary the mother of the younger James and Joses, and Salome. These were the women who followed Me as I walked in Galilee and ministered to Me. And there were many other women there who had also come up to Jerusalem for the festival.

The Burial of My Body

It was Friday evening of the day of Passover preparation, before the Sabbath. Joseph from Arimathaea, a member of the Sanhedrin, who believed the kingdom of God was about to come, went to Pilate to ask for My body. Pilate was surprised that I was dead already and he sent for the centurion to ask whether I had been dead long. On hearing the centurion's report, he gave Joseph My body. So Joseph brought a linen sheet, took Me down and wrapped Me in it, and then put Me in his own tomb which had been hewn out of the solid rock. Then Joseph rolled a stone over the entrance to the tomb. Mary Magdalene and Mary, the mother of Joses, watched and saw where I was laid.

There will always be "observers" who believe in Me, who will verify the "faith" for you.

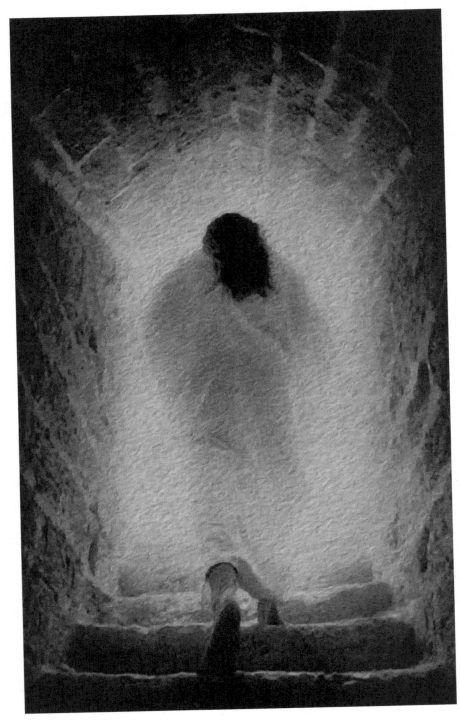

SIXTEEN

MY TEMPORARY TOMB

Early Sunday morning Mary Magdalene, Mary the mother of James, and Salome bought spices to anoint My body. Before sunrise they came to the tomb. They were asking, "Who can roll away the stone from the tomb for us?" Then they saw that the stone had been rolled away. They went into the tomb and saw a young man sitting to the right, dressed in white, and they were scared. But he said, "Do not be afraid! You are looking for Jesus the Nazarene, who was crucified. He is risen; He is not here; come see the place where He was laid. Then go, tell His disciples and Peter that He will be going before you into Galilee; You will see Him there, just as He said."

Just as the women had to obey to see Me, so you will obey so you can see Me and worship Me.

Quickly they ran from the tomb, fearful and terrified; they spoke to no one.

After I had risen early that morning, I appeared first to Mary Magdalene from whom I had cast out seven demons. She went and told My disciples who were grieving and weeping. When they heard that I was alive and she had seen Me, they did not believe it. But later on I appeared in a different form to two of them on their way home. They went and told the others; again they did not believe them.

The Upper Room One Week Later

Afterward, I appeared to the eleven as they sat at the table and I rebuked their unbelief and hardheartedness, because they did not believe the report of those who had seen Me.

You can believe in My resurrection because of the Scriptures, but you can mostly believe because I, the resurrected God the Son, live in your heart.

I commanded them, "Go into all the world and preach the gospel to every person. Those who believe and are baptized shall be saved; but he who does not believe shall be lost. And these signs shall follow those who believe: In My name they shall cast out demons; they shall speak with new tongues; they shall pick up serpents and not be harmed, and if they drink anything poisonous, it shall not kill them. They shall lay hands on the sick and heal them."

Do your part to carry out this great commission into all the world.

After I had talked with them, I was received up into heaven and sat down at the right hand of God.

Then My disciples went out and preached everywhere. I was with them and confirmed their message with signs.

PART THREE

I AM GOD THE SON
OF MAN

Based on the Gospel
of Luke

ONE

THE BIRTH OF JOHN
THE BAPTIZER

In this book are written different aspects of the key events of My life on the earth. You will learn about the disciples that followed Me, and the people whose life I changed. You will learn how to live your life here on earth, and you will learn of the life to come in Heaven. You can have confidence that what I say is truth for I am the Way the Truth and the Life.

You can have confidence in the things that are taught in My Word, so study it carefully to know what I said.

I Promise Zechariah a Son

During the reign of King Herod, Zechariah, a priest of the Abijah corps, had married Elizabeth who was from the priestly family; so he had impeccable qualifications to serve God. Zechariah and Elizabeth were spiritually minded, and they carefully obeyed every aspect of religious law. Because Elizabeth was barren, they had no children. When it finally came Zechariah's turn to offer evening prayers in the temple for all Israel, he also burned incense, a symbol of prayers ascending up to God. A great multitude was outside praying at the tenth hour, which was 4 p.m.

An Angel From God Announces the Birth of John the Baptizer

The appearance of an angel standing by the altar of incense frightened Zechariah; however, the angel said, "Don't be afraid, God has heard your prayers, your wife Elizabeth will have a son and you must name him John. Your son will give you joy and happiness, and multitudes will rejoice with you."

I will help you receive My message when I come to speak to you.

The angel told Zechariah, "Your son will be a great man for God, he must never drink intoxicating liquor, and the Holy Spirit will fill him for service. Your son will convince many to turn to God; he will be rugged like Elijah and will prepare people for the coming Deliverer by softening the hearts of fathers to be like children and convincing the disobedient to return to Your wisdom."

Zacharias Unable to Speak

Zechariah objected, saying he was an old man and his wife was beyond child-bearing years.

Stay long in My presence when I am speaking to you. Do not question what I promise you.

The angel Gabriel reminded Zechariah that he heard this good news standing in the presence of God, and that God sent him to tell it to Zechariah. Because Zechariah didn't believe God would do the things for which he prayed all his life, the angel said that Zechariah wouldn't be able to speak until the child was born.

May you be quick to believe and quick to obey all I tell you to do.

The waiting crowd got anxious because Zechariah tarried; and he couldn't speak when he appeared, so they realized he saw a vision. When his days of service were over, he then returned home. Elizabeth became pregnant and she hid herself from public view. Elizabeth proclaimed, "Lord, You are gracious to take away the embarrassment of having no children."

Gabriel Promises Mary a Son

When Elizabeth was six months pregnant, the angel Gabriel appeared to Mary, a virgin who was engaged to Joseph; they were both in the family line of King David. Gabriel greeted Mary, "Rejoice, Mary, you are highly favored of God, the Lord is with you." Mary was confused with this greeting; she didn't know what it meant.

Gabriel said, "Do not be afraid, God has decided to use you to be a blessing to all the world. You will conceive and deliver a Son, you must call His name Jesus. He will have great influence on the world and He will be the Son of the Most High God. God will give your Son the throne of David and He will rule over Israel forever."

A Miraculous Conception

Mary replied, "How can this happen, I am a virgin, and have not known a man?"

Gabriel answered, "The Holy Spirit will come on you, power from the Most High God will make it happen, and you'll have a child who is the Son of God." Gabriel continued, "Your Aunt Elizabeth has become pregnant with a child in her old age; with God, nothing is impossible."

Mary answered. "I will be the Lord's handmaiden; I am willing to be what the Lord wants me to be; let it happen, as you said."

May you yield your body to Me as Mary did. I will accomplish My purpose in your life, as I did in Mary's life.

Mary Visits Elizabeth

Mary left her home and went to Judah to visit Zechariah and Elizabeth. She greeted Elizabeth as she entered the house; the baby leaped in Elizabeth's womb because he knew he was in the presence of the Messiah. Elizabeth was filled with the Holy Spirit and said, "Blessed are you among women and blessed is the child you'll bear. But why this honor that the mother of our Lord should visit me? As soon as I heard your voice, the baby leaped in my womb. You believed the promises of our Lord, that's why you've been given this great privilege."

Mary's Song—The Magnificat

Mary responded to the Lord, "You are great, my God;

My spirit rejoices in You, my Savior.
You look on this lowly servant,
> now all generations will call me blessed.
For You—the Mighty God—have done great things,
> Holy is Your name.
Your mercy extends to those who reverence You from one generation to another.
You have done mighty works by Your arm,
> You have cast down the proud of heart.
You have brought down mighty kings from their thrones, and You lift up the lowly.
You have filled the hungry with good things,
> and sent the arrogant away empty.
You have come to help Israel, Your people, and You have remembered to be merciful to Abraham and his descendants forever."

Mary stayed with Elizabeth three months, and then returned to her home.

May you ever praise Me for using you, just as Mary who magnified Me in song.

The Birth of John the Baptizer

Elizabeth gave birth to a son at the appointed time and the relatives and neighbors rejoiced with the parents. When they came to circumcise him on the eighth day, the relatives tried to name him after his father. Elizabeth protested saying, "Call him John," but the relatives said no one in the family had that name. When they asked the father about the child's name, Zechariah asked for a tablet and wrote, "His name is John." Immediately Zechariah was able to speak again. He praised God and all the relatives joined him.

Everyone who heard about it wondered, "What will this child be?" for the hand of the Lord was with the child.

I will help you to obey My instructions just as Zechariah did, and then show Myself strong when you obey, just as I healed Zechariah.

Zechariah's Song: The Benedictus

Zechariah was filled with the Holy Spirit and he spoke this prophecy,

"Blessed is the Lord God of Israel,
　　for He visited and rescued His people.
He has sent a mighty Deliverer to the people
　　of His servant, David,
as promised by the holy prophets.
And the Deliverer will save us from our enemies,
　　and from the hand of those who hate the Jews,
to give mercy promised to our fathers
　　and perform His holy covenant,
the promises sworn to our father Abraham,
　　and to grant to us deliverance
　　　　from the hand of our enemies
so that we may serve Him
　　without fear in holiness and righteousness
　　　　in His presence all the days of our life.
And you my child, John, shall be called the prophet
　　of the Most High God.
John shall go before the Deliverer
　　to prepare the way for His coming.
John will tell the people about His salvation
　　and preach the forgiveness of sins,
　　　　showing us His tender mercies
　　that will come to us like the daybreak of the sun.
The Deliverer will give light to those living in darkness,
　　and guide their feet in Your way."

And the child, John, grew strong physically and spiritually, and lived in the desert until his time to preach publicly to Israel.

TWO

MY JOURNEY ON EARTH BEGINS AT MY BIRTH

Caesar Augustus had commanded everyone to return to their hometowns to register for a census for tax purposes. This happened when Quirinius became governor of Syria in 4 BC. All went to be registered to his own city. Then Joseph left Nazareth to return to Bethlehem because he was in the royal line of David; his wife Mary was also in that line. Mary was pregnant and the birth was imminent, so she gave birth while in Bethlehem. I was born in a stable because there was no room in any of the inns. Mary wrapped Me in strips of cloths, swaddling clothes, and laid Me in a feed trough.

Shepherds Visit Me

The same evening I was born, shepherds were in an open field watching over their sheep. Suddenly the sky lit up with an overwhelming light, and a shining angel appeared to them; the shepherds were scared out of their wits. The angel announced to them, "Don't be frightened, I have a wonderful message for you, and for everyone else in the world. Tonight, the Deliverer—the Lord—was born in Bethlehem. You will recognize Him because He will be wrapped in swathes of cloths, and will be lying in a feed trough."

Suddenly, the angel was joined by a gigantic angelic choir praising God saying,

"Glory to God in the highest,
    peace to those who enjoy God's good will."

When the angelic choir returned to heaven, the shepherds said to one another, "Let's go see this baby God told us about." When they ran to Bethlehem, they found Mary, My mother, and Me. I was lying in a manger.

After they saw Me, they went and told others the story that was told them about Me. Those who heard it were astounded by what was told them by the shepherds, but Mary kept all these things to herself and pondered them in her heart. Then the shepherds told everyone about Me, and people were astonished at what they heard.

May you embrace the story of the Baby, and worship Me with all your heart. May you tell everyone about the Baby, and how I came to forgive their sins.

My Dedication by Simeon

I was circumcised eight days after I was born, and they called My name Jesus, just as the angels instructed them.

Love My name for it means Savior; I am your personal Savior.

Later My parents and I returned to the temple for the ritual cleansing of the mother as required by Moses in the law,

"Every male that opened the womb shall
be dedicated to the Lord."

They did this with the offering of the poor, two young turtledoves or two pigeons.

In the temple was an elderly man named Simeon who looked for the restoration of the kingdom. Simeon lived blamelessly, and served God continually, and he was filled with the Holy Spirit. The Lord had revealed to Simeon that he would see the Deliverer before he died. Simeon was led by the Spirit into the temple on the day I was to be dedicated. Simeon took Me into his arms and blessed Me, saying, "Lord, I have seen what You promised, now I am ready to die. For my eyes have seen Your salvation, which all people will see one day. The Deliverer will be a light to the Gentiles, and will bring glory to Your people Israel."

I am your salvation, just as Simeon testified I was his salvation.

Joseph and Mary marveled at Simeon's words. Then Simeon said to Mary, "This child will be rejected by many in Israel, and God will judge their unbelief. But the child will also be received by many in Israel, and they will be saved and rewarded by God."

My Dedication by Anna

There was also a prophetess named Anna who was very old and had lived with her husband only seven years after they were married. She lived in the temple, worshiping God, praying, and very often fasting. She came along as Simeon finished his blessing; she gave thanks to God for Me, telling everyone the Deliverer had come.

At Twelve Years old I was busy in the Temple in Jerusalem

I went with My parents to Jerusalem for the annual Passover Festival when I was 12 years old. As My parents left Jerusalem for home, I stayed in Jerusalem, but My parents didn't know it. After a day's journey they went looking for Me, thinking I was walking toward home with relatives. When they failed to find Me, they returned to Jerusalem to search for Me. After three days they found Me sitting among the teachers, listening to them and asking questions. All who heard Me were greatly impressed at My level of comprehension and the difficult questions I asked them. Joseph and Mary were astonished when they saw Me, and Mary asked Me, "Son, why have You treated us like this? Your father and I have been worried to death."

I answered, "Why were you searching for Me? Didn't you know that I had to be about My heavenly Father's business?" I spoke to them but they did not understand.

Just as I naturally went to the temple, so you naturally go to church. One day, you will go to the place where I dwell.

I returned to Nazareth with them and was under authority to them. My mother didn't forget any of these incidents and meditated on them often. I grew in mental ability and physical strength and was respected by God and men.

THREE

THE MINISTRY OF JOHN THE BAPTIZER

In the fifteenth year of the reign of the Emperor Tiberius, Pontius Pilate was governor of Judea, Herod was governor of Galilee, his brother Philip was governor of the territory of Iturea and Trachonitis, Lysanias was governor of Abilene, and Annas and Caiaphas were in the high priesthood; the Word of God came to John, the son of Zechariah, in the desert. And he preached all over the Jordan valley the need for baptism of repentance to obtain the forgiveness of sins. He fulfilled what is written in the book of the prophet Isaiah,

"The voice of one crying in the desert,
prepare the road for the Messiah.
Make the paths straight for Him.
Every valley must be filled up,
and every mountain and hill leveled.
The crooked places must become straight,
and the rough roads must be made smooth,
and all people must know
about the salvation of God."

So John the Baptizer said to the crowds that were coming to be baptized by him, "You den of snakes! Who warned you to hide from the judgment that is coming? Produce fruit that shows your repentance, and do not justify yourselves saying, 'We have Abraham as our ancestor,' for I say to you that God can raise up children of Abraham out of these stones. Now the axe is already cutting at the roots of the trees. Every tree, then, that will not bring forth good fruit, will be cut

179

down and cast into the fire."

So the crowds asked John, "What must we do?"

He answered, "The one who has two coats must give to him who has none, and the one who has food must do the same thing.'"

Even tax-collectors came to be baptized by John, and said to him, "What must we do?"

So he answered, "Stop collecting more money than is required of you."

Some soldiers asked him, "What must we do?"

So he answered them, "Don't extort money from anyone, don't make false accusations, and be satisfied with your wages."

The people were excited and were arguing whether John was the Messiah. John answered them, "I am only baptizing you in water, but there is coming One after me who is stronger than I am. I am not fit to untie His shoe strings. He will baptize you with the Holy Spirit and with fire; His pitchfork is in His hand, and He will gather His wheat and store it in His barn; and He will burn up the chaff with eternal fire."

John continued to proclaim the good news with many explanations. But Herod the governor was repeatedly reproved by John, because he married Herodias his brother's wife. So Herod later put John the Baptizer in prison.

My Baptism

On a particular day when all the people had been baptized, I was also baptized and as I was praying, heaven opened and God the Holy Spirit came down on Me in bodily form as a dove. Everyone heard a voice out of heaven. "You are my Beloved Son. In You I am well pleased!"

Here is my Genealogy through Mary

I was about thirty years old when I began My ministry; I was the son legally of Joseph, the son of Eli, the son of Matthat, the son of Levi, the son of Melki, the son of Jannai, the son of Joseph, the son of Mattathias, the son of Amos, the son of Nahum, the son of Esli, the son of Naggai, the son of Maath, the son of Mattathias, the son of Semein, the son of Josech, the son of Joda, the son of Johanan, the son of Rhesa, the son of Zerubbabel, the son of Salathiel, the son of Neri, the son of Melki, the son of Addi, the son of Cosam, the son of Elmadam, the son of Er, the son of Jesus, the son of Eliezer, the son of Jorim, the son of Matthat, the son of Levi, the son of Simeon, the son of Judah, the son of Joseph, the son of Jonam, the son of Eliakim, the son of Melea, the son of Menna, the son of Mattatha, the son of Nathan, the son of David, the son of Jesse, the son of Obed, the son of Boaz, the son of Sala, the son of Nahshon, the son of Amminadab, the son of Arni, the son of Hezron, the son of Perez, the son of Judah, the son of Jacob, the son of Isaac, the son of Abraham, the son of Terah, the son of Nahor, the son of Serug, the son of Reu, the son of Peleg, the son of Eber, the son of Shelah, the son of Cainan, the son of Arphaxad, the son of Shem, the son of Noah, the son of Lamech, the son of Methuselah, the son of Enoch, the son of Jared, the son of Mahalalel, the son of Cainan, the son of Enosh, the son of Seth, the son of Adam, the son of God.

FOUR

I AM TEMPTED BY SATAN IN THE DESERT

I was filled with the Holy Spirit, and returned from the Jordan. I was led by the Spirit into the desert where I was tempted by the devil for 40 days.

I will fill you with God the Holy Spirit, and lead you by the Holy Spirit, just as I was led.

I fasted for 40 days, and when the fast was over, I was hungry. So the devil said to Me, "If You are God's Son, turn these stones to bread."

I answered, "It is written, 'Man shall not live on bread alone; (but by every word of God).'"

The devil then leading Me up to a high mountain, showed Me in an instant all of the world kingdoms and told Me, "I will give all the power and splendor of these, because it has been given over to me and I bestow it on whomever I please. If You will kneel to me and worship me, it will all be Yours."

I answered, "Get behind Me, satan, for it is written, 'You shall worship the Lord your God and worship Him only.'"

Then the devil brought Me to Jerusalem to the summit of the temple and told Me, "If You are God's Son, throw Yourself down, for it is written, 'The Lord will command His angels to protect You,' and 'They shall carry You in their hands so that You will not dash Your foot against a stone.'"

I answered him. It has been written, "You shall not tempt the Lord your God."

So the devil, after fully tempting Me, left Me until another opportunity came about.

I Face Unbelief in Nazareth

I came back to minister in My home region, Galilee, and the power of the Holy Spirit was on Me. Everyone in the region heard about Me, and when I preached in the synagogues, everyone was glad to hear Me.

Then I went to Nazareth, My boyhood home; and because it was My custom on the Sabbath, I went to the synagogue. An elder handed Me the scroll of Isaiah; I unrolled it to a certain place and read,

"The Spirit of the Lord is upon Me,
because the Lord has anointed Me to preach the gospel to the poor.
The Lord has sent Me to preach that prisoners shall be free,
    and the blind shall see, and the oppressed shall be released,
and to proclaim that God will bless those who come to Me.
Amen."

Then I rolled up the scroll and returned it to its place and took My seat. Every eye in the synagogue stared at Me, then I said, "This Scripture was fulfilled today."

And everyone was amazed at what I said. They said, "Is not this Joseph's son?"

I told them, "You will probably want Me to prove Myself, like the proverb, 'Physician, heal yourself.' You want Me to do miracles here in Nazareth as I have done in Capernaum, but I know your unbelief. You have not accepted Me, but rather you have rejected Me. I say that no prophet is accepted in His hometown. Remember how Elijah did a miracle to help the widow of Zarephath, even though she was a foreigner? There were many needy widows in Israel because there was a famine. It hadn't rained for three and a half years, yet Elijah was not sent to them. Elijah also healed Naaman of leprosy even though there were many lepers in Israel."

The people in the synagogue were furious when they heard what I said. The people mobbed Me and pushed Me outside toward the edge of the cliff near town. But I walked through the midst of the mob and returned to Capernaum.

I will give you boldness to face unbelief, and give you the wisdom to do what is right.

I came down to Capernaum, a city of Galilee, and taught them on the Sabbath. The people were enthusiastic at My teaching, for I spoke with authority. There was a man in the synagogue who was demon-possessed, who cried out loudly, "What do You want with me, Jesus of Nazareth? Have You come to destroy me? I know who You are: The Holy One of God." But I rebuked him: "Be quiet and come out of him!" Then the demon threw the man down. The demon came out of him without hurting him.

They were amazed and said to one another, "What word is this? For with authority and power He commands unclean spirits and they come out." And reports of Me went everywhere in the surrounding country.

You can believe everything written about Me for it is truth, and praise Me for My power.

I then arose and left the synagogue and went to Simon's home where his mother-in-law was suffering from a high fever and they asked Me about her. I stood over her, and rebuked the fever and it left her. Immediately she arose and waited on them.

At sunset all who had any who were sick brought them to Me, and I laid hands on each one of them and healed them. Even demons came out of many people, shouting, "You are Christ, the Son of God." But I stopped them and did not allow them to speak, because they knew that I was the Christ.

At daybreak I went out to an isolated spot to pray, but the people were looking for Me and found where I was. They tried to keep Me from leaving; but I told them, "I must preach the kingdom of God to other cities because this is the reason I was sent."

And I preached in the synagogues of Galilee.

FIVE

I CALL MY DISCIPLES

The multitude crowded around Me to hear the word of God as I stood by the lake of Gennesaret. I saw two boats on the shore; but the fishermen had left them and were cleaning their nets. I got into one of the boats that belonged to Simon and asked him to push out a little from the shore; then I seated Myself and began to teach the crowd from the boat.

When I had finished teaching, I told Simon, "Push out into deep water and lower your nets for a catch."

Simon answered, "Master, we worked hard all night without catching anything; however, at Your request I will lower the net." And when they did so, they caught a great catch of fish, so that their nets began to break. They signaled their partners in the other boat to come and help them. They filled both boats until they almost sank.

Seeing this, Simon Peter fell at My knees saying, "Depart from me, Lord, for I am a sinful man." He was astonished at the catch of fish and so were his partners—James and John, the sons of Zebedee.

I said to Simon: "Fear not, from now on you will catch men!" They brought their boats to shore, left everything, and followed Me.

I want you to be a "fisher of men and women, boys and girls." I want you to influence people for Me.

In one of their towns, a man with leprosy saw Me and begged Me, "Lord, if You will, You can cleanse me!"

Reaching out My hand, I touched him saying, "I will, be cleansed!" And the leprosy was gone. I told him to tell no one; but, "Show yourself to the priest, and make offerings for cleansing as Moses commanded."

But more people heard about Me and large crowds gathered to hear Me and be healed.

I withdrew often into the desert for prayer.

Seek the quiet places of solitude so you can pray to Me.

I Heal a Paralytic Man

As I was teaching, Pharisees and scribes from the villages of Galilee, Judea, and Jerusalem were sitting there. The power of the Lord was present for Me to heal the sick. Some men brought a paralytic on a bed to lay him before Me. But there was no way to get him to Me because of the crowd. So they went up on the roof and let him down through the tiles in front of Me. Seeing their faith, I said, "Your sins are forgiven."

The scribes and the Pharisees reasoned, "He is speaking blasphemies. Who is able to forgive sins except God only?"

I was aware of their thoughts, and said, "Which is easier to say: 'Your sins are forgiven,' or to say, 'Arise and walk?' But so you may know that I, the Son of Man, have power to forgive sins," I said to the paralytic, "Rise, pick up your mat, and walk."

I have the authority to forgive sins. If you confess that you are a sinner; I will forgive you and cleanse you.

Immediately he stood up in their presence, picked up his mat, praised God, and went home. Everyone praised God and said, "We have seen astonishing things today!"

My Call to Matthew

Going outdoors, I saw Levi a tax collector sitting at the collection table and said to him, "Follow Me!" Rising up, he left everything and followed Me.

Then Levi prepared a great banquet at his home for Me. A large group of tax collectors and others reclined at the table. But the

Pharisees and scribes complained to My disciples, "Why does Your Master eat and drink with tax-collectors and sinners?"

I answered, "Healthy people do not need a physician; but those who are sick. I have not come to call the righteous but sinners to repentance."

They also said to Me, "John's disciples fast and pray frequently, and the Pharisees do so as well, but Your disciples eat and drink."

I said, "Can the wedding guests fast while the bridegroom is with them? But the time will come, when the bridegroom will be taken from them; then they will fast."

I gave this parable to them: "No one patches an old coat with new cloth or else it will tear the new. Also, the patch from the new does not look like the old. And no one pours new wine into old wine skins, else the new wine will burst the skins and the wine is lost and the skins are ruined. But new wine is poured into new wine skins. And no one wants new wine after drinking the old, for he says, 'The old is preferable!'"

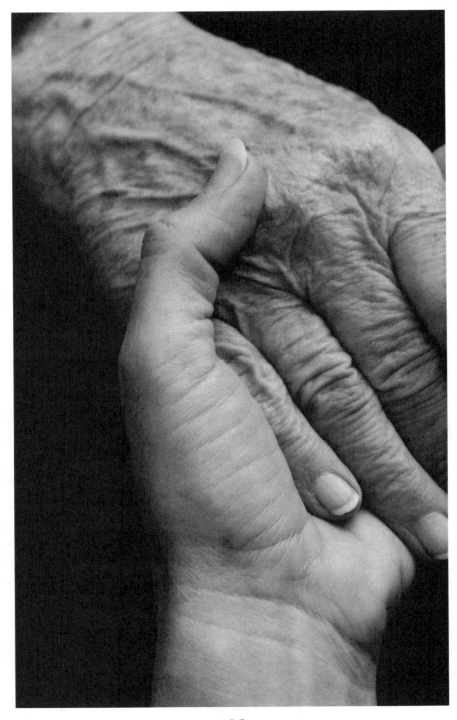

SIX

I QUICKLY END THE DEBATE ABOUT THE SABBATH

As I journeyed home from the Passover at Jerusalem, I went past the grain fields on the Sabbath and My disciples picked the grain and ate it. The Pharisees criticized them because they broke the Sabbath law. I answered, "Have you not read that David when he was hungry and those with him, how he went into the tabernacle and ate the show-bread, and gave some to those with him. They were not allowed to eat the bread; only the priest could eat it." Then I said, "I, The Son of Man, am Lord of the Sabbath."

I will help you properly observe My Lord's Day, not as the religious leaders legalistically observed it. You will worship Me properly on Sunday.

I Heal a Man With a Shriveled Hand

When I got to Capernaum, I entered the synagogue, and a man was there with a shriveled-up right hand.

The Jewish leaders watched Me closely whether I would heal on the Sabbath day so they could charge Me with breaking the law. I said to the man with the shriveled-up hand, "Stand in front of the people." Then I asked, "Is it right to help or hurt on the Sabbath day? To kill or save lives?" I looked at them with anger, then said to the man, "Stretch out your hand." The man did as commanded, and it was completely restored.

The Jewish leaders were angry and discussed how they might get rid of Me.

Don't be critical of anyone who comes to Me for help or healing like the Jewish leaders who criticized Me. Marvel at My compassion on those who hurt or need My help. Marvel at My patience with those who reject Me.

Choosing the Twelve

I went up into the hill country and I continued all night in prayer to God.

The next day I called My disciples to Myself and from them I chose twelve whom I named apostles. Simon, whom I called Peter, was the leader of the first group of four that also included Andrew, James and John. The second group of four apostles was led by Philip, and included Bartholomew, Matthew, and Thomas. The third group of four was led by James, the son of Alphaeus, also called the short one, and included Simon, the former terrorist fighter, Judas, later called Jude, also the son of James, and Judas Iscariot, the one who betrayed Me.

Multitudes Healed

I came down and stood with My disciples on level ground with a large crowd of people from all over Judea, Jerusalem, and from the Tyre and Sidon coast who came to hear Me teach, and to be healed of their diseases. Those who were demon-possessed were also healed. Everyone tried to touch Me because power flowed from Me to heal the sick.

The Beatitudes

Then I looked on My disciples, and began to speak; "Blessed are you who are poor, for the kingdom of God is yours! Blessed are you who are spiritually hungry, for you will be completely filled. Blessed are you who are weeping over sin, for you will rejoice!

"Blessed are you when people hate you and despise you and attack you, and call you evil for the sake of Me, the Son of Man. Rejoice and leap for joy for great is your reward in heaven; for this is the way the prophets were treated. How terrible it will be for all who are rich, for they now receive comforts in full. How terrible it will be for all who now live in luxury, for they will be hungry. How terrible it will be for all who now laugh, for they will mourn and weep. How terrible it will be for all those who are well spoken of for this is the way false prophets were treated.

"But I say to you, love your enemies, do good to those who hate you, bless those who curse you, and pray for those who abuse you. When a man strikes you on one cheek, offer him the other; and when a man takes away your coat, offer him your shirt also. Give to everyone who asks, and do not demand your goods back from him who takes them away.

"Deal with others as you would have them deal with you. If you love only those who love you, what credit do you get for that? Even big sinners love those who love them. And if you do good only to those who do good to you, what credit is that? Even big sinners do that. And if you lend to people expecting to get it back, what credit is that? Even big sinners lend to one another, expecting to get back a full payment. But you must practice loving your enemies. That way your reward will be great, and you will be sons of the Most High. Remember, He is kind to the unlikable and evil person. Be merciful, just as your Father in heaven is merciful.

"Stop criticizing others, so you will not be criticized; stop judging others, so you will not be judged. Forgive others, so you will be forgiven. Give to others, so you will receive good measure, pressed down, shaken together, and running over, and poured into your lap. For the measuring cup you use with others will be used with you."

Then I told them a parable. "One blind man cannot lead another. They will both fall into the ditch. A pupil is like his teacher. Will not everyone when fully trained be like his teacher? Why do you look for a tiny speck in your brother's eye when there is a heavy timber in your own eye? Can you say, 'Brother, let me get that tiny speck out of your eye,' when you have a timber in your own eye? You hypocrite! First get the timber out of your own eye, and then you may get a tiny speck out of your brother's eye.

"A good tree does not bear bad fruit, nor will a bad tree bear good fruit. For every tree is known by its fruit. People do not pick figs from thistles, or gather grapes from a weed. A good man, out of his good character, bears good fruit and a bad man, out of his bad character, produces bad fruit. Out of a man's mouth speaks the things that are in his heart."

I will transform you to be like Me. May good fruit come out of your life, and may good words come out of your mouth.

"So why do you call Me 'Lord, Lord,' but do not practice the things I tell you? Everyone who follows Me and does the things I teach is like a man who is building a house. He digs deep and lays a foundation on bedrock. When the floods come to burst on that house, it will stand because it was built on a rock. But the man who merely hears My words, and does not do them, is like a man who builds a house on the sand. When the floods burst upon it, it will collapse because it has no foundation."

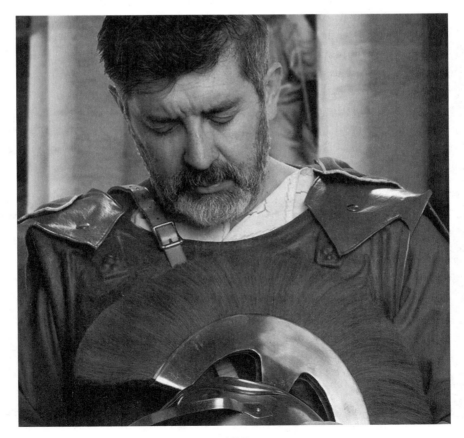

SEVEN

THE GOOD NEWS OF MY MIRACLES STARTS TO SPREAD

When I had finished My sermon in the hearing of the people, I entered Capernaum. There I met a Roman centurion whose servant was very dear to him. The servant was sick at the point of death. When the centurion heard about Me, he asked the Jewish elders to go see Me and ask Me to come and heal his servant of his illness. So they went to Me and urged Me saying, "The centurion deserves this for he loves our nation, and has built our synagogue."

Then I walked with them, but when I approached the house, the centurion sent friends to tell Me, "My Lord, do not trouble yourself about this because I am not worthy for You to come into my house. I do not think myself worthy to even ask You for anything. But simply speak the word, and my servant will be cured. For I too understand authority. I have soldiers under me, and when I order one to go, he goes; another to come, he comes. My servants do what I command."

I was astounded when I heard this and turning to the crowd that was following Me said, "I tell you, I have not found faith this great among the Jews." The messengers returned to the house and found the servant well.

I will give you faith like this army officer, so you can act on My words instantly.

Afterwards I went to the town called Nain. My disciples and a great multitude went with Me. As I approached the gate of the town, I saw a dead man being carried out, a widow's only son. A large crowd from the town was following her.

When I saw this, I was moved with compassion for her, and I said, "Stop weeping." Then I went and touched the coffin, and said, "Young man, I tell you, arise." Then the dead boy sat up and began to speak. I gave him back to his mother.

The crowd began to praise God, saying, "A great prophet has come to us!" and "God has visited us!" News about Me spread over Judea and the surroundings areas.

The Doubts of John the Baptizer

Now John the Baptizer's disciples told him about what I was doing. So John sent two disciples to Me to ask this question, "Are you the One who was to come, or should we look for another?"

So the disciples came to Me and said, "John the Baptizer sent us to ask You, 'Are you the One who is to come, or should we continue looking for another?'"

Even John the Baptizer had doubts, so don't punish yourself when you have doubts. I will forgive you and strengthen your faith to believe Me for greater things.

At that time, I cured many people of diseases and cast out evil spirits, and gave sight to many blind people. And so I answered them, "Go and tell John what you have seen and heard: The blind are seeing, the crippled are walking, the lepers are being cleansed, the deaf are hearing, the dead are being raised and the poor are having the gospel preached to them. And blessed is the one who does not stumble over Me."

After John's messengers left, I spoke to the crowd about John: "What did you go out into the desert to see? A reed blown about by the wind? Really, what did you go to see? A man dressed in fancy clothes? No. Those who dress in fancy clothes and live easy lives are found in the palaces. Really, what did you go to see? A prophet? Yes, I tell you John is far more than a prophet. John is the one the Scriptures predicted: 'Listen, I will send My messenger before You; he will prepare the road for You.' I tell you, of all men born of women, no one is greater than John; and yet anyone who becomes least in the kingdom of God will be greater than John."

I said John the Baptizer was the greatest in My kingdom, yet you can be greater if you are humble. It's hard to humble yourself, yet if you want to be used, I will make you humble.

Many people, even tax-collectors, when they heard John, did what he commanded. They submitted to John's baptism. But the Pharisees rejected God's purpose when they refused to be baptized by him.

"So, what are the people of this age like? They are like little children sitting in the marketplace playing games, and singing, 'We played the wedding song, but you did not dance; we sang the funeral song, but you did not mourn.' John the Baptizer came fasting and many said, 'He has a demon!' I, the Son of Man, have come eating and drinking, and many say, 'He is a glutton and a wine drinker, and a friend of tax collectors and sinners!' But true wisdom is recognized by her children."

A Sinful Woman Anoints My Feet

A Pharisee invited Me to dinner. So I came to the Pharisee's house and took My place at the table. There was a woman in the town with a sinful reputation. When she heard that I was eating at the Pharisee's house, she brought a bottle of perfume and stood behind Me at My feet, continually weeping. Then her tears began to fall on My feet. So she wiped them with the hair of her head, and she kissed My feet. Then she anointed them with the perfume from her bottle. When the Pharisee who invited Me saw it, he said to himself, "If He were really a prophet, He would know that the woman who is anointing His feet has a sinful reputation."

Then I spoke to him, "Simon, I have something to say to you."

So he said, "Teacher, go ahead and say it."

I told this parable: "Two men were in debt to a rich man. One owed him a hundred dollars, the other ten dollars. Neither could pay him, so he generously canceled the debts for both. Now which one of them will love the rich man more?"

Simon answered, "I suppose the one who had the largest debt canceled."

Then I said, "You are right."

And turning to the woman I said to Simon, "Do you see what this woman has done? I came to your house but you did not give Me water to wash My feet, but she has washed My feet with tears and wiped them with her hair. You did not give Me a kiss of greetings, but from the time I arrived, she has not stopped kissing My feet. You did not anoint My head with oil, but she anointed My feet with her sacrifice. Therefore her sins which are many are forgiven because she has loved much. But the one who was forgiven little, loves little."

And I said to the woman, "Your sins are forgiven!"

The guests at the table began to ask themselves, "Who is this man who forgives sins?"

But I said to the woman, "Your faith has saved you; go on in peace."

You can believe Me, just as this woman believed. Your total faith in Me is all I ask. I will forgive your sins.

EIGHT

PREACHING THE GOOD NEWS

Then I went through Galilee from town to town and village to village, preaching the good news of the kingdom of God. The twelve disciples were with Me and also some women who had been cured of diseases and had evil spirits cast out of them. Among these were Mary, who was called Mary Magdalene, out of whom I cast seven demons, and Joanna, the wife of Cleophas, Herod's household manager, Susanna and many other women. They were contributing to the needs of the group out of their personal resources.

Parable of the Sower

A great crowd came together from several towns. I spoke a parable to them:

"A sower went out to sow his seed. As he was sowing, a handful of seeds fell along the path at the edge of the field and the seeds were trampled on, and wild birds ate them up. Another handful of seeds fell into the rocks and as soon as they sprang up, they withered because they had no roots in fertile ground. Still more seeds fell into the thorns that grew up with them and choked the seeds. Finally, some seeds fell into rich ground and grew and yielded a hundredfold harvest."

I said, "Let him who has ears to understand, hear and learn."

My disciples asked Me what the parable meant.

I said to them, "You have the privilege of knowing the secrets of the kingdom of God, but I speak in parables because they look and do not see; they hear and do not understand. This is what the parable means: The seed is God's Word. The seed on the path illustrates those who hear God's Word, but the devil comes and steals the message from their hearts, so that they will not believe it and be saved. The seed sown on the rock illustrates those who accept the message with joy but the seed takes no real root. They believe for a while, but when persecution comes, they fall away. And the seed that falls into the thorns illustrates those who hear it, but they are choked by sin, money, and pleasures, so that it yields no fruit. But the seed sown in rich soil illustrates those who listen to the message, do it honestly, and yield fruit." .

Find good soil in your heart. Let the seed of the gospel grow into a harvest that will glorify Me.

Parable of the Lamp

"No one lights a candle and then covers it up or hides it under a bed, but they put it on a candlestick, so that others may have light. For there is nothing hidden that shall not be revealed, and nothing kept secret that shall not be manifested by the light. So take care that you hear and believe, for whoever receives more will have more given to him, and whoever does not receive more will even have that taken away from him."

My mother and brothers came to see Me, but they could not get to Me because of the crowd. So someone told Me, "Your mother and brothers are standing outside waiting to see You."

Then I said to them, "My mother and my brothers are those who hear God's Word and do it."

I Calm the Storm

I got into a boat with My disciples, and said to them, "Let us go over to the other side of the lake." As we were crossing the sea, I fell asleep. A furious storm swept over the lake and the boat filled with water and we were threatened. So they went to Me and awakened Me and said, "Master, Master, we are in danger!"

Then I got up and rebuked the wind and waves, and immediately the winds and waves were calm.

Then I said to them, "Where is your faith?"

But they were both scared and amazed and said to one another, "Who is He? For He commands even the winds and waves, and they obey Him."

I will calm the storms of your life so you can serve Me.

Demons are Cast into Swine

We landed in the neighborhood of Gadera, which is across the lake from Galilee. As soon as I stepped on shore, a man met Me who was demon-possessed. He had worn no clothes for a long time and lived in the tombs.

When he saw Me, he screamed and threw himself down before Me, and cried out in a loud voice, "What do You want from me, Jesus, Son of the Most High God? I beg You, do not torture me!" On many occasions the demon had seized him. When he had been bound with chains and fetters, he would break his bonds, and the demon drove him into the wilderness.

I asked him, "What is your name?" The man answered, "Legion!" for many demons had possessed him. The demons begged Me not to send them into the bottomless pit. There was a field full of hogs feeding there. So the demons begged Me to let them enter into those hogs. And I let them do it.

Then the demons came out of the man and entered the hogs, and they rushed over the cliff into the lake and were drowned.

When the men who fed the hogs saw what happened, they ran to tell the news in town and the surrounding country. So the people went out to see what had happened. They found the man who had previously had demons now sitting at My feet, fully dressed, and in his right mind. They became frightened when they saw what happened. Those who saw what happened, told how the demon-possessed man had been healed. Then all the people of that country asked Me to leave because they were afraid. So I entered the boat and returned to Capernaum.

The man who was cleansed of the demons begged Me to let him go with Me, but I sent him away saying, "Go back to your home, and tell what great things God has done for you."

The man then went off to tell throughout the city what great things I had done for him. Now when I returned to Capernaum, a crowd welcomed Me, for they were all waiting for Me.

A Woman Is Healed

Jairus, who was the leader of the synagogue, came and fell down at My feet, begging Me to come to his house because his only daughter, about 12 years old, was dying. As I was going, crowds of people continued to press on Me.

Then a woman who had a hemorrhage for years, and had spent all her money on physicians and was not healed, came up behind Me and touched the hem of My tunic. Her hemorrhage stopped immediately. Then I asked, "Who touched Me?"

Everyone denied touching Me. Then Peter said, "Master, the crowds are pressing on You and thronging You."

I said again, "Someone touched Me because I felt power go out from Me." The woman knew her actions were uncovered, so she came forward trembling, and she fell down before Me to tell why she had touched Me. So I said to her, "My daughter, your faith has cured you; go in peace."

Her touch didn't heal her, it was her faith. I will Give you that kind of faith.

Jairus' Daughter Is Raised

While I was still speaking, someone came from Jairus' house to tell him, "Your daughter is dead; don't trouble the Teacher any longer." But I heard what was said, and told Jairus, "Do not be afraid; have faith, and she will be healed."

When I reached the house, I did not allow anyone to go in with Me except Peter, James, and John, and the child's father and mother. Professional mourners were weeping and wailing over her. But I said, "Stop weeping! For she is not dead but asleep."

Then they laughed, for they knew that she was dead. Then I held her hand and said, "My child, get up!" Her life returned and she immediately got up, and I directed that some food be given her to eat. And her parents were amazed, so I ordered them not to tell anyone what had happened.

Thank Me for healing all: a young girl and an older woman; an immediate problem and a lingering one; the rich and the poor; so you know My healing will reach you.

NINE

THE TWELVE DISCIPLES ARE COMMISSIONED

I called the twelve together and gave them power and authority over demons and to cure diseases. Then I sent them out to preach the kingdom of God and to heal. I said to them, "Take nothing for the journey; neither staff, nor purse, nor bread, nor money; and don't take a spare tunic. When you enter a house, stay there until you leave to go on your way. If they don't welcome you, when you leave their town shake the dust from your feet as a testimony against them."

So they set out and went from village to village, preaching the good news and healing everywhere.

The Murder of John the Baptizer

Meanwhile Herod the tetrarch had heard about all the things I was doing, and he was puzzled, because some were saying that John had risen from the dead. Others were saying that Elijah had reappeared. Still others said that one of the Old Testament prophets had risen from the dead.

But Herod said, "I beheaded John. Who is this that is responsible for these reports?"

And he wanted to see Me.

Miracle of the Loaves

When the apostles returned, they gave Me an account of all they had done. Then I took them with Me and went privately to a town called Bethsaida. But the crowds found out and followed Me. I welcomed them and talked to them about the kingdom of God. Then I cured those who needed healing.

It was late afternoon, so the twelve said, "Send the people away so they can go find lodging and food; for we are in an isolated place."

I replied, "You give them something to eat."

But they said, "We have only five loaves and two fish. We need to go buy food to feed this many people."

I will help you share the bread of life with hungry people, just as My disciples did.

For there were about five thousand men. But I said to them, "Make them sit down in groups of fifty." After they did so, I took the five loaves and two fish, and raised My eyes to heaven, and blessed them; then I broke them and handed them to My disciples to distribute among the people. Everyone ate as much as they wanted. What was not eaten was collected, and the disciples filled twelve baskets.

I Visit Caesarea Philippi

Once when I was praying alone with My disciples, I questioned them, "Who do the people say I am?" And they answered, "John the Baptizer; or Elijah; or another Old Testament prophet raised from the dead." But I asked, "But who do you say I am?" Peter spoke up and said, "The Christ of God." Then I gave them strict orders not to tell this to anyone.

Then I said to all, "I, The Son of Man, must suffer many things and be rejected by the elders, chief priests, and scribes and be put to death. But on the third day I will be raised to life." Then I said, "If anyone wants to be My follower, he must deny himself and take up his cross daily and follow Me. For those who hang on to this earthly life for Me will lose it. And anyone who loses his life for My sake, will save it. Is it any profit to gain the whole world, yet his soul is destroyed and lost? Those who are ashamed of Me and My words, I will be ashamed of him when he comes into glory before the holy angels and My Father? I tell you the truth, some who are standing here will not taste death before they see the kingdom of God.

Peter and John Witness My Transfiguration

About eight days later I took Peter and John and James up a mountain to pray.

Will you set aside times to pray, just as I did?

As I was praying, the appearance of My face was changed and My clothing became brilliant as lightning. Suddenly two men appeared to talk with Me, Moses and Elijah. They were speaking of My death which was to happen in Jerusalem. Peter and his companions were sleeping soundly. When they woke up they saw My glory and the two men standing with Me.

As we were leaving, Peter said to Me, "Master, it is wonderful to be here, let's make three tents, one for You, one for Moses, and one for Elijah." He did not know what he was saying.

As he spoke, a cloud covered them; and the disciples were afraid. But a voice came from the cloud saying, "This is My Son, whom I have chosen. Listen to Him."

And after the voice had spoken, they saw only Me. The disciples kept this incident to themselves and told no one what they had seen.

The Disciples Can't Heal

The next day when we came down from the mountain a large crowd came to meet Me. A man in the crowd yelled out, "Master, I beg You, help my son; he is my only child. Without warning, a demon will take hold of him, and he will cry out and become convulsive and foam at the mouth. This happens for a long time, but when it is over it leaves the boy worn out. I begged Your disciples to cast the demon out, but they couldn't."

You don't want to be like these powerless disciples. You want to help those who come to you for help. I will give you power to serve Me and help people.

I said, "Faithless and stubborn generation! How much longer must I be among you and put up with you? Bring him here." The boy was still walking toward Me when the demon threw him to the ground in convulsions. But I ordered the demon out of him, cured the boy, and gave him back to his father.

They were all amazed at the greatness of God. While everyone was marveling at what I did, I said to My disciples, "Listen to Me and remember what I say, for I, the Son of Man, am going to be handed over into the hands of the enemy." But they did not understand Me when I said this because they were spiritually blinded so that they could not understand the meaning of what would happen, and they were afraid to ask Me about what I had just said.

Childlike Faith

An argument started among the disciples about which of them would be the greatest. I knew their thoughts and I took a little child and had him stand by My side. Then I said to them, "Those who welcome this little child in My name welcome Me: and anyone who welcomes Me welcomes the One who sent Me. For the least among you is the one who is greatest."

Mistaken Zeal of John the Apostle

John spoke up. "Master, we saw a man casting out demons in Your name. We told him to stop because he is not with us.

But I said, "You shouldn't have done that; anyone who is not against you is for you."

Now as the time drew near for My return to heaven, I steadfastly set My face to go to Jerusalem. Then I sent messengers ahead of Me. They went into a Samaritan village to make preparations for Me, but the people would not receive Me because I was going to Jerusalem.

When the word came back to them, James and John said, "Lord, do You want us to call down fire from heaven to burn them up?"

I will keep you from making wrong requests of Me, such as these. I will give you compassion for unbelievers and save them through your ministry.

But I turned and rebuked them, "You do not know the spirit that is in you! I, the Son of Man, did not come to destroy men's lives, but to save them." And we went to another village.

Giving Up Everything for Me

As we were walking, we met a man on the road who said to Me, "I will follow You wherever you go."

I answered, "Foxes have holes and the birds of the air have nests, but I, the Son of Man, have no place to lay My head."

I said to another, "Follow Me."

The man replied, "Let me go and bury my father first."

But I answered, "Leave the dead to bury their dead; but you go spread the gospel of the kingdom of God."

Another said, "I will follow You, but first let me go and get permission from my family at home."

I said to him, "No one who puts his hand to the plow, and looks back is fit for the kingdom of God."

If you will be My disciple, you will not look back or turn back. You will follow Me.

TEN

THE SEVENTY ARE SENT OUT IN MY NAME

After this I appointed seventy disciples, and sent them ahead of Me, in pairs, to all the towns and places where I was to visit. I commanded them, "The harvest is great and plentiful but there are few laborers, so pray to Me, the Lord of the harvest to send laborers to My harvest. Start off for now, but remember, I am sending you like lambs among wolves. Do not take a purse, or suitcase, or shoes. Don't waste your time on the road. Whatever house you enter let your first words be a blessing on those who live there. And if a man of peace lives there, your blessing will rest on him; if not, it will return to you. Stay in that house and eat and drink what they give you because the workman deserves his pay. Do not move around from one house to another. When you are entertained, eat what is set before you. Cure those who are sick. Preach 'the kingdom of God is coming.' But if you enter a town that does not make you welcome, go out into the streets and shake the dust of that town off your feet and know that 'the kingdom of God is very near.' I tell you, Sodom will not be judged as severe as that town."

I will teach you how to react to people who are both receptive and non-receptive. I will use your ministry to further My Kingdom.

"How terrible it will be for you, Chorazin! How terrible it will be for you, Bethsaida! For if the miracles done in you had been done in Tyre and Sidon, they would have repented long ago in burlap clothing and ashes. And still, it will not be as severe for Tyre and Sidon at the judgment as with those towns. And as for Capernaum, you want to be exalted high as heaven? No! You shall be thrown down to hell. Anyone who listens to the lessons you illustrate, listens to Me; anyone who rejects your lessons, rejects Me, and those who reject Me reject the One who sent Me."

The seventy disciples came back rejoicing, saying, "Even the demons submit to us when we use Your name." I said to them, "I saw satan fall like lightning from heaven. Yes, I have given you power to walk over the enemy, nothing shall hurt you. Yet do not rejoice that the demons obey you, rather rejoice that your names are written in heaven." At that time I was filled with joy by the Holy Spirit, and said, "I bless you, Father, Lord of heaven and earth, for hiding these things from the intellectuals and the worldly, but You reveal them to Your children. Yes, Father, for that is Your pleasure. Everything has been given to Me by My father; and no one understands the Son, except the Father, and no one understands the Father except the Son and those to whom the Son chooses to reveal to them." Then turning to My disciples, I said privately, "Blessed are the eyes that see what you see, for I tell you that many prophets and kings wanted to see what you see, but they were never able to see it; or to hear what you hear."

The Good Samaritan

A lawyer stood up to test Me with questions, asking, "What must I do to inherit eternal life?"

I said, "What is written in the law and how do you read it?"

The man responded, "You must love the Lord your God, with all your heart, soul, strength and mind;" then he added, "And love your neighbor as yourself."

Then I concluded, "Do this, and you will live."

But the lawyer tried to justify himself asking, "And who is my neighbor?"

I answered with a parable, "A Jewish man went down from Jerusalem to Jericho. He was attacked by bandits who beat him, and stripped him of his clothes and money, and left him half dead in the road. A Jewish priest came down the road and passed by the wounded man. Next a temple assistant passed by on the other side of the road, looked at the man and did nothing. When a despised Samaritan saw the man; he knelt beside him, cleansed the wounds with oil, and bandaged them up. Then the Samaritan put the man on his donkey, took him to an inn and took care of him. The next day the Samaritan gave the innkeeper money to take care of the man, and promised; 'If you need more, I'll pay next time I'm here.'"

Then I asked the lawyer, "Which of these three was a neighbor to the one who was attacked by the thieves?"

The lawyer answered, "The one who showed mercy."

I said, "Yes, now go do the same thing."

I will make you sensitive to the needs of people, then give you initiative to do something about it.

Mary and Martha

When I entered a village near Ephraim, Martha received Me into her house. Her sister Mary sat at My feet to listen to the things I said. But Martha was busy working in the kitchen, so she complained to Me, "It's unfair for Mary to listen to You when I'm doing all the work."

Martha said, "Tell her to help me in the kitchen."

But I answered, "Martha, Martha, you are upset over these trivial things. There is only one thing to be concerned with. Mary has found the main thing and it can't be taken from her."

May you know when to work with your hands and when to sit at My feet to learn from Me. When you come and sit at My feet, I will teach you what you need to know, and I will build character in you, that you need to serve Me.

ELEVEN

I TEACH MY DISCIPLES THE LORD'S PRAYER

After a few days I prayed all night and when I finished, the disciples asked, "Lord, teach us to pray!"

I gave them this prayer as their example, as I had previously given it in the sermon on the mount. I said, "When you pray say,

'Our Father, who is in heaven,
  Holy be Your name.
Your kingdom come.
Your will be done in heaven as on earth.
Give us day by day our daily bread,
    and forgive us our sins
          as we forgive everyone who is indebted to us;
and don't allow us to be overcome by temptation.'"

The act of forgiving someone who has offended you means that you forgive that person by "God's grace," because now God can work in your life and theirs. Your forgiveness means their offense can no longer dominate your life. You treat their offense as nothing, and you are no longer separated from them. But also, it redeems the offender; he is no longer bound to you, and their offense no longer binds them. Forgiveness frees you. You don't forgive for their sake, you forgive for your sake. You forgive others for your freedom, health, and victory. If you won't forgive, it means you are still in bondage to them. You want to be free to love Me, serve Me, and be used by Me.

213

I did not finish the prayer as I did on the previous occasion. I said, "What if you went to a neighbor's house in the middle of the night to borrow bread. You would yell to wake up your neighbor, saying, 'A friend has just arrived for a visit, and I don't have any bread to give him.' Suppose your neighbor yelled back, 'I am in bed, my family is asleep, I can't help you.'"

I said, "Though he won't do it as a friend, if the man kept begging and knocking, his neighbor would get up and give him bread, because of his persistence. So you can do the same with prayer, keep on asking and you will receive. Keep on seeking and you will find, keep on knocking and the door will open. For everyone who keeps on asking—receives; everyone who keeps on seeking—finds; everyone who keeps on knocking—the door opens.

"If your son asks for bread, will you give him a stone—No! If he asks you for a fish, will you give him a serpent—No! If he asks for an egg, will you give him a scorpion—No! If fallen people like yourselves give good gifts to your children, how much more will your heavenly Father give you good gifts?"

I will give you faith to believe Me for the things you need; so pray to me daily for the small things and the large things that you need.

The Long Day

I was casting a demon out of a man who couldn't speak. When the demon had gone out, the dumb man spoke and the people were amazed.

But some of them said, "Jesus does these miracles by Beelzebub, the prince of demons."

Others asked Me for a sign from heaven to prove who I was. But I knew their unbelief and what they were thinking, so I said, "Any kingdom divided against itself will collapse, and a household divided against itself will also collapse. The same thing will happen with satan: if he is divided against himself, he will be defeated. Since you claim that I cast out demons by Beelzebub, let's test that idea. If it is through Beelzebub that I cast out demons, through whom do your own leaders cast them out? Does this prove they are filled with demons? But if the power is of the finger of God, then realize that the kingdom of God has come to you."

I am stronger than all the might of everyone who has ever lived. I will give you strength in your ministry to people.

"When a strong man has armed guards in his palace, his goods are undisturbed; but when someone stronger attacks and defeats the strong man, he takes away all his weapons and his goods. He who is not for Me is against Me; and he who does not help Me, hurts My cause. When a demon goes out of a man, it wanders through dry places looking for a home, and not finding one it returns to the home from which it came. But when he returns, he finds it swept and clean. It then goes and brings seven other demons more wicked than himself. They set up housekeeping, so that the man ends up being worse than he was at first."

Now as I was speaking, a woman in the crowd yelled out, "Blessed is the womb that bore You and the breasts that nourished You."

But I replied, "Far happier are those who hear the Word of God and obey it!"

The crowds got even bigger and I spoke to them, "This is an evil generation that is asking for a sign. The only sign I will give them is the sign of Jonah. For just as Jonah was a sign to the Ninevites, so I, the Son of Man, will be a sign to this generation. On judgment day the Queen of Sheba will rise up to condemn this generation because she came on a long journey to hear the wisdom of Solomon. But there is something greater than Solomon here. On judgment day the men of Nineveh will stand up to condemn this generation because when Jonah preached they repented. There is something greater than Jonah here today.

Parable of the Lighted Lamp

"No one lights a lamp and hides it under a tub, but they put it on the candle holder so that people may have light when they enter a room. Your eye is the lamp of your body. When your eye is healthy, your whole body has light; but when the eye is diseased, your body can't see to walk. See to it then that the light inside you is not darkness. Therefore, if your whole body is filled with light, you can walk confidently because the lamp shines on you with its rays."

Woe to the Pharisees

When I finished speaking, a Pharisee invited Me to eat at his house. I went in and sat down at the table. The Pharisee noticed this and was surprised that I had not first washed before the meal. But I said to him, "You Pharisees clean the outside of your cup and plate, while inside you are filled with extortion and greed. You are foolish. Did not he who made the outside also make the inside? Instead, give to the poor from your inner heart and then indeed everything will be clean for you. Woe to you Pharisees! You who pay your tithe of mint and rue and all sorts of garden herbs and overlook justice and your love of God! You should have practiced these tithes without leaving out your love for God. Woe to you Pharisees who take the good seats in the synagogues and love to be greeted in the market squares. Woe to you, because you are like tombs that men walk on without knowing it!"

A lawyer asked, "Why are you insulting us?"

I said, "How terrible it will be for you, lawyers; you strangle people with religious demands, but you don't do what you require of others. How terrible it will be for you lawyers because you load people down with burdens they can't carry, and then you don't do anything to help them. How terrible it will be for you because you build monuments to the prophets, but it was your ancestors—men like you—who killed them. You honor your ancestors, but they killed the prophets and you built monuments to them. God said, 'I will save prophets and apostles, but you will kill and persecute them.' And this generation will kill God's servants, just as your fathers killed them in the past, from the blood of Abel to the blood of Zechariah. How terrible it will be for lawyers, who hide God's truth from the people; you won't believe it yourself and you prevent others from believing it."

The Pharisees and lawyers tried to trip Me up with questions and did everything they could to oppose Me. They wanted some way to destroy Me.

TWELVE

WARNINGS AND ENCOURAGEMENT FOR MY FOLLOWERS

Meanwhile a crowd so large it couldn't be counted gathered so that they were stepping on one another. So I began to preach, first to My disciples, "Be on your guard against the yeast of the Pharisees—which is hypocrisy. Their hypocrisy is not covered; everyone knows they are filled with pride but their true motives will be uncovered. At the same time, godly people you don't know about will be seen by all. Whatever you have said in the dark will be heard in the daylight, and what you have whispered behind closed doors will be proclaimed on the housetops.

"To My followers I say: Do not be afraid of those who kill the body; that is all they can do. I will show you whom to fear: fear God the Father, who can kill the body but also has the power to cast you into hell.

"Yes, I tell you, fear Him. Are not five sparrows bought for two pennies? And yet not one is forgotten in God's sight. Also, every hair on your head has been numbered. Don't be afraid: you are worth more than many sparrows.

"I tell you, whoever declares himself for Me in the presence of people, I, the Son of Man, will acknowledge him in the presence of God's angels. But the one who disowns Me in the presence of men will be disowned in the presence of God's angels. Everyone who speaks a word against Me, the Son of Man, will be forgiven, but he who blasphemes God the Holy Spirit will not be forgiven. When you are brought before synagogues and authorities, do not worry about how to defend yourselves or what you will say, because when the time comes, the Holy Spirit will teach you what you must say."

Parable of the Rich Fool

Someone in the crowd said to Me, "Master, tell my brother to give me a share of our inheritance."

"My friend," I replied, "who appointed Me a judge, or the arbitrator of your claims?"

Then I said to them, "Watch, and be on your guard against greed, for a man's life does not consist of what he owns."

Yield all your belongings to Me. May your belongings not possess you; rather, may I be your possessor.

Then I told them a parable: "There was once a rich man who had a good harvest from his land. He thought to himself, 'What am I going to do?' I do not have enough room to store my crops.' Then he said, 'This is what I will do; I will tear down my barns and build bigger ones, then I will store all my grain and my goods in the new barns. I will say to my soul: Soul, you have plenty of good things laid by for many years to come; take it easy, eat, drink, and enjoy life.' But God said to him, 'You fool! This night your soul will be demanded; and your riches, whose will they be then?' This is how it will be for the man who stores up treasure for himself in place of making himself rich in the sight of God."

Then I said to My disciples: "Stop worrying about your life, what you will eat, or what you will wear. Your life is more than food, and your body is more than clothes. Think about the ravens. For they neither sow grain nor reap a harvest, they have no storehouses nor barns, and yet God continually feeds them. You are worth more than the birds! Which of you by worrying can add a single thing to his life? So if you cannot add a very little thing, why should you worry about anything else? Watch the lilies grow. They do not work hard nor try to grow. I tell you that not even Solomon in all his glory was ever dressed as elegantly as one of them. Now, if God wonderfully dresses the fields with wild grass, which today is green but tomorrow is thrown into the furnace, how much more will He clothe you who have so little faith?

So stop worrying about what to eat and what to drink. These are the things the Gentiles seek. Surely your Father knows what you need. Seek continually My will, and these things will be added to you.

"Live for today; yesterday has passed, learn from it. Tomorrow is not here, so all you can do is prepare for it. You will not live in the past with its failures and successes. You will not live in the future with its hopes and fears. You will live for today. NOW is all the time you have.

"Stop being fearful, My little flock, for your Father has gladly chosen to give you the kingdom. Sell your property and give to the poor. Get a wallet that will never be empty. Your riches will never fail in heaven where a thief cannot steal nor a moth destroy. For where your treasure is, there will your heart be."

Parable of the Expectant Steward

"You must keep ready for service and keep your lamps burning; be like the servants waiting for their master to come home. When he comes and knocks, they will open the door for him. Those servants will be happy when the master comes. Will he find you watching for him? I say to you, he will prepare to serve them and have them sit at a table, and he will wait on them. Whether he comes before or after midnight, they will be happy when he gets there. But be prepared because if the master of the house knew when the thief was coming, he would not have allowed his house to be broken into. So you must always be ready, for at an hour you are not expecting Me, I, the Son of Man, will come."

Parable of the Faithful Steward

Peter asked Me, "Lord, do You mean this parable for us, or for the multitude?"

Then I answered, "The master will put in charge a faithful manager and give him the task of giving out supplies at the proper time. Happy is that slave who has done what he was supposed to do when his master comes. I tell you the master will put him in charge of all his property. But if that servant says to himself, 'My master will not be coming back for a long time,' and he begins to beat the slaves, and eats and gets drunk; his master will come back when he is not expected, and at an hour that the servant didn't know about. He will judge him severely, and give his share to a faithful worker. That slave who knows his master's wishes and is not ready will be severely punished. But the one who does wrong without knowing it will be lightly punished. Much will be demanded from those to whom much has been given."

You will act on the information I have given you. As a faithful servant, you will be greatly rewarded here on earth as well as in Heaven for eternity.

"I come to bring fire on the earth, and I wish it were already burning! I have a baptism to administer, and I am in anguish until it comes. Do you think that I came to give peace on earth? No! But rather strife. Five in a family will be divided, three against two, and two against three. Father will be against son and son against father, mother against daughter and daughter against mother, mother-in-law against daughter-in-law and daughter-in-law against mother-in-law."

Then I said to the crowd, "When you see a cloud rising in the west, you think, 'It's going to rain,' and it does. And when you feel the south wind blowing, you say, 'It is going to be hot' and it is. Hypocrites! You know how to interpret the weather, the earth, and sky. Why can you not interpret the times? Why can you not decide what is right? When you are being sued in court, do everything you can to satisfy the one suing you. Don't let him crush you before the judge, or the judge will turn you over to the sheriff, and the sheriff will put you in prison. I tell you, you will never get out until you have paid the last cent you owe!"

THIRTEEN

NEWS FROM JERUSALEM

Some in the crowd told Me about the rebellious Galileans who were executed by Pilate and mixed their blood with the sacrificial blood that was offered in the temple.

I answered, "Were these men the greatest sinners among all the Galileans because of their crimes?"

Then I explained, "No, they were not! All men are sinners, and all must repent or they will likewise perish."

Then I referred to the tower in Siloam that fell and killed people. "Were they greater sinners than these who live in Jerusalem?"

Again I answered, "No, they were not! All men are sinners, so all must repent or they will likewise perish."

Then I told a parable, "A man planted a fig tree in his garden, then came looking for fruit, but he found none. The man said to his gardener, 'I have been looking for figs on this tree for three years, but haven't found any; cut it down, why should it take up valuable space?' The gardener answered, 'Leave it alone for a year; I will dig around its roots and use fertilizer. If it bears figs next year, fine! If not, then we will cut it down.'"

In the same way I give people an opportunity to get saved; the Holy Spirit "digs" away at their hardened sin and He adds the nourishment of the Word of God and Christian witness, but each person must eventually trust Me for salvation or suffer the consequences. Pray for the salvation of your hardened friends.

I Heal a Cripple on the Sabbath

As I was teaching in the synagogue on the Sabbath, there was a severely crippled woman present who had been bent over double for years. When I saw her, I called out, "Woman you are healed!"

Then I laid My hands on her and she immediately stood up straight and began glorifying God.

The leader of the synagogue got mad because it was the Sabbath, and said to the crowd, "There are six days for work, and men ought to work during the week. People ought to come get healing during the week, but not on the Sabbath day."

I answered, "You are a hypocrite! Everyone on the Sabbath looses his ox from the stall and leads the animal to water. Ought not this Jewish woman who has been bound for years be loosed from her bondage on the Sabbath?"

The leader and his fellow Jewish officials were put to shame, and the crowd shouted for joy.

I will help you keep your eyes on My ministry to people, and help you overlook religious traditions that don't matter.

Parable of the Mustard Seed

So I continued speaking, "What does the kingdom of God look like? How can I compare it? It is like a mustard seed which a man planted in his garden, and it grew until it became a tree, and wild birds roosted in its branches."

Parable of the Leaven

Again I said, "To what can the kingdom of God be compared? It is like yeast that a cook puts in a bushel of flour until it had risen."

As I was traveling and teaching through the towns and villages, someone asked, "Will only a few be saved?"

I answered, "You must strive to enter through the narrow door; many will try to enter, but will not make it. Once the owner of the house arises and shuts the door, you will find you're standing on the outside and knocking continually and saying, 'Lord, open up for us;' but he will answer, 'I do not know you.' Then you will say, 'We ate and drank with you, as You taught us.' But he will say, 'I do not know you.

Depart from Me, all you evildoers!' You will weep and grind your teeth, when you see Abraham, Isaac, Jacob, and all the prophets in the kingdom of God, but you're locked outside. People will come from the east and west, from the north and south, to take their seats at the banquet in the kingdom of God. Those who are last will be first, and those who are first will be last."

Just then, some Pharisees came warning Me, "Run away quickly, for Herod wants to kill You!"

But I said, "Go tell that fox I am here, casting out demons and healing the sick, today and tomorrow, and on the third day I will finish this ministry. I will continue on my way to Jerusalem, for it is not possible that a prophet will be killed outside that city. O Jerusalem! Jerusalem! You who continue to martyr the prophets, and stone those who are sent to her, how often I have desired to gather your children around Me, as a hen gathers her chicks under her wings. But you said, 'No!'"

I will give you a love for Jerusalem, as I love that city. Pray for the peace of Jerusalem.

"Now you are abandoned to your fate! I say to you, you will never see Me again until you say, 'Blessed is the One who comes in the Lord's name.'"

FOURTEEN

I HEAL A MAN ON THE SABBATH

Later I went to the house of a religious leader for a meal; there was a man there with greatly swollen arms and legs. The leaders watched Me closely to see what I would do; I said to a lawyer, "Is it lawful to heal on the Sabbath?" But the lawyer and the leaders refused to answer Me. So I took the man by the hand and healed him, then sent him away; then I asked, "If your ox falls into a well on the Sabbath, will you not get him out immediately?" The religious leaders had no answer for Me.

I noticed that some guests were trying to get the best seats at a banquet. So I told them this parable. "When you are invited to a wedding banquet, don't sit in the best seats, lest someone who is more important be given those seats and you are moved lower; you will be embarrassed because you must take a lower seat. But when you go to the banquet, take the lower seat; then your host will see you and move you to a higher seat. As a result, you will be honored in front of the guests. Those who try to honor themselves will be humbled, and those who humble themselves will be honored."

Take the humble seat in life, because you want to be in the center of My will.

I told a second parable of a man planning a banquet. "Don't invite your friends, relatives, or rich neighbors, thinking they will invite you to their banquet. But invite the poor, the sick, the lame, and blind and God will bless you because these people can't return the favor, and God will remember you when He passes out rewards."

A Jewish leader thought I had a good point, so he said, "I would consider it an honor to eat in the kingdom of God."

But I answered him with a parable. "A man prepared a great banquet and sent out many invitations. When the banquet was ready, he sent a servant to get the guests, but everyone began making excuses. One man said he bought a field and had to go inspect it. Another man said he just bought a pair of oxen, and had to go try them out. Still a third man said he just got married, so he explained, 'I'm sure you'll understand.' The host was extremely angry and said to his servant, 'Go quickly into the streets and back roads and invite the poor, the sick, the blind and the lame.' Even then there was more room, so the host said, 'Go into the rural roads and look in the woods and urge as many as you can find to come to the banquet.' I want my house full. None of those I first invited came, so they won't even taste the meal I prepared for them."

Count the Cost

Follow Me no matter how hard life gets. Don't turn back when the way gets difficult.

A great crowd was traveling with Me, so I challenged them to follow Me even though it is difficult and tiring. "Those who follow Me must love Me more than they love their father, mother, sister, or brothers, even their own life. You cannot be My disciples unless you pick up your own cross and follow Me."

You will pick up your cross for today and you will follow Me. You will deny yourself.

"Don't begin following Me until you have counted the cost; no one begins building a house but first determines the cost of materials and labor and if he has enough to complete the project. Otherwise, when you lay the foundation, you find out you don't have enough money to complete the project. Then you are embarrassed because you can't complete the house.

"Any general planning a battle will first determine if his 10,000 soldiers can win a battle against 20,000 soldiers. If a general doesn't plan well, he will have to send a delegation to arrange conditions of peace or surrender. So following Me is a struggle with the world, the flesh, and the devil; so you must renounce all that you have to be My disciple.

"Salt is good; but when it loses its taste, how can it season? When it is not good for anything else, it will be thrown away. Let him who has ears, listen and do it."

FIFTEEN

THE PARABLE OF THE LOST SHEEP

The tax-collectors and sinners gathered around Me to hear what I had to say. But the religious leaders were complaining about Me because I received sinners and ate with them. I answered them with a parable, "If you had 100 sheep, and one of them were lost, wouldn't you leave the 99 and go search for the one lost sheep till you found it?"

Count people as you count sheep. Count them because people count.

"When you found it, wouldn't you carry it home in your arms, and tell everyone to celebrate with you because you found the one lost sheep? Even so, there will be more rejoicing in heaven over one sinner who repents, than over 99 self-righteous people who think they don't need to repent."

Rejoice with Me over everyone who comes to salvation.

Parable of the Lost Coin

I told a second parable of a woman who had 10 pieces of silver that was part of her marriage vow. "If she loses one piece of silver, doesn't she search for it with a lamp and sweep the house till she finds it? Then she calls her friends to rejoice with her because she found it. There is joy in the presence of the angels over one sinner who repents."

Parable of the Lost Prodigal Son

I told a third parable of a man who had two sons and the younger son demanded his portion of the inheritance, so the father divided the inheritance between the two sons. The younger son took his money and went to a distant country. There he wasted his money on sinful and luxuriant living, spending everything he had. When a famine came, the boy was hungry, so he took a job feeding pigs. No one gave him anything to eat and he decided to eat the pig's husks because he was starving. The young man came to his senses when he realized his father's servants had more to eat than he had. He decided, "I will go to my father and tell him, 'I have sinned against heaven and against you. I am no longer worthy of being called your son. Will you hire me as a servant?'" The young man returned home to his father. While he was a great distance away, his father saw him coming; he loved him, ran to hug him, and kissed him.

The son said, "Father, I have sinned against heaven and you, I am no longer worthy to be called your son!" But the father told the servants, "Bring the family robe and put it on him, put the signet ring on his finger, and shoes on his feet; kill the fatted calf, and let's have a feast. This my son was dead, but now he is alive; he was lost, but now is found," and they began a family banquet celebration. The older son was working in the field. When he approached the house, he heard music, laughter, and rejoicing; so he called one of the servants to ask, "What's happening?" The servant answered, "Your brother has come home and your father has killed the fatted calf because he returned safe and sound." The older son was angry and would not go into the banquet, so his father came out to invite him in. The older son said angrily, "I have served you many years, I have never disobeyed you, yet you never killed a fatted calf for me or had a celebration for me. Yet, my younger brother squandered his inheritance in sinful living and you throw him a big celebration." The father said, "You are always with me, and everything I have is yours. It is right to celebrate because he is your brother, for he was dead, but now is alive; he was lost, but now he is found."

Never leave Me as did the younger son, and never be bitter over My forgiveness of anyone. Rejoice with Me over the salvation of all.

Sixteen

PARABLES FOR MY DISCIPLES AND FOR THE PHARISEES

I told the disciples a story of a rich man and his deceptive manager who was stealing from him. The rich man told his deceptive manager that he learned what he was doing, so he fired him. So the manager had to get the books in order. The manager thought about where he would work next; he said, "I am not strong enough to dig, and I'm too ashamed to beg." The manager then planned to adjust the books of those who owed money to the rich man so they would take care of him. The manager called the first, "How much do you owe?"

He answered, "One hundred barrels of oil."

The manager said, "Write down 50 barrels." The manager asked the second, "How much do you owe?"

He answered, "One thousand bushels of wheat."

The manager said, "Write down 800 bushels." The rich man commended the fired manager for such a shrewd act. The people of the world work harder at their dishonesty, than the people of the light work to be honest.

I said, "Shall I teach you to act that way—to buy friendship dishonestly? No! If you are not honest in small things, you won't be honest in larger matters. If you have not been faithful in handling the money of others, you will not be entrusted with your own. And if you are unfaithful in handling worldly wealth, who would trust you with the eternal wealth of heaven?"

I will give you a desire to be absolutely honest about money, even to the smallest amount.

"No one can serve two masters. Either you will love the first, and hate the second, or you will love the second and hate the first. You cannot serve God and money."

The Pharisees, who loved to make money, laughed at Me when they heard My principles about finances. I answered, "You make people think you are honest, but God knows your greedy hearts. You pretend to be honest and humble before others, but you are despicable in God's sight. The law of Moses and the messages of the prophets have been your guides in the former ages. Now your guide is the good news preached by John the Baptizer that the kingdom of God is ushering in a new era. That doesn't mean the force of the law has changed, for it is easier for heaven and earth to pass away than for one dot of an 'i' of the law to change.

"That means the marriage law remains the same. Anyone who divorces and marries another commits adultery; anyone who marries a divorced woman commits adultery."

To the Pharisees—the Rich Man and Lazarus

I then told of a rich man who wore expensive clothes and lived in great luxury every day. "A poor man named Lazarus was lying in the street outside his gate covered with sores and the dogs came to lick them; he yearned to eat the leftovers from the rich man's table. The beggar died and the angels carried him to be with Abraham where those who died in faith were located. The rich man also died, and was buried but went to hell; as he was in torment he saw Lazarus far off in the company of Abraham.

"The rich man shouted, 'Father Abraham, have pity on me; send Lazarus to come dip his finger in water and cool my tongue, for I am tormented by these flames.'

"But Abraham said, 'Son, remember on earth you had everything, and Lazarus had nothing. Now he is comforted, and you are in pain. Besides, there is a great divide between us so that those who want to come here from your side can't cross over, and those on this side can't come to you.'

"The rich man begged Abraham, 'Send Lazarus to my home on earth to warn my five brothers so they don't come here.'

"Abraham answered, 'Your brothers have Moses and the prophets to warn them, let them listen to the Scriptures.'

"The rich man answered, 'That is not enough. If someone were to rise from the dead and tell them, they would turn from their sins.'

Then Abraham replied, 'If they will not listen to Moses and the prophets, they will not repent, even though one returns from the dead to tell them.'"

There is a place called hell where unbelievers will go after death. Help me stop your friends and family from going there.

SEVENTEEN

I TALK ABOUT MY COMING BACK TO EARTH

Then I said to the disciples, "It is impossible to keep from being tempted to sin, but how terrible it will be for the one who tempts others to sin. He would be better off if a huge stone were tied around his neck and he were thrown into the sea than to face punishment for tempting a little one to sin! Rebuke your brother when he sins and forgive him when he repents; if he sins seven times in a day, you must forgive him each time he repents."

The disciples asked, "Lord, help us have more faith."

I answered, "If you had the smallest amount of faith, the size of a mustard seed, which is the smallest of seeds, then you could say to a mulberry tree, 'Be uprooted and be cast into the sea,' and it would happen."

I told My disciples another parable, "Suppose you were a servant who plowed in the field or shepherded the sheep, would you just return home, sit down, and eat? No! First you prepare your master's meal and then serve it to him before you eat your own meal. The servant does not deserve thanks for doing what he is supposed to do, No! He is supposed to do those things; those who follow the Lord should have the same response. You do not consider yourself worthy of praise, you simply do what you are supposed to do."

Healing Ten Lepers

As I was heading back toward Jerusalem, I came to the boundary between Samaria and Galilee. Ten lepers stood off at a distance.

As I approached a village, they shouted out to Me, "Jesus, Master, have mercy on us."

I answered, "Go show yourself to the priest, just as it is commanded in the Scriptures." They were healed as they obeyed Me and began the journey.

One came back shouting, "Glory to God for healing me." He threw himself at My feet and thanked Me. The healed man was a despised Samaritan.

You don't want to be unthankful as were the nine lepers. Come and bow at My feet as did the one Samaritan, and "Thank Me for salvation."

I asked, "Did I not heal ten lepers? Where are the other nine?" The only one who has come back to praise God is this foreigner." Then I said to the man, "Stand up, and go home; your faith has healed you."

My Second Coming

One day a religious leader asked Me, "When will the kingdom of God begin?"

I answered, "The kingdom of God won't come with outward signs, so you can't say it began here or there; the kingdom of God stands among you." I was referring to Myself as the King.

You don't just live for the day of the rapture; rather, you live today for Me—the coming One.

Later I talked about this with My disciples, "There is coming a time when you will look for Me to be with you, but I won't come to you physically. Some will proclaim I have returned either here or there; don't believe the report, nor go out looking for Me. Everyone will see Me when I return. It will be as bright as lightning flashing across the heavens; but first I must suffer grievously and be rejected. When I return, the people will be just like those in Noah's days. They ate, got drunk, married, and ignored Noah's warning right up to the day when Noah entered the ark. Then the flood came to destroy them. My coming will be the same as it was in Lot's day. They were eating, getting drunk, buying, and selling, planting and building right up till Lot left Sodom. Then God rained fire and brimstone from heaven to destroy them all. The same will happen when I, the Son of Man, am revealed from heaven to those on earth who reject Me. When the day of judgment comes, those on the housetops must not go in the house for their belongings, neither should those in the field try to retrieve their things. Remember Lot's wife; anyone who holds on to the things of this life will lose his life, and those who give up their life, for Me, will save their life.

At that hour two will be sleeping in the bed; one will be taken and the other left behind. Two women will be grinding corn; one will be taken and the other one will be left behind. Two men will be in the field; one will be taken, the other left behind."

The disciples asked, "What will happen to them?"

I replied, "Wherever there are dead bodies, the buzzards gather."

EIGHTEEN

SETTING MY SIGHTS ON JERUSALEM

As I was preparing to leave for Jerusalem, I used a parable to teach that we should always pray and not give up.

The Story of the Persistent Widow

"There was a judge who was godless, and despised those who came before him for judgments. A widow kept coming to the judge demanding justice against her enemy. The judge kept refusing her. Finally he reasoned, 'I don't fear God or people, but this woman is pestering me to death with her continual begging for me to do something. I will give her justice because she continually asks for it.'"

I said, "Here is what the godless judge said, 'God will see that justice is done to those who continually pray to Me, just as the widow got justice, even when God seems to delay. God will answer persistent prayer and avenge them speedily. And when I, the Son of Man, return, will I find people of faith on earth who continually pray?'"

The Pharisee and the Tax Collector

Then I gave the following parable to those who considered themselves righteous, but who hated others. "Two men went into the temple to pray, one a self-righteous Pharisee, and the other one was an obvious sinner. The Pharisee boasted in his prayer that he was not a cheater, or an adulterous law-breaker; but he fasted twice a week and gave a tenth to God of all he possessed. The obvious sinner did not lift his eyes to heaven, but beat on his chest to express his sorrow for his sin; then he prayed, 'God be merciful to me a sinner.'"

I said, "This obvious sinner—not the Pharisee—was forgiven; those who exalt themselves will be humbled and those who humble themselves will be exalted."

Then people brought their babies to Me to be touched by Me. But when the disciples saw it, they discouraged them. But I called to the children and said, "Let the little children come to me, and do not stop them, for the kingdom of God belongs to children. I say to you, whoever does not accept the kingdom of God as a little child will never enter it."

The Rich Young Ruler

A rich young ruler asked, "Good Master, what must I do to get eternal life?"

I answered, "Why are you calling Me good, only God is good, but if you wish eternal life, keep the commandments."

The young man answered, "Which should I keep?"

I said, "Do not kill, and do not commit adultery, do not steal; do not bear false witness, honor your father and mother, and love your neighbor as yourself."

The young man said, "I have kept all these."

I said, "If you would be perfect, go sell all you have and give it to the poor; you will have treasure in heaven, and then follow Me."

The young man was sad when he heard this, for he had great wealth.

Then I told My disciples, "I say to you it is hard for a rich man to enter heaven; it is easier for a camel to go through a needle's eye than a rich man to enter heaven."

The amazed disciples said, "Who then can be saved?"

I answered, "No one from a human perspective, but all things are possible with God."

Get a vision of a great, powerful, God who can do great, powerful, things for you.

Then Peter added, "We have left all to follow You; what will be our reward?"

I answered, "In the next world when I sit on My throne, you, My disciples, will sit on twelve thrones, ruling the twelve tribes of Israel. Everyone who has left housing, brothers, sisters, father, mother, children, or land for My sake, will receive 100 times more when he receives eternal life."

The Selfish Ambition of James and John

As I was heading toward Jerusalem, I said to My disciples privately, "Behold, we are going up to Jerusalem. The petitions by the prophets concerning Me, the Son of Man, will be fulfilled there. I will be delivered to the Gentiles, mocked, insulted, and spat on. They will whip Me and kill Me, but I will rise again on the third day."

But they could not understand because it was a riddle to them, and they could not grasp what I meant.

The Healing of Blind Bartimaeus

As I came near Jericho, a blind man sat by the road begging. When he heard the crowd passing by, he asked what was happening. They told him, "Jesus of Nazareth was passing by."

He yelled loudly, "Jesus, Son of David, have mercy on me."

Then they tried to keep him quiet, but he yelled even louder, "Son of David, have mercy on me."

So I stopped and told them to bring the blind man to Me. When he got near, I asked, "What do you want Me to do for you?"

The blind man said, "Lord, I want to see."

Then I said, "Receive your sight; your faith has made you well."

Immediately he could see and he followed Me, praising God. When the people saw the miracle, they also praised God.

I will give you spiritual sight so you can see kingdom things. I will help you to praise Me in all you do.

NINETEEN

ZACCHAEUS

As I was walking through Jericho, Zacchaeus, an extremely rich and influential tax-collector, tried to get a look at Me, but he couldn't see over the crowds on the road side. Zacchaeus ran ahead and climbed up into a sycamore tree to see Me when I passed that way. I looked at him and said, "Zacchaeus, come down, I'm going to eat at your home."

Zacchaeus hurriedly came down and prepared a banquet for Me, but the crowd disapproved because Zacchaeus was a backslidden Jewish tax-collector.

Zacchaeus told Me, "I will give half my wealth to the poor, and those I've cheated; I will restore four times what I took from them."

I said, "Today salvation has come to this house because he is a son of Abraham. I, the Son of Man, have come to seek and save those who are lost, such as Zacchaeus."

Some thought the kingdom would come immediately, so I told a parable to correct that wrong impression. "A noble man was called to a distant place to be crowned king of that province. Before he left, he called his ten workers and gave them each $2,000 to invest while he was gone. But some of the workers rebelled and sent the nobleman word that he was no longer their lord. When the nobleman returned, he called the workers to whom he had given money to find out their profit. The first man reported his $2,000 had made a profit of $20,000, ten times the original amount. 'Wonderful,' responded the nobleman, 'you have been faithful; you will be ruler of 10 cities.' The second worker reported he had turned his $2,000 into $10,000, five times the original amount; the nobleman made him ruler of five cities. The third man had only the original $2,000, so he explained, 'Because you are an exacting man, reaping where you don't sow, I was afraid. I hid it safely in linen cloth.' The nobleman called him a 'wicked worker,' saying, 'You are condemned by your own words. You knew I reaped where I didn't sow, therefore why didn't you deposit my money in a bank so I could have drawn interest from it?' The nobleman said to those standing near, 'Take the $2,000 from him and give it to the man with $20,000.'

They answered the nobleman, 'He already has $20,000.'

I answered, "Those who do more with more will get even more, and those who do little with little, it shall be taken from him. But bring my enemies here who did not want me as their king and slay them in my presence!"

I will help you serve faithfully with the spiritual gifts I've given you. Don't hide your "talent" in the ground.

The Triumphal Entry Into Jerusalem

The next day—Sunday—news that I was coming to Jerusalem swept through the crowds of Passover pilgrims. As I came to Bethpage, I sent two disciples into the village telling them they would find a donkey with her young colt tied there. "If anyone asks why you are taking the donkey, tell them the Master needs it to ride into Jerusalem." This act fulfilled Scripture, "Tell the people of Zion, your King is coming to you, humbly riding on a donkey, even on a young colt."

The disciples did as instructed and found the donkey as I said. As they were loosing the animal, the owners asked why they were untying the colt. They answered, "The Lord needs it."

So they put their coats on the donkey and I rode on a colt that had never been ridden by anyone. Great crowds spread their coats on the road, others waved their palm branches as they went to meet Me.

The crowds who marched in front of Me shouted,

"HOSANNA to the Son of David,
blessing on Him who comes in the Lord's name,
HOSANNA in the highest heaven."

The religious ruler said to Me, "Rebuke Your followers for they are blaspheming God and the Scriptures."

I answered them, "If they stopped praising God, the rocks would immediately cry out praise to God."

I approached Jerusalem, and as soon as I saw the city, I wept tears over it, and said, "If you had only known how to have peace! But now peace is hidden from you. For a time is coming when your enemies will build siege towers against you and surround you on all sides. They will kill you and your children. They will not leave one stone upon another, because you did not know your God had visited you."

Cleansing the Temple

When I got to the temple, I began cleansing it; I forced the merchants and their customers to leave. Then I upset the tables of those selling pigeons and stopped workers from bringing in their merchandise. I said, "Do not the Scriptures teach, 'My house shall be called a house of prayer for all people, but it's become a den of thieves?'"

I was teaching daily in the temple; the leaders heard what I said and wanted to destroy Me. But they were afraid to do anything against Me because the people were listening intently to My teaching.

TWENTY

CONTROVERSY IN THE TEMPLE

While I was teaching the people in the temple and preaching the good news, the high priests and the scribes, with the elders, debated Me openly before the people, and said to Me, "Tell us where You get authority to do as You do? Who gave You Your authority?"

Then I answered, "I will ask you a question. Tell Me, did John get his baptism from heaven or from men?"

They discussed with one another, and said, "If we say, 'From heaven,' He will say, 'Why did you not believe John?' But if we say, 'From men,' all the people will stone us, for they are convinced that John was a prophet from God."

So they answered, "We do not know where it was from."

Then I said, "Neither will I tell you where I got My authority for doing what I do."

Parable of the Vineyard Owner

Then I told the people the following parable: "A man planted a vineyard and rented it to tenant farmers, and went on a long journey. At harvest time he sent a servant to the tenants to collect his part of the grape crop, but the tenants beat him and sent him away empty-handed. Again the owner sent another servant and they beat him and insulted him, and sent him back empty-handed. Again they sent a third servant, and they wounded him and kicked him out of the vineyard. Then the owner said, 'I will send my dearly loved son. They will respect him.' But when the tenants saw the son, they said, 'This is the heir; let us kill him so that what he inherits will be ours.' So they threw him out of the vineyard and murdered him. What will the owner of the vineyard do to those tenant farmers? He will come and kill those tenants and lease the vineyard to others." When they heard this, they said, "No!" But I glanced at them and said, "What does this Scripture mean, 'That stone which the builders rejected has now become the cornerstone'? Everyone who falls on that stone will be saved, and the one on whom the stone falls will be crushed to death."

I am the Cornerstone; you bow on this "stone" to worship the Father, the Son, and the Holy Spirit.

The Pharisees' and Herodians' Question

Then the scribes and the high priests wanted to arrest Me at that time, but they were afraid of the people. They knew I meant the parable for them. So they watched closely, and sent spies to catch Me in My conversation, so they could turn Me over to the governor. So they asked Me, "Teacher, we know that You speak and teach what is right, and show no preference to anyone, but You teach the way of God no matter who is listening. Is it right for us to pay taxes to Caesar, or not?"

But I detected their trick and said to them, "Show me a coin. Whose picture and title is inscribed there?"

They answered, "Caesar's"

I said to them, "Then give to Caesar what belongs to Caesar, and give to God what belongs to God!"

They could not twist what I said, and they were astonished at My answer. They said no more.

You will do in this life, what needs to be done; and you will do for Me what needs to be done.

The Sadducees' Question

Next, some of the Sadducees, who claimed there is no resurrection, asked Me, "Teacher, Moses wrote that if a man's brother dies and leaves a wife but no child, the man should take the widow and raise up a family for his brother. Now there were seven brothers. The first brother married a wife and died childless. Then the second, third, up to the seventh who died but left no child. Then the woman died. In the resurrection, whose wife will she be?"

I answered, "The people of this world marry and are married, but those who are worthy of the resurrection from the dead, neither marry nor are married. For they are like the angels of God; they neither marry nor are they given in marriage. Moses at the burning bush demonstrated this when he called the Lord 'the God of Abraham, the God of Isaac, and the God of Jacob.' The Lord is not the God of dead people but of living people, for all live in Me."

Then some of the scribes answered Me, "Teacher, You have given an insightful answer." They were afraid to ask Me any more questions.

Now I Ask a Question

Then I said to them, "How can anyone say that the Christ is David's Son? In the book of Psalms, David said, 'The Lord has said to my Lord, Sit at My right hand, until I make Your enemies the footstool of Your feet.'" Since David called Messiah Lord, then how can the Messiah be David's son?"

I Denounce the Scribes and Pharisees

Then I spoke openly so everyone could hear, but directed My words to My disciples, "Beware of the scribes who walk about in long robes and love to be greeted with praise in public places; they love to be seated in the best seats in the synagogues and to be recognized with honors at a banquet—these men take widows' houses and cover up their greed with long prayers! They will receive a much greater sentence."

TWENTY-ONE

TEACHING ABOUT THE FUTURE

I looked to see rich people dropping money into the treasury. Then I saw a poor widow drop two small coins into the treasury. And I said, "Verily, this poor widow has dropped in more than all of the rich, for they gave out of their abundance, but she gave out of her poverty all that she had."

The Mount of Olives Discourse

Some were talking about the temple and how beautiful it was decorated with stones. I said, "You may admire it, but the time is coming when one stone will not be left on another. Everything will be torn down."

Then My disciples asked Me, "Teacher, when will these things happen and what is the sign that will predict it?"

So I said, "Be careful and do not be misled! Many will come claiming to be Messiah, and saying, 'I am He,' and 'The time is near.' Do not follow them. You will hear of wars and rumors of wars; don't be panic stricken. These things must happen first, then the end will come."

Then I said to them, "One nation will go to war against another, and one kingdom against another. There will be earthquakes, pestilences, famines and dreadful events, and threatening signs in the sky. But before these things take place, they will arrest you, persecute you, and turn you over to synagogues to be put in prison. You will be brought before presidents and governors for My name's sake. This will be your opportunity to testify for Me, so you must determine in your hearts how to make your defense. I will tell you what to say, then your opponents will not be able to resist you and refute you. You will be betrayed by parents, brothers, relatives, and friends. They will kill some of you and you will be continuously hated by everyone because you bear My name. And yet not a single hair on your head will perish in hell. If you stand firm, you will establish your souls."

Jerusalem Will be Destroyed

"When you see Jerusalem surrounded by armies, then understand that tribulation is near. Let those in Judea flee to the mountains, and those within the city flee from it. These are the days of tribulation when its predictions in the Scriptures will be fulfilled. Woe to pregnant women and those with nursing babies. There will be great tribulation in the land and persecution on this people. They will be killed by the edge of the sword, or carried off as captives among the nations. Jerusalem will be trampled under the feet of the pagan, until the times of the Gentiles come to completion."

The Second Coming

"And there will be signs in the sun, moon, and stars. On earth the nations will give up hope with no direction like the roaring of the sea and its waves. Men will faint with fear because of the things that will come on the world. Then they will see Me, the Son of Man, coming on a cloud with great power and glory. When these events begin to happen, look up and lift your heads, for your deliverance is near."

Parable of the Fig Tree

Then I told them a parable. "Look carefully at the fig tree; when you see new branches shooting from their buds, you know that summer is near. So when you see these signs taking place, know that the kingdom of God is near. Verily I say to you, this generation will not pass away before these things take place. Heaven and earth will pass away, but My words will never pass away."

I have told you of all the destruction in the future. Trust Me to hold you in My hand in the future.

"Be on your guard so that you are not loaded down with self-pleasures, drunkenness, and worldly concerns. That day can catch you unawares like a trap. It will come on all who are living anywhere on the earth. So watch and pray that you will have strength to escape all these things that will take place. Make sure you take your stand in the presence of Me, the Son of Man."

During the days I taught in the temple, but I spent the nights on the Mount of Olives. The people rose early in the morning to come listen to Me in the temple.

TWENTY-TWO

MY FINAL DAYS
ON EARTH

Events on Wednesday

The Festival of Bread without Yeast, also called the Passover, was drawing near. So the high priests and scribes sought how they could put Me to death, but they were afraid of how the people would respond. Satan entered into Judas Iscariot, one of My apostles. Judas went to discuss with the high priests and temple police how he could deliver Me to them. They were thrilled and agreed to pay him for it. Judas in turn accepted the deal and began to look for ways to deliver Me to them without getting the people involved.

Events on Thursday

Then the day of the Festival came, the day when the Passover lamb was sacrificed. So I sent Peter and John on a mission with these directions, "Go and prepare a place for us to eat the Passover meal."

They asked Me, "Where should we prepare it?"

I answered, "When you enter the city you will see a man carrying a pitcher of water; follow him to a house. Then say to the owner of the house, 'Our Teacher says to you, "Show us the room where He can eat the Passover supper with His disciples."' Then the owner will show you upstairs a large room. Make preparations there."

I know about small things like a man carrying a jar of water; so I know about the small things that will happen to you. Commit the small things of your life to Me.

So they went and it happened as I had said, and they prepared the Passover meal.

Celebrating the Passover

When it was time, I took My place at the table with the apostles about Me. I said, "I have a great passion to eat this Passover meal with you before I suffer. I will never again eat this meal with you until we are in the kingdom of God." Then I received a cup, gave thanks, and said, "Take this and taste because I will not again drink from the vine until we are in the kingdom of God."

Then I took bread, gave thanks, and broke it, and gave it to them saying, "This is My body which is broken for you. This is a memorial to Me." After supper I took a cup and said, "This cup represents the new covenant to be established by My blood, which is poured out for you."

My Betrayer Is Predicted

"The hand of the one who betrays Me is on the table! Because I, the Son of Man, am going away, as it has been predetermined. How terrible it will be for that man who is My betrayer." Then the apostles began to discuss among themselves which one was going to betray Me.

Then there arose a contention as to who should rank as greatest. But I said to them, "The kings of the Gentiles rule over people and those who exercise authority are given the title of 'Benefactor.' But don't do that. Rather, the greatest among you must be like the youngest and must lead by serving people. Who is the greater, the one sitting at the table or the servant who waits on him? Is it not those who sit at the table? I come to you as a servant who waits on you and you have continued to support Me in my trials. Therefore as My Father has given Me a kingdom, so I give you the privilege of eating and drinking at My table in My kingdom. You will sit on thrones to rule the twelve tribes of Israel."

I Predict Peter's Denial

"Simon, Simon, satan has asked for your soul to sift you like wheat, but I have prayed that your own faith should not fail. And Peter, after you have returned to Me, you must strengthen your brothers."

But Peter protested, "Lord, I am ready to go to prison or death for You!"

But I said, "I tell you, Peter, the rooster will not crow before you deny three times that you know Me!"

Then I said to them, "When I sent you out without money or suitcase, or shoes, did you need anything?"

They answered, "We didn't need anything."

Then I said to them, "But now the man who has money must take it with him and a suitcase too. And the man who does not have a sword must sell his coat and buy one. For I tell you, what has been written about Me must be accomplished: 'I was numbered with the transgressors.' That prediction has to be accomplished."

So they said, "Lord, we have two swords!"

And I answered them, "That is enough!"

Agonizing Prayer in Gethsemane

Then I left to go up the Mount of Olives, as it was My habit of praying there. My disciples followed Me. When I reached the place, I said, "Pray that you may not be tempted."

I withdrew about a stone's throw from them to kneel down and pray, "Father, if You are willing, take this cup from Me. Yet not My will but Yours be done!"

There comes a time when you must say with Me, "Not my will, but Yours be done. I knew the terrible suffering that lay ahead, but there was no other way to save humans, so I submitted to the inevitable. You too come to situations where you must submit your will to God's will. I know best and I have a perfect will for your life. You must abandon your will and submit to do My will. May My will always be done in your life.

An angel came to Me from heaven to strengthen Me. But I, being in agony, prayed earnestly so that My sweat became like drops of blood that dripped on the ground. I rose from prayer to go to the disciples but found them sleeping. I asked them, "Why are you sleeping? Rise and pray that you enter not into temptation."

I Am Betrayed, Arrested, and Forsaken

While I was still speaking, a crowd came with Judas, one of the twelve, as their guide. He approached Me to kiss Me, but I replied, "Judas, do you betray Me, the Son of Man, with a kiss?"

The apostles saw what was about to take place, and asked, "Lord, shall we defend You with our swords now?" Then one of the apostles slashed the high priest's servant and cut off his right ear.

But I intervened, "Permit Me to be arrested!" So I touched his ear and healed him. Then I said to the high priests, temple guards, and elders, who had come to arrest Me, "Have you come out with swords and clubs and treated Me as if I were a robber? When I was with you daily in the temple, you never tried to arrest Me! But in this darkness is your chance to do it."

My Second Trial—Before Caiaphas

After they arrested Me and led Me away, they brought Me to the house of the high priest. Peter followed at a distance. A fire was kindled in the middle of the courtyard. Peter was sitting among those gathered for warmth.

A servant girl saw Peter sitting by the fire and said, "This fellow was with Jesus."

But he denied it and said, "Woman, I do not know Him."

On another occasion a man recognized Peter and said, "You are one of them too."

But Peter said, "Man, I am not."

About an hour later another man confidently said, "He certainly was with Jesus, for he is a Galilean!"

But Peter said, "Man, you don't know what you are saying."

While he was speaking, a rooster crowed.

Then I turned and looked at Peter. Peter remembered what I had said to him, "Before a rooster crows, you will deny me three times." So Peter went out and wept bitterly.

Do not deny Me as Peter did. I will give you strength and courage to keep this pledge.

Then the soldiers who had Me in custody whipped Me and mocked Me. They blindfolded Me and then said to Me, "Prophesy, who struck You!" And they continued to abuse Me.

The Third Trial—Before the Sanhedrin

As soon as light came, the elders, high priests and scribes assembled to bring Me before the Sanhedrin. They demanded, "Tell us if You are the Messiah."

But I answered, "If I tell you, you will not believe Me, and if I ask you a question, you will not answer Me. But after this I, the Son of Man, will be seated at the right hand of God."

Then they yelled at Me, "Are You the Son of God?"

And I answered, "Yes, I am."

Then they concluded, "What further evidence do we need? We have heard blasphemy ourselves from His own mouth!"

TWENTY-THREE

MY CRUCIFIXION

The Fourth Trial—Before Pilate

Then all the Jewish leaders led Me to Pilate and brought the following charges against Me: "We have found this man destroying our nation and stopping people from paying taxes to Caesar and He claims to be a king Himself."

Then Pilate asked Me, "Are You the King of the Jews?"

And I answered him, "I am."

Then Pilate said to the Jewish leaders and the crowd, "I find nothing worthy of a trial for this man."

But they insisted, "He is starting a rebellion all over Judea. He began in Galilee and now He is teaching here."

Hearing this, Pilate asked if I were a Galilean. When he learned that I was under Herod's jurisdiction, he sent Me to Herod because Herod was in Jerusalem at that time.

The Fifth Trial—Before Herod

Now Herod was anxious to see Me for he had wanted to see Me because of what he had heard about Me. Herod was hoping to see some miracle done by Me.

I don't do miracles for the curious, or to entertain people. I do the miraculous for those who believe. I will give you faith to believe.

So Herod continued to question Me for a long time, but I did not answer him at all. Meanwhile the high priests and the scribes were waiting to accuse Me. Then Herod and his soldiers tried to embarrass Me and made fun of Me. He put a royal robe on Me and sent Me back to Pilate. That day, Herod and Pilate became friends for they had previously been enemies.

Then Pilate called to himself the high priests, the leaders of the council, and the crowd, and said, "You brought this man to me on a charge of religious rebellion against the temple. I have examined Him in your presence and find Him not guilty of your charges. Nor does Herod, for he sent Him back to me. Indeed, Jesus has done nothing to deserve the death penalty. I will beat Him and let Him go."

It was the custom for him to release one from prison at the festival. But the crowd began to shout, "Away with this fellow; give us Barabbas!" He was a man who had been put in prison for starting a riot and for murder.

Again Pilate appealed to them to let Me go.

But they continued shouting, "Crucify Him, crucify Him!" So Pilate spoke to them a third time, "Why, what is His crime? I find nothing that deserves the death penalty. I will beat Him and let Him go."

But the crowd and religious leaders continued to demand with loud voices that I be crucified. Then Pilate allowed their demands to be carried out. Pilate released Barabbas who had been put in prison for riot and murder, but turned Me over to be crucified.

I was crucified instead of Barabbas. In the same way, I died instead of you. That's how much love I have for you!

I Am Crucified

As they were leading Me away, they grabbed a man, named Simon from Cyrene, as he was entering the city from the rural area, and made him carry My cross on his shoulders. A vast crowd of people followed Me and women were mourning and weeping. I turned and said to the women, "Women of Jerusalem, stop weeping for Me, but weep for yourselves and for your children. A time is coming when it will be said, 'Happy are the childless women and women who have never given birth and nursed babies!' Then people will cry out to the mountains, 'Fall upon us, and cover us up!' If they do this evil when the wood is green, what will they do when it is dry?"

Two others, criminals, were also led out to be crucified with Me. When we came to the place called Golgotha, "The Skull," they crucified Me and the criminals, one on My right hand and the other on My left hand. They cast lots to divide My clothes among them. All the while people stood around looking on.

The members of the Sanhedrin scoffed at Me and said, "He saved others, now let's see if He can save Himself. Let's see if He really is God's Messiah, His Chosen One!"

The soldiers also made fun of Me offering Me vinegar, and saying, "Save Yourself if You are the King of the Jews!" A shingle was nailed above My head with these words, "THE KING OF THE JEWS."

One of the criminals on his cross kept abusing Me saying, "If You are the Christ, then save us and Yourself."

But the other criminal rebuked him, "You should fear God because you are suffering the same penalty as He. We suffer justly because we are getting what we deserve. But this man has done nothing wrong."

Then the criminal asked, "Jesus, remember me when You come in Your kingdom!"

I answered him, "This day you will be with Me in paradise."

Aren't you glad that all the thief had to do was believe in Me to be saved. That means you're saved because you believe in Me.

It was about noon when darkness covered the area and it stayed dark until three o'clock. The sun failed to shine. At that time the curtain before the Most Holy Place in the temple was torn in two. Then I cried with a loud shout, "Father, I commit My spirit to You." Then I breathed My last.

The captain of the soldiers saw what had happened and prayed to God, "Certainly He was innocent!" When the crowds who had come to view the crucifixion had seen what took place, they returned to the city. All My friends, and the women who also followed Me from Galilee, stood at a distance.

My Burial in Joseph's Tomb

A man named Joseph, a good and upright man, a member of the Sanhedrin who had not voted to condemn Me, was there. He came from the Jewish town, Arimathea, and he was waiting for the kingdom of God. Joseph went to Pilate to ask for My body. Then he took the body down from the cross, wrapped it in a linen sheet, and laid it in a tomb carved out of rock, where no one had yet been laid. It was the preparation day, and the Sabbath was just beginning. So the women, who had followed Me from Galilee, watched Joseph closely to see where the tomb was located and where My body was laid.

In the Grave

Then they went home to prepare spices and perfumes. They rested on the Sabbath according to the Old Testament commandment.

TWENTY-FOUR

MY ASCENSION BACK TO HEAVEN

The Visit of the Women to the Tomb

On the first day of the week before the sun came up, they went to the tomb with spices to prepare My body. They found the stone rolled back from the entrance to the tomb. When they went inside, they did not find My body. And as they were looking around, two men in glistening robes suddenly stood beside them. The women were afraid, and turned their faces to the ground. The two men said to them, "Why are you looking for Jesus among the dead? He is alive. He is not here but has risen. Remember, He told you that while He was still in Galilee. He said that He, the Son of Man, was going to be turned over to evil men to be crucified, but that He would rise again on the third day."

Then the women remembered My words and returned to Jerusalem from the tomb and told all those things to the eleven and then told the others. The women were Mary Magdalene, Joanna, and Mary, James' mother; but because their report seemed to be nonsense to them, they didn't believe the women.

Peter ran to the tomb and stooped down to see the linen clothes lying there, but nothing else. Then Peter went home, wondering what happened.

An Appearance on the Road to Emmaus

That afternoon, two of My followers were on their way home to their village called Emmaus, about seven miles from Jerusalem. They were talking together about all those things that had taken place that day. As they were discussing the events of the day, I joined them as they continued their journey. But their eyes were blinded to Me and I kept them from recognizing Me.

How many times have I come alongside you and you didn't recognize My presence? I will open your blind spiritual eyes to see My presence.

Then I said to them, "What is this news that you are talking about as you walk?"

The one named Cleopas answered, "Are You the only visitor to Jerusalem who did not know about the things that have happened these past few days?"

And I said to them, "What things?"

They answered, "The talk of the town is about Jesus of Nazareth. All the people believe He is a prophet, mighty in deed and word. The high priests and religious leaders turned Him over to be sentenced to death to be crucified. But we kept hoping Jesus is the Messiah who was coming to set Israel free. Today is the third day since His death occurred. But this morning some women who follow Him have astounded us! They went to the tomb early and could not find His body. They came and told us that they had seen a vision of angels who told them He was alive. Then some followers went to the tomb and found it exactly as the women described, but they didn't see Him."

Then I said to them, "O slow of mind and heart to believe all that the prophets have said! Did they not teach that the Messiah had to suffer and then enter His glory?" Then I began with Moses and taught My way through the prophets and explained to them all the passages in the Scriptures about Myself.

As we approached their village, I made as though I were going farther, but they urged Me, "Come and stay with us, for it is getting toward evening and the day is almost over."

So I entered in to stay with them. Then I took My place at the table. I received the loaf, and blessed it and broke it, and handed it to them. Then their spiritual eyes were opened and they recognized Me. Then I vanished from them.

They said to each other, "Did not our hearts burn as He talked to us on the road, as He explained the Scriptures to us?"

Immediately they got up and returned to Jerusalem and found the eleven and other followers all together.

They told the couple that I had risen from the dead and had been seen by Simon. Then the two told what had occurred on the road, and how they recognized Me when I broke the loaf.

The Upper Room on Sunday Evening

While they were discussing these things, I stood among them and said, "Peace to you!"

They were startled and fearful; some even thought they saw a ghost. But I said, "Why are you so upset, and why do you have doubts in your hearts? Examine My hands and My feet, for it is I, Myself. Touch Me to see for yourselves, for a ghost does not have flesh and bones, as you see I have."

After this, I showed them My hands and My feet. So while they were still doubting and wondering, I asked, "Have you anything to eat?" They gave Me a piece of broiled fish. They saw Me take it and eat it.

I Ascend Back to Heaven

Then I said to them, "Let Me tell you again what I said while I was with you; that everything that is written about Me in the law of Moses, in the prophets, and in the Psalms, had to be fulfilled." Then I opened their spiritual eyes so they might understand the Scriptures.

Then I said to them, "The Scriptures say the Christ would suffer for sins, rise from the dead on the third day, and that repentance in My name as the condition for the forgiveness of sins should be preached to all nations. You are to begin at Jerusalem as witnesses to these things.

"I will send on You the promise of My Father. But you must stay right here in the city and pray until you are anointed with power from on high." Then I led them out of the city as far as Bethany, and I lifted up My hands and blessed them. While I was blessing them, I was lifted up from them, and was taken up to heaven. And with joy, they went back to Jerusalem; and continued in the temple praying and praising God.

PART FOUR

I AM GOD THE SON
OF GOD

Based on the Gospel
of John

ONE

I AM GOD THE SON

I Am God the Son, who is from the beginning. I tell all about God, the heavenly Father. I was face to face with God throughout eternity because I am God.

And without Me nothing was created. I do all the things that God, My heavenly Father, will do. I have all life in Myself and give life to all My creation. I am the life of God who is the Light to all who are lost in a dark, forbidding world. I shine in the hostile darkness but the darkness doesn't even know I exist.

Commit yourself to My message, which is written in the Word of God. It is eternal and perfect. You will learn My message, believe My message, and share it with others.

John is My Witness

John the Baptizer was a prophet sent by Me, who came to tell all about the shining Light, that through Me, the Light, all might be saved. John the Baptizer was not the saving light, but was the human sent to point everyone to Me, the Light of the world.

I am the true saving Light who offers spiritual light to everyone in the world. I came to the world that I created, but those living in the world did not recognize Me as their Creator Savior. I came to My own people—the Jews—and they refused to recognize Me.

But as many as recognize Me, and receive Me, I will make them children of God, simply because they believe in the authority of My name. They will be born again by My power, which is not a birth of blood, or the choice of people, or of flesh.

I had all the celestial glory of heaven, but I clothed My heavenly glory with human flesh. God living in flesh was the greatest glory of all. I am the uniquely begotten Son and have all the grace and truth of God. John the Baptizer said of Me, "This is the Messiah whom I introduced to the world. Jesus comes after me, but is preeminently before me."

I AM the Eternal Word, who created the universe, who had eternal fellowship with God the Father, and who became flesh when I was born of the Virgin Mary. You should worship and praise Me for all I am and do. I created you and everything in this universe. Worship Me for My unlimited power and greatness.

My grace was offered and your need of grace was fulfilled. The law of Moses condemned you to death, but grace and truth, by Me, gave you life. You could never have seen the eternal Father, but I came from His heart to show you what your Father is like.

Commit your life to Me. I became flesh and lived among the mortals I created. I am the truth and spoke the truth to you. You can experience the riches of eternal life because of Me.

Religious Leaders Question John the Baptizer

The religious establishment sent delegates to ask John the Baptizer this question, "Who are you?" John told them he was not the Messiah. Then they asked, "Are you Elijah or the prophet who will come at the end of the age?"

John said, "No."

They said, "Give us an answer to report to our authorities."

John quoted Isaiah, answering, "I am a voice crying in the wilderness; prepare the way for the Messiah." They were Pharisees who questioned him. The religious delegates asked why he was baptizing with water. He answered, "I baptize with water, but there is One standing among us who will baptize with the Spirit of God. He who is coming after me is preferred before me, because He lived before me. These things happened on the banks of the Jordan River, but I came baptizing so He might be revealed to Israel."

My Baptism

The next day John saw Me coming to him and told the crowd, "See that Man. He is the Lamb of God who takes away the sin of the world." He said this to let everyone know I was the One coming after him. John said, "I didn't know who He was." John the Baptizer added, "I didn't know Jesus was to be the Messiah until I saw the Spirit come upon Him like a dove. But the Lord who sent me to baptize with water told me, 'The One on whom the Spirit comes, and stops there, this is the One who is the Messiah. He will baptize with the Holy Spirit.'" Then John said, "I then noted and believed He is the Son of God."

I Meet Six Disciples

The next day John the Baptizer stood with two of his disciples; as they saw Me walking, he said, "Behold the Lamb of God."

As Andrew and John were following Me, I turned to ask, "What do you want?" That evening Andrew and John talked at length to Me.

The next day Andrew told his brother Simon, "We have found the Messiah," and Andrew brought his brother to Me. I changed Simon's name to Peter, which means he was firm and solid as a stone.

Be zealous to tell your family and friends about Me, and bring them to know Me as their Lord and Savior. You can find answers to all of your questions in Me. Focus your sight on Me, and see the greatness of My character.

The next day when I saw Philip, I said, "Follow Me." Philip was from the same hometown as Andrew and Peter.

Philip told his friend Nathaniel, "We have found the Messiah."

Nathaniel was skeptical, "Can any good thing come out of Nazareth?"

Philip just said, "Come and see."

When I saw Nathaniel I said, "You are a sincere Israelite, you are an honest seeker."

Nathaniel asked, "How do you know me?"

I revealed My divine omnipresence by saying, "I saw You talking under the fig tree to Philip when he told you about Me."

Nathaniel responded, "Jesus, You are the Son of God; You are the

King of Israel."

Nathaniel believed in Me because of what Philip told him; but I said, "You'll see much greater things than this. You'll see heaven opened and the angels of God going up and down upon Me, the Son of Man."

TWO

MY FIRST MIRACLE

On the seventh day after My baptism, I was in Cana where a marriage ceremony was held; My mother was also there. My six disciples and I were invited to the meal. When the wine ran out, My mother said to Me, "There is no more wine."

I answered, "Why do you turn to Me for help? It is not the time to reveal who I am."

My mother told the servants, "Do whatever He tells you."

There were six stone water pots available to them, each one held 20 to 30 gallons. I said to the servants, "Fill them to the brim with water." Then I said, "Take them to the master of ceremonies." The servants carried the water to the one in charge. When they had arrived, the water had turned to wine; then the master of ceremonies toasted the wine. The servants who carried the water pots knew what happened. "Why have you kept back the best wine until now? People usually serve their best wine first. When the guests have drunk a lot, then a poorer quality is served."

This was the first miracle I did that manifested My glory, and My disciples believed in Me.

After this I changed My base of operation from Nazareth to Capernaum, which is located by the Sea of Galilee.

I Cleanse the Temple

When the Passover came in the spring of A.D. 26, I went up to Jerusalem with My disciples. I found people in the temple selling animals and birds for sacrifice—cattle, sheep, and pigeons. Money changers had set up tables to exchange foreign coins into Jewish money, because the foreign coins had images of false gods. I made a whip out of some rope, and drove the animals out of the temple, and overturned the tables of the money changers. I commanded, "Stop turning my Father's house into a market to sell your sacrifices."

The disciples were amazed at My anger and said, "His devotion to the Lord's house burns in Him like a fire."

The Jewish leaders challenged Me, "What miracle can You show us that gives You authority to do this?"

I replied, "Destroy this temple, and I will raise it up in three days."

They said, "It has taken 46 years to build this temple. Do You think You can rebuild it in three days?" But I was speaking about the temple of My body. After the resurrection, My disciples remembered I spoke about this event earlier; it was not about rebuilding the temple. While I was in Jerusalem for the Passover, many believed in Me, because they saw the miracles I did. But I did not entrust Myself to them, because I knew what was in their hearts.

There comes a time when you must no longer tolerate heresy and evil, but you must confront evil by prayer and action. That's what I did when I cleansed the temple at the beginning of My ministry and the end of My ministry.

THREE

A NIGHT INTERVIEW WITH NICODEMUS

Nicodemus was a Jewish leader who observed the law. He came to Me at night to compliment Me, saying, "Jesus, You are a Teacher who comes from God, because You perform miracles that couldn't be done without God's help."

I told him, "I say to you, you must be born again to see the kingdom of God."

Nicodemus replied, "How can a man be born when he is old? Can he go back into his mother's womb to be born again?"

I answered, "I say to you, unless you are born again of water and the Spirit, you will not enter the kingdom of God. What is born of flesh is flesh, and what is born of Spirit is Spirit. Do not be surprised when I say you must be born again. The wind blows anywhere it pleases; you can hear its sound, but you can't tell where it comes from or goes. That describes those who are born of the Spirit, and how the Spirit bestows life on them."

Nicodemus asked, "How can this happen?"

I answered, "You are a respected teacher, yet you do not understand these things." I continued, "I say to you, I am telling you what I know, but you will not believe Me. If you do not believe what I say about this world, how can you believe heavenly things? Since I have come to earth from heaven, I can explain heavenly things to you. As Moses lifted up the serpent in the wilderness, so people could repent by looking to the serpent. In the same way I, the Son of Man, will be lifted up so that everyone who looks to Me in belief will be saved. The Father loved everyone in the world so much that He gave Me, His only begotten Son, to die for each of them. Now everyone who believes in Me will not perish, but will have eternal life. For the Father did not send Me to condemn the people of the world, but that they might be saved through belief in Me. No one who believes in Me will be condemned, but those who refuse to believe in My name are condemned already. The verdict of death is handed down because light has shined on the people of the world, but people love darkness more than light, because of their love of evil things. Everyone who continually does evil things hates the light and rejects it, because it exposes their motives and actions. Those who believe the truth and come to the Light will be saved. Their deeds verify their faith that they are of God."

The death I talk about is eternal separation from God the Father in a place called Hell, where the fire never dies and is never put out. But God loved you so much that He sent Me to die, for your sins, on the cross. Now, if you place your complete trust in me, you will never perish, but you will have eternal fellowship with Me in Heaven. I want you to know that you can have this eternal life just as I said to Nicodemus, "You must be born again." Live by My truth, so everyone can see what I do for you.

My Baptism and John the Baptizer's Baptism

My disciples and I left Jerusalem for the countryside where many people were baptized by My disciples. John the Baptizer was baptizing nearby at Aenon, for he had not yet been thrown into prison. Many also came there for baptism. The Jewish leaders tried to tell the disciples of John the Baptizer that My baptism was better than their baptism, and there arose a dispute.

John's disciples came to tell John, "The man you baptized—the One you called Messiah—He is baptizing more than you are."

John the Baptizer answered, "God in heaven gives each man the work he is to do. I told you I am not the Messiah, I am sent to prepare the way for Messiah. The crowds—the Bride of Christ—will naturally go where Christ the Bridegroom is located. I am a friend of the Bridegroom, I rejoiced when I answered His voice calling to me.

He—Jesus—must increase, I—John the Baptizer—must decrease. He comes from heaven, and He is greater than all. We who are born on this earth only understand the things of earth. He testifies what He has seen and heard, and no one receives His testimony. Those who believe in Jesus have discovered the truth of God that has come from heaven. He speaks the words of God, because He has the Spirit of God on Him. The Father loves Jesus, the Son, and has given everything to Him. Those who believe in the Son already have eternal life, and those who have not believed in the Son do not have eternal life, but the punishment of God rests on them."

FOUR

THE STORY OF THE SAMARITAN WOMAN

I learned that the Pharisees were told that I was winning and baptizing more followers than John the Baptizer, although I didn't actually baptize, My disciples did it, so I left Judea to go home. When I left Jerusalem, I surprisingly went home through Samaria, because the Jews have no dealings with the Samaritans. When I came near Sychar, I sat on Jacob's well because I was worn out from the hot journey, and it was noon. A Samaritan woman came to draw water from the well. I was sitting there and said, "Give Me a drink." The disciples had gone into the town to get food.

She was surprised that a Jew would ask, because the Jews despised the Samaritans. She said, "Why would You, a Jew, ask water from me, a Samaritan?"

I said, "If you only knew God's gift and who it is that offers you water, you would have asked Me for a drink, and I would have given you living water."

The woman replied, "You don't have a bucket; how could You get water from this deep well?" She continued, "Are You greater than Jacob who drank from it with his family and cattle?"

When you are thirsty, I will come and fill your cup. You can drink of My presence. That water satisfies and refreshes your spirit.

I answered, "Whoever drinks this water will get thirsty again, but those who drink of the water that I give will never be thirsty again. The water I give will be an artesian well inside them that gushes up into eternal life."

The woman said, "Give me some of that water so I will never get thirsty again, and have to come to this well for water."

I abruptly said, "Go call your husband!"

She answered, "I have no husband."

I replied, "You have correctly answered, because you have had five husbands, and now you're not married to the one you're living with."

She exclaimed, "You must be a prophet to know this." Then she argued, "Our fathers worshiped here. The Jews say Jerusalem is the place to worship."

I interrupted to say, "The hour is coming when no one will worship on this mountain or in Jerusalem. You don't know whom you worship; but the Jews know whom they worship. In fact, the hour is already here when true worshipers will worship the Father in Spirit and truth. God is Spirit, and those who worship Him must worship in their hearts and truthfully."

The woman said, "I know that Messiah is coming; He will tell us everything when He comes."

I answered, "I am He."

Then My disciples came and saw that I talked with a woman. "Why are You talking with her?"

The woman left her water pot and hurried off to tell the men in the village, "Come see a man who told me everything I've ever done." She asked, "Could this man be the Messiah?" They left the town to go meet Me.

I will give you a passion to share your testimony with needy people, like the Samaritan woman. You will tell your non-Christian friends, "Come see a Man who knows everything about me."

Meanwhile the disciples told Me to eat, but I said, "I have food to eat that you don't know about." The disciples thought someone else had brought Me food. I said, "My food is doing the will of the Father and completing His work. People say, 'Harvest comes four months after planting,' But I say, 'Look around at the fields, they are already ripe for harvest.' Everything is ready for the reaper to go to work to bring in the 'grain' of eternal life; then the sower and reaper will rejoice together." Then I explained, "One sows, another reaps; I send you to reap where you didn't sow, and you get rewards for their effort."

Many Samaritans believed in Me because the woman said, "Come see a man who told me everything I've ever done." The Samaritans begged Me to stay with them and I stayed two days, and many got saved.

The Samaritan men told the woman, "Now we believe because of what we have heard for ourselves, not just because of what you said."

After two days I left and continued to Galilee. But that was My home area, so I said, "A prophet is not respected in his home country." But when I got to Galilee, the crowds welcomed Me.

Healing the Nobleman's Son

I returned to Cana where I had turned water to wine. There, an official from Herod's court came begging Me to heal his son. The official had sought to find Me in the area because his son was very sick. I said, "Why is it that none will believe in Me unless they see miracles?"

The official answered, "Come down to Capernaum and heal my son before he dies."

I answered, "Go home, your son will live." The official believed My words and turned to start his journey home. While he was on the road, his servants met him to say his son had recovered. The official asked what time had the fever broke; the servant told him, "4 p.m." The father realized that was the same hour when I said, "Your son will live." This was the second sign-miracle I did in Cana, and the official and his family believed in Me.

FIVE

PROOF THAT I AM GOD

I obeyed the Old Testament command to attend the Festival of Passover at Jerusalem at the end of My first full year of ministry. I went by the pool of Bethesda, a name that means "House of Mercy." There were five porches where a great number of sick invalids were waiting for an angel to come stir the waters in the pool. The sick believed that the first one into the water would automatically get healed. There was a man who had waited unsuccessfully for 38 years. I went only to him because he had been there a long time. I asked, "Would you like to be healed?"

The lame man answered, "I don't have anyone to put me in the waters after it is stirred up. When I am going to the water, someone jumps in before me."

I said, "Take up your bedroll and walk!" Immediately, the man was healed and he picked up his bedroll and walked.

The healed man walked through the crowd to the temple; the Jews told him it was wrong to carry any burden—even a bedroll—on the Sabbath. The man told them, "The One who healed me said, 'Take up your bedroll and walk.'"

The Jews asked, "Who healed you and told you to break the Sabbath law?" But the healed man did not know who healed him because I left him to walk through the crowds.

Later, I found the healed man in the temple and told him, "Go and don't do the sin any more that was responsible for this lame condition, because a worse thing will happen if you do." The healed man went and told the Jews that it was Me who healed him. The Jews confronted Me, because I told the healed man to carry his bedroll on the Sabbath.

I answered the Jewish leaders, "My Father, who is just like Me, has worked up until now, but now I work." The Jewish leaders sought to kill Me because I said I was just like the Father, and because I had broken their law, and I said the Father and Son are equal in nature.

I AM Equal in Nature, Power, and Authority

I answered the Jewish leaders, "I say to you, I do nothing by Myself. But when I see the things God the Father does, I do the same things. God the Father and God the Son are equal in power." Then I said, "The Father loves Me as His Son and shows Me everything He does. The Father will do greater miracles than healing the lame, so you'll marvel. As the Father raises the dead and gives them life, so I, the Son of God, will also raise the dead. The Father and Son are equal in authority.

"The Father does not judge the sins of everyone, all judgment is given to Me. He who does not honor Me, honors not the Father."

I said, "He who receives My Word, and believes on Me, has eternal life and will not be judged for his sins, but has passed from death unto eternal life.

"I tell you, an hour has been coming, but now it has arrived, when spiritually dead people will hear My words and receive eternal life. The Father has this life in Himself and I also have it, and give it to those who believe in Me. The Father has given Me the authority to execute judgment; therefore the time is coming when all in their graves will hear My voice and be raised. They who have obeyed the Father will be raised to the resurrection of life. They who have disobeyed the Father will be raised to the resurrection of the damned." I told them, "I can do nothing by Myself, but I do the will of the Father who sent Me."

Four Proofs That I Am God

John the Baptizer

I said, "No one can bear witness of himself, and have other people believe him. If I only tell how great I am, don't listen to Me. John the Baptizer told you about Me, and he told the truth. The Old Testament said at the mouth of two witnesses shall every testimony be established.

The testimony of John the Baptizer was a light that shined so people believed what he said about Me.

My Miracles

"But the testimony of My miracles was even greater; they proved that the Father sent Me into the world.

God The Father's Voice

"A third testimony is the voice of the Father that thundered at My baptism. No one has seen God, but you heard My voice, but you didn't believe it, because you do not have the Word of God dwelling in you. You do not believe the words the Father said."

The Scriptures

I told them, "Search the Scriptures, these words testify of Me that I am from the Father, but you will not come to Me to have eternal life. You think you have eternal life, but you don't. Because you refuse to believe in Me you do not have the love of God in you." I said, "I have come in the Father's name, and you will not receive Me, yet you receive others coming in their own name. You seek glory from other Jewish leaders, and do not seek the glory that comes from the heavenly Father. I will not accuse you in the final judgment. Moses whom you revere, he will accuse you in the judgment. If you believe Moses—and you don't—then you would believe Me, because Moses predicted my coming."

I told you to search the Scriptures to know Me in salvation, and to know Me in order to grow in grace. I will open your spiritual eyes as you study the Bible. May you find My presence concealed in the written Word. May you know Me more intimately as you go deeper into My Word.

SIX

TWO MIRACLES
AND A LESSON

There was a great multitude following Me, so I went up into a mountain near Tiberias. The multitude followed Me because of My miracles, and because I healed the sick. I then went up into the mount to sit with My disciples. We were on our way to Jerusalem to celebrate the springtime festival of Passover. I surveyed the multitude, and then said to Philip, "Where can we buy food for them?" I knew that I would feed them with a miracle. I was testing Philip's faith in Me.

Be faithful when you are tested. Those who endure testing for a season know that joy comes in the morning.

Philip answered, "If we had the day's wages of 200 servants there would only be a little bit for each one."

Andrew heard the conversation and found a young boy with five loaves of bread and two small fish. Then Andrew said, "This isn't enough for all the crowd."

I said, "Make the men sit down in groups of 50 and 100 to make distribution easy." They sat on grass in the area. I looked to heaven to bless the food, then I gave it to the disciples, and they distributed it to the multitude. Everyone had as much as they could eat. Then I said to My disciples, "Gather the food that is left over." So they gathered up 12 full baskets.

After the people saw the miracle, they said, "This is the One whom the prophet Jeremiah predicted was coming into the world to feed us bread."

*I will feed you, when you are spiritually hungry, just as I fed the
5,000 by the sea.*

I Walk on the Water

The multitude rushed toward Me. They wanted to make Me King,
but I went into the hills to pray. When evening came, the disciples
went down to the lakeside and got into a boat heading toward the
other side toward Capernaum. It was dark and I was not with them. A
storm came up and the winds blew threateningly. They rowed three or
four miles but were not making headway. Then they saw Me walking
on the sea towards them. I said, "It is I, do not be afraid." They received
Me into their boat and immediately we were at land.

Sermon on the Bread of Life

The next day the crowd walked around the sea toward Capernaum,
and they saw only one boat the disciples used. However, there were
other boats that came from the place where I fed the multitude. People
had gotten into these boats to follow Me. So they asked Me, "Rabbi,
how did You get here?"

I answered and said, "You seek Me because you saw the miracles.
Yesterday you ate of the bread and fish." I told them, "Don't work for
food that perishes, but work for the bread of eternal life which I, the
Son of Man, offer you."

The crowd asked, "What must we do to perform the works of God
which You do?"

I answered, "The work of God is to believe in Me, the Son whom
the Father has sent."

The crowd answered, "Do a miracle for us so we can believe in You
and follow You. Our fathers ate the manna in the wilderness that Moses gave to them during the 40 years of wilderness wanderings."

Then I said to them, "I say to you, it was not Moses who gave you
bread from heaven. My Father gives true bread out of heaven. I am the
bread of God who comes from heaven to give life to the world."

The crowd said, "Please give us this bread."

I said, "I am the Bread of Life. He who comes to Me will never
hunger. He who believes in Me will never thirst, but you don't believe

in Me. All the Father gives Me shall come to Me, and I will not turn them away, because I come from heaven to do the will of the Father, and not My will. It is my Father's will that I should lose no one who believes in Me, and I should raise them up in the resurrection. And this is the will of the Father that everyone who believes in the Father will have eternal life and that I will raise them up in the last day."

The Jewish leaders complained because I said, "I am the bread who comes from heaven." They argued, "Is not this Jesus, the son of Joseph? We know His father and mother; how can He say, 'I come from heaven?'"

I answered, "Don't complain! No one comes to Me except the Father draws him, and I will raise him up in the last day. It is written in Isaiah, 'All will be taught by God, everyone who believes what I say will come to Me.' No one has seen the Father except Me, the One who comes to you from the Father. I have seen the Father. I say to you, the one who believes has eternal life. I am the Bread of Life. I am the Bread who comes from heaven that you may eat and not die. The Jewish forefathers ate manna in the wilderness, and they died. If you eat of My bread, you will live forever, and the bread I give you is Myself, it is given for the world."

The Jewish leaders argued among themselves saying, "How can this man give us Himself to eat?"

I answered them, "I say to you, except you believe in Me, and accept Me as Savior, you will not have eternal life. He who believes in Me and accepts Me as Savior has eternal life, and I will raise him up from the dead in the last day. I am true spiritual meat to eat, and true spiritual water to drink; and the one who believes in Me, and accepts Me as Savior, will live in Me and I will live in Him. I live, because the living Father sent Me, and the one who believes in Me and accepts Me as Savior, will live because of Me. This is the Bread Who comes from heaven. It's not like the bread the forefathers ate and died. He who eats this Bread will live forever." I ended these things I taught in Capernaum.

I Am the Creator, God the Son, and I Am the Bread of Life. I will provide physical food for you when you are hungry. I will fill you spiritually with the Bread of Life when you are weak. Accept Me today as your Savior, and live forever with Me in Heaven.

Many of My disciples said this sermon was too difficult to believe. But I knew they were complaining, so I said, "If this sermon causes you problems, what will you think when you see Me ascending back to heaven where I was previously? The words I spoke are Spirit and life; the Spirit will give you eternal life, the flesh cannot help you. Some of you have not put your faith in Me." I knew from the beginning those who believed in Me, and who would betray Me. So I said, "No one can come to Me except the Father draws Him." Therefore many disciples stopped following Me.

Then I said to the twelve, "Will you also stop following Me?"

Peter answered, "Who else can we follow? You have the words of eternal life. We believe and know You are the Messiah."

I answered them, "I chose all twelve of you; yet one of you is a devil." I was referring to Judas Iscariot, the one who would betray Me.

SEVEN

THE COMING OF THE HOLY SPIRIT

After this I stayed in Galilee, because the Jewish leaders sought to kill Me in Judea. The Festival of Shelters was approaching and every Jewish male was to attend once. My unsaved brothers counseled Me to go to the Festival of Shelters in Jerusalem. They said, "Go do miracles so the multitude will believe You and follow You. A person who wants to be known doesn't do things in secret, but he manifests himself to the world."

My Unbelieving Brothers

My brothers did not believe in Me. I told them, "This is not the hour for Me to manifest Myself. The world does not hate you, but it hates Me, because I tell them their works are evil. It's not time for Me to manifest Myself," so I didn't do what they suggested. After My brethren went to the festival in Jerusalem, I privately went on an out-of-the-way road, arriving in the middle of the week.

I Attend the Festival of Shelters

The Jewish leaders were looking everywhere saying, "Where is Jesus?" The crowd was confused, some said, "Jesus was a good man." Others said, "He leads the multitude astray." Yet no one supported Me publicly, because they were afraid of the Jewish leaders.

I went into the temple on Wednesday and taught. Everyone marveled at My knowledge, because I hadn't graduated from the best schools. I answered, "I don't think up the things I teach, this doctrine comes from My heavenly Father. If anyone is yielded to do the Father's will, he shall understand this doctrine whether this is My idea or the Father's. He who does his own will, also seeks his own glory, but he who seeks to glorify the Father, there is no unrighteousness in him. Moses gave you the law, but none of you keeps it; none of you is righteous before God." I said, "Why do you want to kill Me?"

The Jewish leaders said, "You have a demon, because You think someone is trying to kill You."

I said, "I healed a lame man on the Sabbath eighteen months ago, and you hate Me for it. Moses gave you the law to circumcise a boy and you circumcise on the Sabbath, yet you are angry with Me because I healed on the Sabbath day. Aren't healing and circumcision both a work of God? Let's judge according to God's perfect judgment; did we not both do right on the Sabbath?"

The crowd began talking among themselves, "Isn't this the man the leaders want to kill; yet they say nothing when He speaks openly? Maybe they think He is our messianic Deliverer so they don't do anything to Him."

I preached loudly to the crowd, "You think you know Me, and you think you know where I come from, but you don't really know Me. The Father who sent Me, knows Me and I know Him, because I come from Him."

The crowd wanted to take Me to the Jewish leaders, but no one laid a hand on Me, because My hour had not come. Yet many in the crowd believed on Me saying, "The Messiah won't do more miracles than this man has done."

When the Jewish leaders heard I was preaching to the multitude, they sent officers to arrest Me. I responded, "I will be with you for only a little while, then I'll go to the One who sent Me. You will look for Me, but not find Me because I'm going where you can't come."

The crowd talked among themselves asking, "Where is He going that we can't find Him? Is He going to the Jews in the dispersion or is He going to teach Gentiles?" Also they asked, "What does He mean when He says we can't go where He is going?"

God The Holy Spirit

On Sunday, the last day of the Festival of Shelters, when thousands of priests were parading with pots of water to pour out as a drink offering to God, I shouted to the crowd, "If anyone is thirsty, come to Me for satisfaction. He who believes on Me will have living water flowing out of his inner being." I was referring to the indwelling Holy Spirit, but the Holy Spirit had not yet been given, because I had not yet gone to glory.

Someone, who had been in the crowd, said of Me, "Jesus is a true prophet!"

Others said, "He is the Messiah!"

But the crowd argued, "The Messiah doesn't come from Gentiles, but from Bethlehem, the village where David was born." The crowd was divided because of Me, and no one laid a hand on Me.

The Jewish leaders asked the officers why they didn't arrest Me. They answered, "No one speaks like Him." Some said, "This man is not the Messiah. We know this man comes from Nazareth, but we don't know where Messiah comes from."

The leaders rebuked them, "Are you also deceived by this Man? Have any of our leaders believed Him?"

The Pharisees said, "The crowd is cursed, because they don't know the law."

Nicodemus, by this time a believer, said to them, "Does our law judge a man before we hear Him?"

The leaders ridiculed Nicodemus, accusing him of coming from Galilee, "Search the record; no prophet comes out of Galilee." After the festival was over, they all went home.

I invite you to come to Me, and drink of the Water of Life freely, to find energy and satisfaction. When you are weak, come to drink of Me for strength to continue on. When you can't find happiness or satisfaction, come to Me to drink and to find purpose in life, and peace. I will fill you with My presence.

EIGHT

AN ARGUMENT WITH RELIGIOUS LEADERS

I went to the Mount of Olives for the night, but early the following morning I went to the temple and sat down in the middle of the multitude to teach. The religious leaders threw a woman in the middle of the crowd who was caught in the very act of adultery. The leaders said to Me, "This woman was caught in the very act of adultery. The law demands that she be stoned, but what do You say we should do?"

The Jews used this occasion to try and trap Me so they would have an accusation against Me. I stooped to write with My finger in the ground, but the leaders continued to question Me. Then I stopped to say, "He who has not committed this self-same sin, let him cast the first stone." Again I stooped to write on the ground, then the eldest leader left first and eventually all the other leaders left. Then I said to the woman, "Where are those who accuse you of sin?"

She answered, "They are not here to accuse me."

I said, "Neither do I accuse you, go from here and sin no more."

There will be times when you don't know what to do, and you don't know which way to turn. I will shine light in your soul, so you will know the plan I have for your life. I AM the light that brightens your path. Come walk with Me and I will show you where to go. With My light, you will see dangers on the path as well as safe places when you need protection from danger.

I Argue with the Religious Leaders

I said, "I am the light of the world, those following Me shall not walk in darkness, but shall have the light of life."

The religious leaders snarled, "You bear witness to Yourself. You are bragging and lying."

I answered them, "My claim is true, I know where I came from, and I know where I am going. But you don't know anything about Me. You judge according to the flesh; you don't know the facts. I will not judge you now, but I will in the future. The law says to accept a statement if two agree about what happened. Then I am one witness to My claims, and My Father is the other witness."

"Where is the Father?" they asked.

I answered, I answered, "If you had known that I AM God the Son, you would have known God the Father." Later, I was sitting where money was received, but the officials didn't arrest Me, because My hour had not yet come. I said to the crowd, "I am going away; you will search and not find Me, because you can't come to where I'm going."

The Jews didn't understand, so they asked, "Will You commit suicide?"

Then I said to them, "I am from above, you are from this world, and you shall die in your sins unless you believe that I am the Messiah."

The Jews asked again, "Who are You?"

I answered, "I am the One I claim to be. I could teach you much, but that would condemn you. I am the One the Father sent to you, the One who sent Me is true." But the Jews still didn't understand I was telling them I came from God, and that I AM God the Son. Then I said, "When you have lifted up the Son of God, then you will realize I am the Messiah from heaven. The One who sent Me is with Me, He has not deserted Me. I do always the things that please the One who sent Me into the world." Many people believed the words I spoke. Then I explained to them, "If you abide in My words, then you are truly My disciples, and you'll know the truth, and the truth will set you free."

Then the Jewish leaders answered, "We are Abraham's descendants, we have never been slaves to anyone. How can You make us free?"

I answered, "I say to you, everyone who commits sin is a bond slave to sin. A slave does not live in the house forever, but a son lives there forever. If the Son shall make you free, you shall be truly free. Yes, you are descendants of Abraham, but some of you are trying to kill Me, because My words have not set you free. I speak what My Father tells Me to say, but you speak what your father tells you."

The Jews answered, "Our father is Abraham."

I answered, "No, if Abraham were your father, you would do what Abraham told you to do. Instead, you are planning on killing Me just because I told you the truth."

The Jews said sarcastically, "We were not born out of wedlock," suggesting I didn't have a father. The Jews bragged, "Our Father is God."

I answered, "If God were your father, you would love Me, because I come from the Father." Then I told them plainly, "Your father is the devil and you do the lustful sins of the devil. The devil is a murderer from the beginning and doesn't have any truth in him. The devil is a liar and doesn't speak the truth. I tell you the truth and you do not believe Me. None of you can point out any sin that I have ever done. If you were of God, you would listen to My words, but you don't understand them, because you are not of God." The Jews accused Me of being a Samaritan and being possessed with a demon. I answered, "I do not have a demon, and I honor the heavenly Father. I have no desire to make Myself great; the Father will do this for Me." Then I said, "I say to you, if you will obey My words, you will never taste death."

"Now we know you have a demon," the Jews answered. "Even Abraham died, and You claim if a man obeys Your words he shall never die." The Jews asked, "Who do You think You are—God?"

Then I answered them, "If I am just bragging, it doesn't mean anything; it is the Father who will glorify Me. But you do not know the heavenly Father. If I said you knew the Father, I'd be lying as you lie. Your father Abraham rejoiced to see My day; he knew I would come into the world and Abraham rejoiced to see My day."

The Jewish leaders said, "You aren't even 50 years old, and You said You've seen Abraham."

I answered, "You're right; before Abraham was even born, I existed." The Jewish leaders picked up stones to kill Me, but I hid Myself and walked past them out of the temple.

There is a battle between the kingdom of light and the kingdom of darkness. I knew the religious Jews were agents of satan, and I knew their strategy to defeat Me. Therefore, you must study Scripture to understand satan's strategy, and then follow God's principles to lead a godly life, and serve God successfully.

I HEAL A MAN BORN BLIND

As I left the temple, I saw a blind man, and My disciples asked, "Who sinned, his parents or this man that he was born blind?"

I answered, "Neither did this man nor his parents, but his blindness demonstrates the power of God. Each of us is given a task in life. We must do it in the daylight because the night comes when work ends. While I'm still in this dark world, I am the light of the world."

Then I spat on the ground to make clay and then rubbed it on the blind man's eyes and told him, "Go wash in the Pool of Siloam." So he went and washed, and came back seeing.

The neighbors who knew he was blind were dumbfounded. "Is this the same one we knew who begged?"

Others said, "It looks just like him."

The healed man said, "I'm the one who was blind!"

They said, "How were you healed?"

He answered, "A man named Jesus made clay, and rubbed it on my eyes and said, 'Go wash in Siloam.' I did, and now I see."

They asked, "Where is this Jesus fellow?"

He answered, "I don't know!" The crowd brought the healed man to the religious leaders; it was the Sabbath. They also asked how he was healed. The healed man answered, "Jesus put clay on my eyes, and now I see."

The religious leaders criticized, "This Jesus is not from God, because He breaks the Sabbath."

But someone in the crowd answered, "How can a sinner do such a great miracle?"

The religious leaders asked the healed man what he thought of Me. He answered, "Jesus is a prophet!"

The religious leaders said, "This man wasn't blind." So they asked his parents if the man was born blind.

The parents answered them, "We know that he is our son, and that he was born blind, but we don't know what happened to him. Ask him, he is old enough to speak for himself." The parents were afraid of the Jewish leaders, because anyone saying I was the Messiah would be excommunicated from the temple.

His parents again said, "Ask him, he is of age."

Then the Jewish leaders asked the man a second time, "Give glory to God, not to this Jesus fellow; we know He is a sinner."

The healed man said, "I don't know if Jesus is evil, all I know is that I was blind, and now I see."

The religious leaders kept demanding, "How did Jesus heal you?"

The healed man became exasperated. "I told you once, do you want to hear it again? Do you want to become Jesus' disciple?"

They cursed him, "You are His disciple, but we are Moses' disciples. We know God spoke to Moses, but we don't know this fellow."

The healed man was incredulous, "Why, here is a miracle, and you don't realize Jesus opened my eyes. We know God does not hear the prayer of sinners, but He answers those who worship Him and do His will. Since the world began, no one has opened the eyes of a blind man. If this Jesus is not of God, He could do nothing."

The religious leaders shouted, "You were born in sin. Are you trying to teach us anything?" So they excommunicated him from the temple.

Spiritual Blindness

I heard they excommunicated him, so I found him and asked, "Do you believe in the Son of God?"

The healed man answered, "Who is He?" I answered, "You are looking at Him. I am the One who healed you."

The blind man said, "Lord, I believe," and then he worshiped Me.

Then I announced to the crowd, "I come to judge so that those who think they see will become blind, and those who are blind will see."

The religious leaders asked, "Do you think we are blind?"

I answered, "If you were blind, you would want Me to heal you. But because you don't understand who I AM, you are blinded to the truth of God."

Healing a man who was born blind was proof that I AM God, but there is something worse than physical blindness. I will give you eyes to see My truth, and I will take away your spiritual blindness. I will give you a heart to obey My commands, and I will take away any doubt. When the healed man saw Me, he recognized I did a miracle in his life. Then he worshiped Me. I can give you eternal life, and you too can worship Me.

I AM THE GOOD SHEPHERD

I said, "Those who don't follow Me, but climb over the wall into the sheepfold are thieves. My sheep enter by the door, because I am the Shepherd of the sheep. The sheep hear My voice, and I call My own sheep by name and lead them out."

"I go before them and call them, and they follow for they know My voice, but will not follow a stranger." When I used this extended metaphor the crowd didn't understand what I meant. So I said, "I am the door for the sheep; those who came before are thieves and robbers, but My sheep didn't obey their voice." I repeated Myself, "I am the Door, all who enter by Me will be saved, and they will go in and out to find pasture. "The thief comes to kill and destroy the sheep, but I come to give sheep the fullness of life."

I promised that everyone who enters the door of salvation will enjoy the freedom of going and coming into My sheepfold. Also, I promised that they would eat abundantly, and would enjoy life more abundantly. Those who pray salvation's request will enjoy fellowship with Me forever.

I said, "I am the Good Shepherd who gives His life for His sheep. A hired man will run away when the wolf attacks, because the sheep don't belong to him, and he isn't their shepherd. The wolf attacks the sheep and scatters the flock. The hired man runs away because he is hired; he doesn't really care about the sheep." I said, "I am the Good Shepherd and know My sheep, and My sheep know Me and follow Me. Just as the Father knows Me, and I know the Father, I know My sheep and will lay down My life for them. I have other sheep who are not in this fold, they are the Gentiles who will believe on Me. I will lead them also. These other sheep will listen to My voice, and then all My sheep will be one flock and all will live in one sheepfold—heaven."

I said, "The Father loves Me, because I lay down My life, but I will take back My life. No one can take My life from Me; I willingly die, and I have power to raise Myself from the dead. This is the assignment I was given by the Father."

You received physical life when you were born physically. Then you received spiritual life when you prayed to receive Me as your Savior. God intended for you to make your physical life a dwelling place—sanctuary—for Me to live in you. You must keep your body separated from sin, while God makes you holy by living in you. As you immerse yourselves in Scripture, fellowship with the Father, and attempt to follow Me, you become transformed into God's image.

The crowd was divided over what I said. Some said, "He raves like a man possessed by a demon. Why should we listen to Him?" Others said, "Can a demon-possessed man cause the blind to see? He doesn't sound like one possessed by a demon."

Winter in Jerusalem

When winter settled on Jerusalem, it was time for Hanukkah; I returned to the temple near Solomon's Porch. The crowd surrounded Me, asking, "How long will You keep us in suspense? Tell us if You are Messiah."

I answered, "I did tell you, but you didn't listen; I did miracles, but you wouldn't believe them. You didn't believe because you are not sheep of My flock. My sheep know My voice and obey Me. I know them and they know Me and follow Me. I give My sheep eternal life and they shall never perish, no one can snatch them from Me. My Father has given them to Me, and He is more powerful than anything else, so no one can steal them from Me." Then I said, "I and the Father are One."

The Jewish leaders then picked up stones to kill Me. I responded, "The Father has directed Me to do many miracles to help people who are hurting; for which one of these miracles do you stone Me?"

They answered, "Not for works of mercy, but for blasphemy. You are a mere man like us, but You have said You are God."

I quoted Scripture, "Your law says men are gods, so if the Scripture is always right, why did it call mere men gods? How can You say I blasphemed God when the Father who sent Me said I am the Son of God? Even if you refuse to believe who I am, at least believe the miracles I do. Then you will realize the Father is in Me, and I am in the Father." They tried to arrest Me, but I walked away from them and crossed over the Jordan to stay near the place where John the Baptizer first baptized.

My disciples said, "John didn't do miracles, but everything he said about You is true." At that time many people believed in Me.

ELEVEN

I RAISE LAZARUS FROM THE DEAD

I received a message from Mary and Martha telling Me that Lazarus was sick. This is the same Mary who anointed Me with oil and wiped My feet with the hair of her head. The sisters reminded Me that I loved Lazarus. Actually I loved all three of them. When I received the message, I told My disciples, "This sickness will not end in death, but I, the Son of God, will be glorified through it." Now I loved Martha, her sister Mary, and Lazarus. I stayed where I was for two more days, then I told My disciples, "Let's go to Judea." They cautioned Me against making the trip, because the Jews tried to stone Me the last time I was there. I replied, "There are 12 hours of daylight for walking so you won't stumble when there is light to see by. Those who walk in darkness stumble, because there is no light to guide them." I then said, "Our friend Lazarus sleeps, I go to awaken him."

The disciples answered, "It's good if he sleeps."

They didn't understand what I meant, so I said plainly, "Lazarus is dead. Now I'm glad I wasn't there when he died, because now you will believe completely in Me."

Then Thomas—the twin—said to the other disciples, "Let us go with Him, and die with Him."

When I arrived, I found out Lazarus had been dead four days. Bethany was about two miles from Jerusalem, so many Jews had come to sympathize with Mary and Martha. When Martha heard that I had arrived, she went out to the graveyard to meet Me. Mary stayed in the house grieving. Martha accused Me, "If You would have been here, my brother would not have died. But now I know that whatever You ask from God, He will give it to You."

I told Martha, "Your brother will rise again."

Martha said, "I know he'll arise in the resurrection at the last day."

I said to her, "I am the resurrection and the life, and those who believe in Me will never die."

Martha answered, "Yes, I believe You are the Deliverer-Messiah, the Son of God Who was sent into the world." Martha ran to whisper to Mary in a low voice, "The Master is here and wants to see you." Mary immediately got up and went to Me outside town. When the Jews, who were mourning, saw Mary leave, they followed her thinking she was visiting the cemetery.

As soon as Mary saw Me, she threw herself at My feet, saying the same thing as her sister, "Lord, if You had been here my brother would not have died."

I saw Mary's tears and the mourning Jews following her. I said with a deep sigh, "Where is the body?" Then I wept.

The Jews responded, "Behold how much Jesus loved Lazarus."

Other Jews said, "This man makes the blind see, why couldn't He keep Lazarus from dying?"

I sighed deeply. When I got to the tomb—a cave—with a stone closing the opening, I said, "Take away the stone."

Martha protested, "Lord, the body stinks; he's been dead four days."

I answered, "Have I not told you that if you will believe, you'll see the glory of God." They rolled the stone away, then I looked into heaven, "Father, I thank You for hearing Me before I pray, so that the people here will believe in Me." Then I yelled with a strong voice, "*Lazarus, come out!*" Lazarus came bound, hands and feet with swaths of cloth, and a cloth wrapped around his face. I cried, "Unwrap him and free him."

I raised Lazarus to life after he had been dead four days. I will do the same for you, so that one day you can live with Me in Heaven forever.

Results from Raising Lazarus

Then some of the Jewish leaders saw it happen, and believed. Therefore many Jews believed in Me, because I raised Lazarus from the dead, but others ran to tell the religious rulers what happened. They gathered in council to decide what to do. One said, "What can we do? This man does miracles."

Another said, "If we don't do something, the Romans will come punish us and the nation, because they will think Jesus is fermenting a revolution."

Caiaphas, the high priest, said, "You're all wrong! Let this man die instead of our people. Why should our whole nation perish?"

This prophecy, that I should die for everyone, came from Caiaphas the high priest when he was inspired by God to make this prediction. So from that time on the religious leaders were convinced that it was right to plan My death. I stopped preaching to the multitudes and went to the desert and stayed on the border of Ephraim and Samaria. People were journeying to Jerusalem for the Passover; they were curious to see Me and kept asking, "Do you think Jesus will come to this Passover?" Meanwhile the religious leaders had announced that anyone seeing Me must report it to the authorities so I could be arrested.

TWELVE

MY TRIUMPHAL ENTRY INTO JERUSALEM

Six days before the Passover meal, I attended a banquet at the home of Martha in Bethany. Lazarus, her brother, sat with Me at the head of the table. Mary poured a jar of costly perfume over My feet and wiped them with her hair. The house filled with the beautiful smell. Judas Iscariot complained that the perfume could be sold and the money given to take care of the poor. He didn't care for the poor, he was a thief who was in charge of the money given to Me. I answered, "Let her alone, she is preparing Me for burial. You can help the poor later, but you won't have Me very long."

Worship Me for My death for your sins, just as Mary worshiped Me at the festival at Bethany.

When the crowds heard that I had come to Jerusalem, they came eagerly to see Me and Lazarus; the one whom I raised from the dead. Then the religious leaders decided to kill Lazarus also, because many believed on Me because of Lazarus.

My Entry into Jerusalem

On Sunday morning many people who had come to the Passover Festival wanted to see Me. When they heard I was coming to Jerusalem they cut palm branches to wave before Me. They shouted "HOSAN-NA, blessed is the King of Israel who is representing the Lord." I was riding on a young donkey that had never been ridden before. I was fulfilling Scripture, 'Fear not daughters of Zion. Your King is coming, riding on a young donkey. My disciples didn't understand what was happening that day, but after I was resurrected, they understood the meaning of the triumphant entry because they saw it predicted in the Scriptures. The people who saw Me raise Lazarus from the dead also witnessed this event. Because of Lazarus' resurrection, many people came to see My triumphant entry.

The Pharisees were not impressed. They said, "We are not getting anywhere; the whole world is following Him."

The Greeks Want to See Me

There were some Greeks worshiping in the temple. They approached Philip asking, "We would like to meet Jesus." Philip told Andrew and they told Me.

Just as the Greeks wanted to see Me in the temple, you too will want to see Me with your spiritual eyes, and experience Me in your heart.

I didn't answer directly but said, "The hour has come for Me, the Son of Man, to return to heaven and be glorified. A grain of wheat must die when it falls to the ground; otherwise it will remain only one grain of wheat. But if it dies, it yields a rich harvest of food. Those who love their life will lose it, and those who don't live for this life will exchange it for eternal life. If anyone wants to be My disciple, including the Greeks, they must follow Me. Then they will be where I AM, and the Father will honor them when they follow Me. Now my soul is greatly troubled. Shall I ask My Father to deliver Me from the house of suffering? No! That is the reason why I came to earth. Father, glorify Your name through My coming death."

Then everyone present heard a voice from heaven, "I have glorified it, and I will glorify it again."

Some who heard the noise thought it was thunder; others thought it was an angel speaking. I answered, "This sound was for your sake, not Mine, the time for judgment of sin has come. Satan—the prince of the world—will be cast out. When I am lifted up—on the Cross—I will draw all to Me." I said this to predict the way I would die.

The crowd was astonished answering, "We thought the Scriptures taught Messiah would live forever. Why are You saying the Son of Man must be lifted up in death? Are You talking about the Messiah?"

I said, "My light will illuminate you only a short time. Learn from the Light while you can, or else darkness will come and you'll be lost in it. While you have the Light, believe the Light, and you'll become children of the Light." Then I left and they couldn't find Me. Despite all the miracles I did, most of the people did not believe I was the predicted Messiah. This fulfilled the prediction of Isaiah, who said, "Lord they don't believe, they don't accept Your miracles." Indeed, they couldn't believe, as Isaiah said in another place, "God has blinded their eyes and hardened their hearts, lest they should see with their eyes and understand with their hearts, and turn to God and I save them."

Isaiah said these words when he saw the Lord glorified, sitting on the throne, and he was speaking of Me. Nevertheless many leading citizens believed on Me, but they didn't confess Me openly for fear of social pressure. They were afraid of being excommunicated from the temple for they desired acceptance by people, more than from God. I proclaimed loudly in the temple, "Those who believe in Me, also believe in the Father who sent Me. And those who understand what I am saying, also understand what the Father wants them to know. I have come as a light to all people, and those who believe in Me will not live in darkness. If anyone hears and understands My teachings, but rejects them, I will not judge them, for I come to save all people. But those who do not accept My teachings and reject Me, will be judged in the last day by what I've said. The Father will judge him, because the Father who sent Me told Me what to say, and My words give life eternal. Therefore, everything I am saying to you comes from the Father in heaven."

Believe in Me and obey My words for they give you eternal life.

THIRTEEN

MY LAST SUPPER WITH MY DISCIPLES

On Thursday night, before the Passover supper, I knew that My hour had come, the time for Me to die for the sins of the world. I would love My followers, having loved them to the end. After the supper, the devil had already put into the heart of Judas Iscariot to betray Me. Knowing the Father had put all things into My hand, and that I had come from the Father, I knew I would return to the Father. I arose from the table, laid aside My tunic, and wrapped a towel around Myself as a servant. I poured water into the basin and began washing the disciples' feet and wiping them dry with the towel. When I came to Peter, the fisherman asked, "Will You wash my feet?"

I answered, "You don't understand now, but you'll understand in the future. If I don't wash you, you'll have no part with Me."

So Peter answered Me, "If that's the case, then not only my feet, but my hands and head."

I answered, "He that is bathed all over, need only to have his feet washed. Now you are clean, but not all of you." For I knew who would betray Me. Therefore I said, "You are not all clean." When I finished washing their feet, I put My tunic back on and sat down with them and said, "Do you know what I have done for you?"

Just as I, God the Son, washed the feet of My followers, I will help you to be humble and serve others, so that you may follow My example.

"You call Me Master and Lord, and so I am. If I, then, Your Lord and Master, have washed your feet, then you ought to be willing to wash one another's feet. I have given you the example to do to others what I have done for you. I say to you, a servant is not greater than his master, neither is the one sent greater than the one who sent him. If you know these things, happy are you if you do them. I have chosen all of you, but not all are of Me, that the Scriptures may be fulfilled, 'He that eats with Me, lifts up his heel against Me.' I'm telling you before it happens, so when it comes to pass, you will know I am your Messiah."

Judas, the Betrayer

I was obviously troubled. Then I said, "I say to you, one of you will betray Me." The disciples looked at one another, not completely understanding what I meant. One disciple was leaning on My chest; he was John, the disciple whom I loved. Peter beckoned for John to find out who I meant.

John, who was leaning on Me, said, "Lord, who is it?"

I answered, "He that dips his hand in the same dish that I dip, he is the one who will betray Me. It is good if that man were never born. When I dip the bread into the lamb stew, the one to whom I give it is the one." Then I dipped the bread into the stew and gave it to Judas. But the disciples didn't understand, because Judas was the honored guest, and it was the custom to give it to that person first. After Judas received the bread, satan entered in him. I said to him, "Do quickly what you are going to do." None of the disciples understood what happened because they thought I said, "Buy what is needed for the Passover festival." When Judas received the bread, he went out into the darkness. The night was spiritually black.

My presence will be with you, so you will never betray Me with any deeds, thoughts, or attitudes.

Peters Request

When Judas left, I was relieved saying, "Now I, the Son of Man, am glorified and God is glorified in Me. Since God the Father is glorified in Me, I will also be glorified in Myself. Children, I am going to be with you only a short time. You will look for Me and won't find Me, because where I'm going you cannot follow Me now. So, I'm giving you a new command, that you love one another as I have loved you. By your love, all people will know you are My disciples."

Everyone has difficulty loving some people. It is humankind's old proud ego. I love everyone in the whole world and died for them. Let Me take control of your heart, and love others through you.

Peter asked, "Where are You going?"

I answered him, "You cannot now go where I am going, but later you can follow Me."

Peter answered, "Why can I not follow You now? I'll lay down my life for Your sake."

I replied, "You only think you'll die for Me. I say to you, you will deny Me three times before the rooster crows."

FOURTEEN

THE UPPER ROOM DISCOURSE

I told the eleven, "Do not let your heart be troubled, hold on to your faith in God and your faith in Me. There are many rooms in My Father's house, if it were not true, I would have told you. I am going to prepare a place for you there, and when I get it ready, I will come back for you, and I'll take you to be with Me. You know the way to the place I am going."

But Thomas responded, "No! We don't know where You are going, nor do we know how to get there."

I said, "I am the way to heaven, also, I am truth and I am eternal life. You must come through Me to go to the Father." "Since you know Me, you should also know the Father, and from now on you'll know the Father."

I said that I would come back to take You where I AM. That's what I want. I want you to live with Me in heaven for all eternity.

Philip disagreed, "We don't know what the Father looks like. Show us the Father so we can believe."

I answered, "I have been with you all this time and I'm surprised you don't know the Father. He who has seen Me has seen the Father. What I say are not My words, but they are from the Father who lives in Me. The Father also does the miracles that I do. Believe that I am in the Father, and He is in Me, or else believe it because you have seen My miracles. I say to you, he who believes in Me shall do the works that I do, and even greater ones, because I am going to the Father. Whatever you pray, asking in My name, I'll do it, so that the Father will be glorified in Me. If you pray for anything in My name, I'll do it."

I want you to come in My name, the name of Jesus, to ask your request. I said that I would do it if you asked in My name. You can ask in my name, because I AM in your heart. My blood has cleansed you and given you access to the Father, because I AM your intercessor.

I told them, "If you love Me, obey My commands, and I will ask the Father to send you another person in My place. He will live in you forever. This other Person is God, the Holy Spirit, the third Person of the Trinity. The unsaved cannot receive Him because they do not believe in Him or know anything about Him. But you will know the Holy Spirit, because you believe in Me. He will dwell with you and be in you. I will not leave you alone in the world, I will come to you. Shortly, I will leave you, because I'm leaving the world. But you will see Me later. Because I live, you shall live also. At that time you'll know I'm with the Father in heaven, but I'll be in you and you'll be in Me. Those who have My commands and keep them are the ones who love Me, and those who love Me will be loved by the Father, and I will love them and I'll show Myself to them."

I promised two things that you can know beyond a shadow of a doubt: first, I would come to live within your heart when you are saved; second, you would be placed in Me in heaven. The first means you have My life in you. The second means you can be as close to God, the heavenly Father, as I AM.

Judas—not Iscariot, but another disciple with that name—asked, "How can You show Yourself to us and not to the world?"

I answered, "Those who love Me will obey My commands, and My Father will love them, and We will come to live in them. Those who don't obey My commands, don't love Me. It's not just My Word they reject, it's the Father's Word. I'm explaining these things to you while I'm with you, but the Holy Spirit, whom the Father will send in My place, He'll explain all spiritual things to you, and will remind you of the things I said to you."

You need the Holy Spirit guiding in your life to help you learn Scripture, and to remember the things I said in My Word.

"I am leaving My peace with you, but not as the world gives, so don't be afraid of anything. Previously I told you I'm going away, but I'm also coming back. Because you love Me, rejoice that I'm going to the Father. I tell you this before it happens so you'll believe in Me when it happens. I'll not be able to talk with you much more. The evil prince of this world is coming to try Me, but don't worry, he has no authority over Me. I am going to do the thing the Father wants Me to do; that will show My love to Him. Now, let's leave this upper room."

I did supernatural miracles such as healing a leper and raising the dead. What could be greater than these miracles? A soul saved for all eternity is greater in an insurmountable measure. Because I went to the Father, you can lead people to Me. I want you to be a soul-winner. I will give you a desire to win people to Me, then help you use every opportunity possible to do it.

I am the Vine, you are the branches

FIFTEEN

I AM THE TRUE VINE

I AM your true vine, My Father is the gardener, He cuts away any branches not growing fruit and prunes back every branch that has fruit. So you are a healthy plant when you live by My words. I will abide in you as you abide in Me. Just as a branch can't bear fruit unless it's attached to the vine, so you can't produce anything unless you are attached to Me. I AM the vine, you are a branch; as long as you remain attached to Me, and I abide in you, you will bear plenty of fruit. Anyone who will not remain attached to Me will be punished. He'll be like dead branches that are collected and thrown into a fire to be burned. When you remain settled in Me, and My words remain in you, you can ask what you want and I will give it to you. I AM glorified when you bear much fruit. Then everyone will know you are My disciple.

I want you to produce more fruit in your Christian life, and more fruit in your service to Me. I want you to abide in Me so you can be fruitful.

As the Father has loved Me, so I love you. You can settle down to rest in My love for you. You will obey My commands to remain in My love, just as I kept the Father's commands to remain in His love. I tell you this so My joy would rest in you and your joy would then be complete. I have commanded you to love one another just as I have loved you. You can't have greater love for others than to lay down your life for them. You are My friend, when you obey My commands. You are no longer My servant, because a servant doesn't know what his master does. But you are My friend, because you know what I AM doing, as I

AM doing what the Father told Me to do. You did not choose Me, but I chose you and challenged you to go bear fruit. Now, whatever you ask the Father in My name, I will gladly give to you. Again, I command you to love one another, because the world will hate you and those who follow Me.

But know this, the world hated Me long before it hated you. You do not belong to this world. I have separated you from it, therefore the world hates you. You will remember what I said, "A servant is not greater than his master. Since they persecute Me, the world will persecute you." They will hate you and persecute you because you are my disciple, and because they do not know the Father who sent Me. If I hadn't given the truth, the world wouldn't experience the guilt of their sin, but now they have no excuse. Those who hate you hate My Father. If I hadn't done miracles among them, they would have been blinded in their sins. Now they see, and hate both Me and the Father. As written in the Scriptures, "They hated Jesus without a cause."

When the Holy Spirit comes—the Spirit of truth who comes from the Father— He will speak plainly to your heart about Me. Then you can also speak plainly about Me, because I will speak through you and remove your blindness. Then you can bear witness because you have been with Me.

I promised that if you would abide in My Word, your prayers would be answered. That means you can live and ask according to Scripture to get your prayers answered.

SIXTEEN

THE TESTING OF
YOUR FAITH

I told them about coming persecution so their faith wouldn't be shaken. I said that they would be excommunicated from their assemblies. There was coming a time when people would kill them, thinking they were serving God by doing so. They would do this because they don't have true knowledge of Me or the Father. I did not originally tell My disciples about persecution because I was walking among them. But now that I was going away, they needed to be reinforced, so they wouldn't be shaken when it happened.

The world will hate you, just as it hated Me. I will give you strength to endure persecution and live for Me. I will help you to do more than endure trials; I will give you victory over them.

Yet none of My disciples asked, "Where are You going?" because they were distressed that I was leaving. But it was a good thing for Me to go away, because if I hadn't left, the Holy Spirit would not have come. But because I left, I would send the Holy Spirit to convict the world of sin, righteousness, and judgment. The Holy Spirit will convict—cause people to see their sin, because they do not believe in Me. The Holy Spirit will convict—cause people to see their lack of righteousness, which will keep them out of heaven. The Holy Spirit will convict—cause people to see coming judgment, because I suffered for them on the cross. Many more things could be said, but the disciples weren't ready to hear.

Then I told what the Holy Spirit would do for believers. "When He comes, the Spirit of Truth, He will reveal to you everything that is truth. Then He'll guide you to understand truth. The Holy Spirit will not be concerned with His own agenda, but He will bring glory to Me, and He will reveal to you things to come. All the Father's glory also belongs to Me; this is the glory the Holy Spirit will reveal. All things the Father has, also belong to Me."

I will send the Holy Spirit to guide you into truth, and to keep you from error. The world, the flesh, and the devil continually try to pull you away from Me.

In a little while I would leave My disciples and they would see Me no longer in the flesh. But a short time later they would see Me. The disciples did not understand what I meant about leaving them and then coming back to them. They were puzzled over My leaving a little while. I knew they wanted to question Me, so I said plainly, "In a short time you'll see Me no longer; then a short time later you'll see Me again." Then I explained, "You will weep when I'm gone, but the world will rejoice. But your weeping will be turned to rejoicing. It'll be like a woman suffering in childbirth, but when her child is born, she forgets about her suffering." I explained that they would be sad, but when they would see Me again, they would be full of joy, a joy that no one could take from them. When that day comes, they won't have any questions; they can go directly to the Father with their questions. I then promised that whatever anyone asks in My name, the Father will give it to them. Up until then the disciples hadn't prayed in My name, now they could ask in My name and they would receive answers so that their joy would overflow. Up until that time I used figures of speech and parables, but the time had now come when I spoke plainly. I explained, "When that day comes—and now is—you can ask the Father in My name and I will pray to the Father for you. The Father loves you because you have loved Me, and you know that I came to the world from the Father."

The disciples said, "Now we believe You came from the Father. You are not using figures of speech. Now we understand."

I said, "You only think you understand. The time is coming when you will be scattered to your homes, leaving Me alone." I said, "I have told you this so you will have peace in the world. But you will also have trials; so have faith, I have conquered the world."

SEVENTEEN

MY PRAYER TO
BE GLORIFIED

After I left the Upper Room, I lifted My eyes to heaven and prayed, "Father, My hour is come. Glorify Your Son, so I can glorify You. I pray that those You have given Me will have eternal life; eternal life is in You, the only true God, and is found in Me, the One You sent to earth. I have glorified You on earth and accomplished the work You sent Me to do. Now Father, glorify Me with the glory I had in heaven which I had with You before the world was created.

A Prayer for My Disciples

"I have given Your name to the men You gave me. They were Your men and You gave them to Me. They have faithfully kept Your Word. They know the things You told Me to do, because I told them what You said to Me. They have received Your Word and they believe it, and they believe I came from heaven to do Your will. I pray for these disciples, I do not pray for the world; I pray for those You have given Me. All things that are Mine are Yours, and I am glorified in these disciples. I am no longer in the world, but they are in the world, so I pray for them. I pray—Holy Father—that You would keep them safe, that they may be one, as We are One. While I was with them, I kept them —guarded them—and not one of them is missing, except the son of perdition who fulfilled Scripture by betraying Me. Now I come to You, Father, that they may have joy. I have given them Your Word, and the world hates them because they reject the world, even as I am not of the world. I am not praying for You to take them out of the world, but that You would keep them from the evil one. They are not of this world, just as I am not of this world. Make them holy by Your Word, Your Word is truth. I am sending them into the world, even as I was sent into the world. I set Myself apart from heaven for them, now may they be set apart to reach others.

"I am not praying for these disciples only, I'm also praying for those who will believe because of their word." I prayed that all believers may be one as I and the Father are One; "And the glory You gave Me I give them, so they may also be one as We are. I am in them, as You are in Me, so that the world may realize You sent Me, and You love Me and You love them. Father, I want them to be with Me in heaven, that they may see My glory that I've had before the foundations of the earth. O Father, the world does not know You, but I have known You, and made You known to these disciples, that the love You have for Me may be in them, and I in them, and they in Me."

EIGHTEEN

I AM BETRAYED, ARRESTED, AND FORSAKEN

After I spoke these words, My disciples and I went over the Brook Kidron and entered a garden. Judas knew the place where I often went to pray, so he led Roman soldiers and officers from the religious leaders with lanterns, torches, and weapons to arrest Me. I knew what was happening so I met them and asked, "Who are you looking for?"

They answered, "Jesus of Nazareth."

I responded, "I am He," This was My statement of deity. Then the Roman soldiers and Jewish guards were driven backward to the ground. Again I asked, "Who are you looking for?"

They said, "Jesus of Nazareth."

I answered, "I told you, I am He. Since you want Me, let these go."

With this, prophecy was fulfilled: "I lost none of those that You gave Me."

Judas had given them a sign that I would be the one whom he kissed. So Judas kissed Me, and said, "Arrest Him!"

I said to Judas, "Are you betraying Me, the Son of Man, with a kiss?" As the guards moved forward to take Me, Simon Peter, having a sword, cut off the right ear of Malchus, the high priest's servant. I answered, "Put up your sword; I must drink the cup of suffering the Father has for Me." Then I touched him and healed him.

They grabbed Me and bound Me, but I responded, "Have you come out in the middle of the night to arrest a thief? I sat daily in the temple, but you didn't arrest Me." This came to pass because it was predicted in Scripture. Then the disciples left Me and fled into the night.

The First Trial—Before Annas, the Former High Priest

The soldiers and guards led Me bound to Annas the former high priest who was deposed for his corruption. Caiaphas, his son-in-law, was put in that office. Now Caiaphas was the one who counseled the Jewish leaders that it was expedient for one man to die for the people. Simon Peter followed Me along with John. Since John was known by the servants in the high priest's home, he was allowed to enter, but Peter was kept out. Then John vouched for Peter and he was allowed to enter the courtyard.

The girl at the door said to Peter, "Aren't you a disciple of Jesus?"

Peter said, "No!" Then Peter warmed himself by a fire, for it was cold. He was standing with the others by the fire.

Annas asked Me about My disciples and what I taught; I answered, "I spoke openly in synagogues and the temple and I kept back nothing secretly. Ask those who heard Me what I taught."

When I answered this way, an officer struck Me with his hand, saying, "Why did You answer the high priest that way?"

I replied, "Tell me if I have spoken evil; if not, then don't strike Me."

So Annas sent Me, still in handcuffs, to Caiaphas the high priest. But Simon Peter was still warming himself when someone said to him, "Are you one of His disciples?"

He denied it and said, "No, I am not."

One of the high priest's servants, a relative of the one whose ear Peter cut off, said, "Didn't I see you in the garden with Jesus?" Again Peter denied it, and immediately a rooster crowed. Peter saw Me and ran away weeping.

The Second Trial—Before Caiaphas

They led Me from Caiaphas to the judgment hall—the courtroom—in Pilate's place. It was early morning and they would not go into a Gentile's house, because that would defile them, and they would be unfit to eat the Passover meal.

The Third Trial—Before Pilate

So Pilate came outside and asked, "What charge do you bring against this man?"

They answered, "If He had not broken the law, we would not have brought Him to you."

Pilate told them, "You take Him and try Him in accord with your religious laws."

But the Jews answered, "It is not legal for us to execute anyone." This fulfilled the prophecy of Me that indicated how I would die.

So Pilate went back into the judgment hall to call for Me and asked, "Are You the King of the Jews?"

I answered him, "Are you asking Me this on your own or have others put this question in your mind?"

Pilate answered, "I don't think like a Jew. Your people and their high priests have brought You here. What have You done?"

I answered, "My kingdom is not in this world. If My kingdom were of this world, My followers would have fought to keep Me from being arrested. So My kingdom is not about this world."

Then Pilate retorted, "Then You are a King?"

I answered, "Yes, I am a King. For this purpose I was born, for this purpose I have come into the world, to give them the truth. Everyone who seeks truth will listen to what I say."

Pilate asked Me, "What is truth?" Then he went outside again to the Jews to tell them, "I have no grounds to try this man."

Pilate told them there was a custom to set one man free at Passover. He asked, "Do you want me to set free the King of the Jews?"

Then they yelled and chanted, "No! Not this man, but Barabbas!" Now Barabbas was a robber.

NINETEEN

MY DEATH ON
THE CROSS

So Pilate had Me scourged. Then the soldiers wove a crown out of thorns to place on My head. Then they put a purple coat on Me, and mocked Me saying, "All hail, King of the Jews!"

Then they slapped Me on the face. And Pilate went outside again to the Jews and said, "I am going to bring Him out so you can see that there are no grounds to try Him." So I was brought out still wearing the crown of thorns and purple coat. Then Pilate announced, "Look at this man!"

But the high priests and temple officers glared at Me and shouted to stir up the crowd, "Crucify Him! Crucify Him!"

Pilate answered, "You take Him and crucify Him for I find no ground to try Him."

The Jews answered, "We have a law, and He has broken God's law; He deserves to die for claiming to be God's Son."

When Pilate heard that statement, he was more afraid than before and went back into the judgment hall to ask Me, "Where are You from?" but I did not answer. Then Pilate said, "Why do You refuse to speak to me? Don't You know that I have the authority to free You or crucify You?"

I answered, "You could have no power at all over Me if authority had not been given to you from above. So the one who betrayed me has the greater sin."

Pilate kept looking for a reason to set Me free, but the Jews shouted, "If you set Him free, you are not a friend of Caesar's. Anyone who claims to be a king is speaking treason against Caesar."

When Pilate heard the charge of "treason," he had Me brought out. Then Pilate sat on the judge's bench at the place called the stone platform, or in Hebrew, *gabbatha*. It was the day of preparation for the Passover and it was about six o'clock in the morning. Then Pilate said to the Jews, "Look at your King!"

But they shouted, "Crucify Him! Crucify Him!"

Pilate said to them, "Do you want me to crucify your King?"

The high priests answered, "We have no king but Caesar." Then Pilate turned Me over to them to be crucified.

My Crucifixion

So they led Me, carrying My cross to a place called "the Skull," or in Hebrew, *Golgotha*. There they crucified Me, with two criminals, one on each side, with Me in the middle. Pilate had the legal indictment written and nailed to the cross: "Jesus of Nazareth, the King of the Jews."

Now many of the Jews read this sign, because I was crucified near the city. It was written in Hebrew, Latin, and Greek. So the high priests of the Jews demanded of Pilate, "Don't write, 'The King of the Jews,' but write, 'He said, I am the King of the Jews.'"

Pilate refused, saying, "What I have written, I have written!"

After the soldiers crucified Me, they divided My clothes into four parts, one for each soldier. But the coat, woven without a seam, was expensive. So they agreed, "Let us not cut it up, but let us cast lots to see who gets it."

This fulfilled Scripture, "They divided My clothes among them, and for my clothing they cast lots."

My mother and her sister, and Mary, the wife of Clopas, and Mary of Magdala were standing near My cross. So when I saw My mother and the disciple, whom I loved, John, standing near her, I said to My mother, "There is your son." Then I said to John, "There is your mother." From that time on, John took My mother to his own home. When I knew that the end was near, I said, "I am thirsty." Some vinegar was there. So they soaked a sponge in some vinegar and put it to My lips. As soon as I tasted the sour vinegar I said, "It is finished!" Then I bowed My head and gave up My life.

It was the day of preparation for the Passover, so they did not want the bodies, including mine, to remain on the crosses during the Sabbath. Therefore the Jews asked Pilate to break our legs and take down our bodies. The soldiers broke the legs of the first and second thieves who had been crucified with Me. But they saw that I was already dead, so they did not break My legs. However, one of the soldiers thrust a lance into My side, and blood and water flowed out. John the Apostle, who saw this testified to it. And his testimony is true, and he knows it is true so that you may believe it. This fulfilled Scripture, "Not a bone of Him was broken." It also fulfilled another Scripture, "They shall look on Him whom they pierced."

My Burial in the Tomb

After this, Joseph of Arimathea, My secret disciple for fear of the Jews, asked Pilate if he could remove My body, and Pilate said yes. So Joseph took down My body. Also Nicodemus, who came to Me by night, brought a mixture of myrrh and aloes about one hundred pounds to anoint My body. So they wrapped My body in swathes of cloth and anointed it with spices, in accord with the Jewish custom of preparing a body for burial. There was a garden near the place where I had been crucified. There was a new tomb in the garden where no one had yet been buried. So, because it was the Jewish Preparation Day and because the tomb was there, they laid My body there.

TWENTY

PETER, JOHN AND MARY VISIT THE EMPTY TOMB

On the first day of the week Mary Magdalene went to the tomb. It was still dark, because it was early in the morning. She saw the stone was removed, so she ran to tell Simon Peter and John, the disciple whom I loved. "Someone has taken away the Lord from the tomb, and we do not know what they have done with the body." So, Peter and John ran to the tomb; the younger John outran Peter. John looked inside the tomb and saw the linen clothes still wrapped together, but he didn't go in. Peter didn't stop, but ran straight into the tomb and also saw the linen clothes together and the death mask lying at another place. Next, John entered the tomb and examined everything. Then he believed that I had risen from the dead; and they returned to their house.

John had faith to believe that I rose physically from the dead. The empty tomb proves that I rose from the dead. You are saved by grace because you put your faith in Me. This faith is not your own doing, but My gift to you. You cannot boast that you had anything to do with it. I have made you what you are, a new person, created in Me, to serve Me by doing good works, which I planned for you to do.

Mary Returns to the Tomb

Later that morning Mary Magdalene returned to the tomb; she wept as she looked into the tomb. Then she saw two angels clothed in white sitting at the head and feet where My body had been laid.

"Woman, why are you crying?" the angels asked.

She answered, "Because they have taken away my Lord and I don't know where He is." I was standing in back of her, but she didn't know who I was. She thought I was a gardener, so she asked, "If you have taken away His body, tell me where it is and I will take Him away."

It was I who said, "Mary."

Her blindness was taken away and she called Me, "Rabboni," an old Hebrew word for "respected master."

I said, "Quit clinging to Me as though things will continue in the future as they were in the past." I explained, "I must go to My Father in heaven. He is also your Father. He is My God and your God."

Mary returned to Jerusalem to tell the disciples, "I have seen the Lord." Then she told them all the things I said to her.

I Appear to the Disciples

In the evening of resurrection day—the first day of the week—the doors of the room were locked where the disciples had gathered for fear of the Jews. I came to stand in the midst of them and said, "Peace to you!" Then I let them examine My hands and My side, and so the disciples were filled with confidence and joy over seeing Me, their Lord. Then I said again, "Peace to you! Just as the Father has sent Me into the world, so, I am sending you into the world." I breathed on them and said, "Receive the Holy Spirit, who will teach you and use you, just as He has done throughout past ages. He will be with you until you are endued with His power. Those you lead to faith will have their sins forgiven; those who reject Me as their Christ will retain their sins."

Thomas, the disciple called Didymas—a twin—was not there. The disciples told him, "We have seen the Lord."

He said, "I must see the nail prints in His hands, and put my hand into the wound in His side; otherwise, I will not believe."

Do not demand physical assurances to believe. Just know that I am the crucified Son of God who died for you.

The Upper Room One Week Later

Eight days after Passover, the disciples gathered again in the upper room on a Sunday evening. Thomas was with them this time. The doors were locked, but I again stood among them and said what I said the previous Sunday, "Peace to you!" I spoke first to Thomas, "Reach your finger to touch My wounds and place your hand in the wound in My side. Don't doubt, but believe."

But Thomas didn't do it, he answered, "You are my Lord and my God."

I said, "God will bless you because you have seen Me and believe. But God will also bless those who haven't seen Me, and yet believe."

I did many miracles that were not written in the gospels, but these miracles are written that people will believe that I am the Messiah, the Son of God, and when they believe, they will receive eternal life.

Believe that I am God the Son, so you can know beyond a shadow of a doubt that you have eternal life.

TWENTY-ONE

I APPEAR ON THE LAKE SHORE

A week later—on Sunday—I appeared to seven of My disciples on the shore of the Sea of Galilee; Simon Peter, Thomas, Nathanael of Cana in Galilee, the sons of Zebedee, and two of My disciples were together. Simon Peter had announced, "I am going fishing." Those who went with him were Thomas, Nathaniel, James and John, Andrew, and Phillip. They got into a boat and fished all night, but caught nothing.

When the day was breaking, I stood on the beach, but the disciples didn't know it was Me. I yelled to them, "Have you caught any fish?"

They answered Me, "No!"

I answered, "Cast the net on the other side of the boat and you will catch fish." They cast on the right side and couldn't draw in the fish because there were so many.

So John said to Peter, "It's the Lord." Peter put on his tunic and dove into the water to swim to Me. The other disciples came in a little boat, for they were 100 yards from the beach.

When they got to shore, they saw a charcoal fire cooking fish; there was also bread. I said, "Add the fish you've caught to these." Simon Peter went and pulled the net to land. It had 153 fish in it, yet the net didn't break. I said, "Come eat, break your fast." No one asked who it was, for they all knew it was Me; I served all of them breakfast. This was the third Sunday that I appeared to them.

Peter Restored

After breakfast I said, "Simon, Son of Jonah, do you love Me more deeply than you love these nets?"

Peter answered, "Lord, You know that I like and admire You."

I answered, "Feed My lambs." I said to him a second time, "Simon, do you deeply love Me?"

Peter answered, "Lord, You know that I like and admire You."

I answered, "Tend My sheep." I said a third time, "Simon, do you really like and admire Me?"

Peter was ashamed I asked him three times, because he denied Me three times, and because he only said he liked and admired Me. So Peter answered, "Lord, You know everything; You know I really like and admire You."

I said, "Feed My sheep." Then I predicted, "When you were young, you were able to dress yourself, and go where you wanted. But when you get old, they will stretch your hands out on a cross and they will clothe you with what they choose, and lead you where they want to go." By this I was saying Peter would die as a martyr. Then I concluded, "Follow Me."

Then Peter turned around and saw John who also leaned on His breast at the supper saying, "Lord, who betrays You?"

Peter turned to John and asked Me, "What about him?"

I said, "If he lives till I return, how does that concern you? You must follow Me."

This statement made many think John would live until I returned to earth. But I didn't say John wouldn't die; I only said, "If he lives till I return, how does that concern you?"

I Ascend Back to Heaven

Then I said to them, "Let Me tell you again what I said while I was with you; that everything that is written about Me in the law of Moses, in the prophets, and in the Psalms, had to be fulfilled." Then I opened their spiritual eyes so they might understand the Scriptures.

Then I said to them, "The Scriptures say the Christ would suffer for sins, rise from the dead on the third day, and that repentance in My name as the condition for the forgiveness of sins should be preached to all nations. You are to begin at Jerusalem as witnesses to these things.

"I will send on You the promise of My Father. But you must stay right here in the city and pray until you are anointed with power from on high." Then I led them out of the city as far as Bethany, and I lifted up My hands and blessed them. While I was blessing them, I was lifted up from them, and was taken up to heaven. And with joy, they went back to Jerusalem, and continued in the temple praying and praising God.

I Want You to Live With Me in Heaven Forever

This is what I did for you. I came down out of heaven and took the form of a man, took the punishment that you deserved and died on the cross. And because your sins are covered by My blood, I no longer hold your sins against you! The really great news is that I didn't stay dead. I rose from the grave and live in Heaven. I want you to live in heaven with Me too. You must only BELIEVE in Me!

Are you Willing to...

- transfer your trust from yourself to Me alone for eternal life?
- believe that I took your place and paid for all your sins on the cross?
- repent of your sins and follow Me?
- receive God The Fathers' gift of eternal life through Me?

Just pray this prayer and believe it in your heart:

Dear Jesus, I believe that you died for me. I admit that I have sinned and cannot save myself. Please forgive me of my sin. Help me to turn from my sin and follow you. Amen.

Psalm 1

Your life will be happier:
> If you don't follow the advice of sinners
> If you don't loiter with the wicked
> If you don't become a part of an evil group

You will discover happiness by obeying My laws
> And thinking right day and night.

You will be like a tree rooted by living waters.
> Bearing fruit at the right seasons

Your leaf will not wither
> And you will prosper in what you do.

The wicked are blown about like worthless trash,
> I will judge them for their rebellion and wasted
> life.

They will not stand with the godly before Me.
> For I take care of those who live right
> But the evil doers will be destroyed.

Psalm 23

I am your shepherd.

I will find a place for you to lie down and rest as comfortable as a green pasture.

I will restore your soul.

I will lead you in right paths, as surely as my name is the Lord.

I will guide you through death's valley and bring you out on the other side.

My rod will protect you from danger, and my staff will rescue you when you are in trouble.

I will prepare a meal for you that will become your favorite.

I will satisfy your thirst with a cup that is full and running over.

My goodness and mercy will be like sheep dogs, will keep you from straying, and lead you to the perfect place of rest.

It is my house, my home in heaven and you can live there forever.

Psalm 100

A Prayer Of Gratitude When Entering My Presence

Shout with joy to Me when entering My presence,
    Everyone from every nation join in.
Worship as you enter My presence with singing
    Because I am the Lord your God.
I made you and you belong to Me;
    You are My people and the sheep of My pasture.
Come into My gates giving thanks;
    Enter My courts with praise.
Bless My holy name
    By giving thanks for all I have done for you.
I, the LORD, am good, My mercy is everlasting;
    And My truth endures forever.

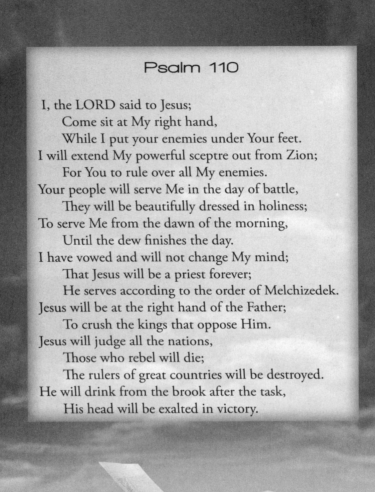

Psalm 110

I, the LORD said to Jesus;
    Come sit at My right hand,
    While I put your enemies under Your feet.
I will extend My powerful sceptre out from Zion;
    For You to rule over all My enemies.
Your people will serve Me in the day of battle,
    They will be beautifully dressed in holiness;
To serve Me from the dawn of the morning,
    Until the dew finishes the day.
I have vowed and will not change My mind;
    That Jesus will be a priest forever;
    He serves according to the order of Melchizedek.
Jesus will be at the right hand of the Father;
    To crush the kings that oppose Him.
Jesus will judge all the nations,
    Those who rebel will die;
    The rulers of great countries will be destroyed.
He will drink from the brook after the task,
    His head will be exalted in victory.

Psalm 117

Praise From All People

Praise Me your Lord, with the different ethnic
    groups of the earth;
    Praise Me with all people of the earth,
For I love you with unending love;
    My faithfulness endures forever.
Praise Me your Lord.

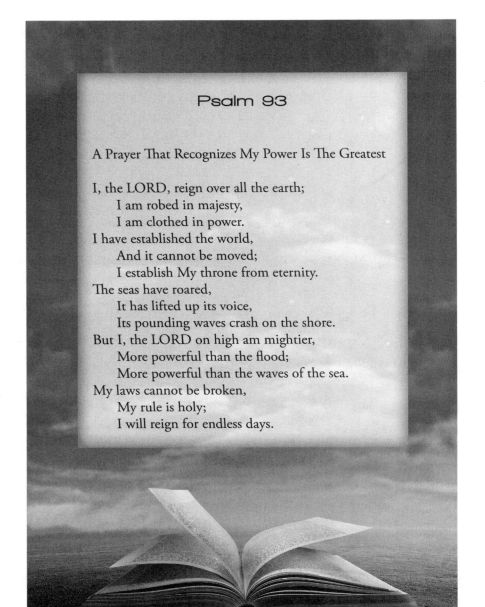

Psalm 93

A Prayer That Recognizes My Power Is The Greatest

I, the LORD, reign over all the earth;
    I am robed in majesty,
    I am clothed in power.
I have established the world,
    And it cannot be moved;
    I establish My throne from eternity.
The seas have roared,
    It has lifted up its voice,
    Its pounding waves crash on the shore.
But I, the LORD on high am mightier,
    More powerful than the flood;
    More powerful than the waves of the sea.
My laws cannot be broken,
    My rule is holy;
    I will reign for endless days.